LONG-DISTANCE REAL ESTATE INVESTING

Praise for

LONG-DISTANCE REAL ESTATE INVESTING

"I've been in real estate my entire adult life, and I have seen many different systems and ideas on how to get rich in the business. David's system is the first solid one I've seen that allows you to choose the market that's best for you and invest where it makes sense, not just where you happen to live and are comfortable. I recommend this book to all my listeners on Real Estate Rockstars."

—Pat Hiban, *New York Times* best-selling author of
6 Steps to 7 Figures: A Real Estate Agent's Guide to
***Building Wealth* and *Creating Your Destiny* and host**
of the award-winning podcast Real Estate Rockstars

"It is a common misperception in real estate investing that you should buy only where you live. David Greene has put that myth to rest. In this book, he shows you the secrets to building your wealth through real estate. This is a must-read for investors who want to expand their real estate empire nationwide."

—David Osborn, best-selling author
of *Wealth Can't Wait*

"David's advice in this book was the catalyst I needed to finally look outside my own backyard for real estate deals. I tripled my rental portfolio by purchasing out-of-state rental properties thanks to the advice in this book. I wish I had read this a decade ago!"

—Brandon Turner, real estate investor, podcast host, and author of *The Book on Rental Property Investing*

"I've found the key to a successful day hinges on putting yourself in a position to succeed before the day starts. The same is true for your financial life. David has found a way to allow anyone to invest in real estate wherever it makes sense to do so, rather than waiting for his or her specific market to be in an ideal state. If you want to experience financial success in the future, you should start preparing now. This book will show you how to do exactly that!"

—Hal Elrod, number one best-selling author of *The Miracle Morning*

"The real beauty of David's system is that the principles apply to scaling your real estate investing business across the board, whether you're looking to pick up a few single-family rentals or acquire large multifamily properties. He systematically disassembles the myths and roadblocks of long-distance real estate investing and in their place provides the path to successfully investing anywhere, whether near or far!"

—Andrew Cushman, real estate investing expert and author on BiggerPockets.com

LONG-DISTANCE REAL ESTATE INVESTING

HOW TO BUY, REHAB, AND MANAGE OUT-OF-STATE RENTAL PROPERTIES

DAVID GREENE

BiggerPockets®
PUBLISHING

Long-Distance Real Estate Investing

David Greene

Published by BiggerPockets Publishing LLC, Denver, CO

Copyright © 2017 by David Greene.

All Rights Reserved.

Publisher's Cataloging-in-Publication data

Names: Greene, David M., author.

Title: Long-Distance real estate investing : how to buy , rehab , and manage out-of-state rental properties / David Greene.

Description: Denver, CO: BiggerPockets Publishing, 2017

Identifiers: ISBN 978-0-9975847-5-2 (pbk.) | 978-0-9975847-6-9 (ebook) | LCCN 2017956004

Subjects: LCSH Real estate investment--United States. | Dwellings--Remodeling. | Dwellings--Remodeling--Planning. | Residential real estate--United States. | House buying--United States. | Rental housing--Management. | Rental hous-ing--Finance. | Real estate management. | BISAC BUSINESS & ECONOMICS / Real Estate / General | BUSINESS & ECONOMICS / Personal Finance / Investing

Classification: LCC HD259 .G74 2017 | DDC 332.63/243--dc23

Published in the United States of America

10 9 8 7 6 5 4 3 2

DEDICATION

For Kyle, my best friend and biggest supporter. You're a lion. For BiggerPockets, because without you, I would never have had the confidence to carve this path, and for GoBundance, whose members encouraged me to think bigger, take more risks, and bet on myself. This is to all those out there who won't accept the status quo and who push the limits of "what's always been."

CONTENTS

CHAPTER 1: **Why Invest Out of State?** 12

    Don't Trust Your Gut 16

    Disrupt the Norm 18

    Investing in Your Own Backyard 20

    The Crop Analogy... 21

CHAPTER 2: **The Power of the Internet** 25

    Finding Homes through the MLS 26

    Finding Property Tax Records 27

    Homeowner's Insurance Online 30

    Ways to Determine an Area's Desirability. 30

    Determining Rental Rates.................................... 34

    Finding Past Permits 35

    Using Your Smartphone to Manage Your Business. 37

    Using Technology to Buy Property Sight Unseen. 38

    Smartphone Apps in Your Business 41

CHAPTER 3: **Rules and Relationships** 46

    Price-to-Rent Ratios 48

    Determine an Area's Price-to-Rent Ratio 50

    Alternative Strategies to Buy-and-Hold 55

    Vacation Rentals 57

    How to Leverage Relationships 58

CHAPTER 4: **The First Members of Your Team** 61

    The Deal Finder 63

    Find High-Producing Agents 64

Agents with a Team 65
Ways to Save Time on Your Search. 69
An Agent and an Investor—My Advice to You 76
The Lender 79
Loans for Investors 83
How to Find a Lender 86
How to Reach Out to Lenders. 88
Alternative Lending Options 91
The Ease of Electronic Payments 93
Supercharging Your Equity Growth, the Easy Way. 94
Electronic Rent Deposits 95
Leveraging Financing 98
Accurately Reporting Rental Income 102

CHAPTER 5: The Rest of Your Team 105
Finding Referrals. 107
What to Ask Before Hiring a Property Manager. 112
How to Negotiate Better Terms 117
Leveraging Your Property Manager's Knowledge 118
The Contractor 120

CHAPTER 6: Understanding Your Market. 135
Tracking Property Values 137
What to Do When Prices Are Rising 138
What to Do When Prices Are Dropping 140
Investing in Down Markets, Wherever They May Be 142
Rental Rates 144
Anticipating Rental Rate Increases 147
Following Employment Trends. 149
Understanding Your Tenant Pool 150

CHAPTER 7: Working with the Market 155
Creating an Apples-to-Apples Comparison. 156
Understanding Return on Equity 159
Timing the Market. 161
The "Headache Factor" and Opportunity Cost. 163
Improving Your Portfolio's Performance. 166
Timing Your Lease Renewals Correctly. 169
Cash for Keys 171
Accept Some Headaches 172
The 1031 Like-Kind Exchange 178

CHAPTER 8: Managing Out-of-State Properties............181

Give Your Contractor Incentive and Maximize Your Results....... 185
Create Accountability through Paying a Bonus 187
Create Accountability through Advertising 188
Paying for Materials Yourself............................... 189
Adding Value by Adding Your Own Time..................... 191
Using Your Contractors' House Accounts to Save You Money..... 194
How to Manage Paying Your Contractor 196
How to Pay Your Contractor 197
The Partnership Mentality 201

CHAPTER 9: Finding Materials............................205

R&D (Rip Off and Duplicate)............................... 207
Finding Design Inspiration 208
Getting Samples from Your Contractor 219
When the Design Idea Is Formed............................ 221
Determining the Value of Upgrades......................... 223
How to "Hack" Your Contractor............................ 230
The Upgrade Hack 231
Four Simple Factors to Determine Value 237
Finance Hacking 244

CHAPTER 10: Maximize ROI................................247

Big Lots Equal Big Opportunity 248
Buying Bad Houses in Nice Areas........................... 252

CHAPTER 11: Tricks to Find More Deals Out of State 259

Real Estate Owned 261
Short Sales 266
NOD 268
Half-Finished Homes 270
Leveraging the Listing Agent 272
Paying Your Real Estate Agent a Bonus 278

CHAPTER 12: The Long-Distance Investor 281

CHAPTER 1

WHY INVEST OUT OF STATE?

Ninety percent of millionaires become so through owning real estate. More money has been made in real estate than in all industrial investments combined. The wise young man or wage earner of today invests his money in real estate.

—ANDREW CARNEGIE

In 1848, Andrew Carnegie immigrated to the United States. As the son of very poor parents, he became one of the first American rags-to-riches stories. Carnegie got his start working in a cotton mill for $1.20 a week and went on to work for a telegraph office and later moved on to the Pennsylvania Railroad.

Smart and hardworking, he began investing in a variety of industries including coal, iron, oil, railroad companies, and a telegraph firm (industries he was familiar with from his past employment). By his early thirties, Carnegie had amassed his first small fortune. This capital was later used to form the Carnegie Steel Company, one of the most dominant businesses the world had ever seen at that time.

Carnegie ran the company successfully until he eventually sold it to a banker for $480 million, making him one of the world's richest men of his time. It allowed him to become the father of philanthropy. He penned "The Gospel of Wealth" and spent the rest of his life giving away the better part of his fortune while living a life many of us aspire to emulate.

It is safe to say Andrew Carnegie dominated the competition in his time. To go from a dirt-poor immigrant to one of the world's richest men is no small feat, and yet with all his experience, success, knowledge, and business brilliance, Carnegie encouraged those who desired to grow their wealth to invest in real estate.

Powerful stuff, right? It's tough to ignore the advice of a man who had seen so much, won so often, and grown to be so large. His quote above saying that more money has been made in real estate than through all industrial investments combined is powerful, and it speaks to the unique ways real estate works to grow wealth. I am one of those examples. Much like Carnegie, my family also emigrated from Scotland, and I worked in several different vocations before I began investing my wages. Like Carnegie, I have invested the profits from my endeavors in real estate for seven years. And I've got to say, it's been one of the very best decisions I have made in my life.

I'm not very big on reinventing the wheel, and I've never been the most creative guy. My skill set is much less exciting, but I am good at being taught how to do something, mastering it, and then finding a more efficient way to do it. Some might call it laziness, but others will say it is industriousness. However you define the motive, the fact remains that I don't like wasting time, money, or effort. You shouldn't either.

How did I get here? I took what I learned and applied it to each job I had, from being a sandwich maker at Togo's, a waiter at steakhouses, a police officer on the streets, and now a real estate agent in California. Part of this process has always been asking, "Why?" Why does everyone do it that way? Why is that the best? The "why" behind the "what" has always fascinated me. If you can understand the "why," the underlying mechanics behind the result, you can find ways to improve your results.

What I've found through every profession, game, challenge, or undertaking is the longer you consistently seek to understand the process, not just the result, the better you will be at understanding patterns that emerge. If you study it long enough and commit to understanding its inner workings, you will start to see these patterns for yourself, and then you can begin to anticipate them and their actions. From there, you can make adjustments to capitalize on these patterns.

We see this phenomena in sports most clearly as rookie mistakes. What we are really referring to is someone's lack of experience causing them to misread or overlook a pattern a more experienced player would have seen, like a quarterback who throws an interception because the safety baited him into believing he was headed in a different direction or the basketball player who gets caught up and chooses to shoot the ball instead of passing it to a wide-open teammate.

Yet for some reason, we don't afford this same process to ourselves as new real estate investors. We expect ourselves to be perfect, to perform as the experienced ones do. When we don't, we quit and assume we just weren't cut out for this. Can you imagine how catastrophic this would be if professional athletes did the same? Peyton Manning would have realized he just threw too many interceptions to be a good quarterback and would never have broken the records he did.

Great players play long enough to allow their brains to start sensing patterns emerging more quickly to anticipate changes and beat the opposition. If you want to be a great investor, you have to go through this same process. You have to make mistakes and commit yourself to a learning process. If you understand the inner workings that make the whole thing tick, that will lead to you gaining the confidence to apply your skills anywhere.

A huge problem for many investors is that their mind is trained to look for reasons *not* to do something, especially with out-of-state investing. They see it as unsafe, unstable, and dangerous, so they don't look much deeper and miss out on all the opportunities it brings to build wealth faster and more efficiently than traditional models.

I am going to discuss the objections, address the valid concerns, answer all the tough questions, and put the outdated and misguided assumptions about out-of-state investing to rest. I'm here to tell you that you can invest out of state in a way that is almost identical to how you invest in your own backyard.

If you are reading this book, it is safe to assume that one of your goals is growing wealth through real estate. As Carnegie said, real estate has created millionaires more than any other profession. You don't have to be a genius or a wealthy hedge fund manager to recognize that real estate is manageable, controllable, and follows patterns. Real estate comes in many shapes and sizes, which can work for anybody.

It's not reinventing the wheel but more so making sure to invest where it makes sense for *you* and your personal situation, not where it's convenient, close, or comfortable. Wealth isn't going to fall in your lap. You have to go build it. If you're going to do that, you need to know where to find it.

Maybe you're at the top of your market. Maybe prices are too high to find rental property. You want to know how to use real estate to grow your wealth when buying in areas that may not be close to you. For years, this has been considered foolish. They have been warned not to set sail for the far end of the sea, for surely they would fall off the other side when they reached the end. The key is, some of us have learned the world isn't flat.

It is wise to listen to the advice of men and women who have gone before you. I also believe we can easily fool ourselves into taking advice from someone who sounds smart but who has no firsthand experience. Don't continue to believe something just because others say it may be so. Don't continue to operate under assumptions that haven't been tested, the "why" behind the "what" that explains how things work.

Let's take a second to explore how out-of-state investing came to be known as risky, why at one time this made perfect sense, and how the world has changed to make this no longer the case.

DON'T TRUST YOUR GUT

Curiosity will conquer fear even more than bravery will.

—JAMES STEPHENS

When I tell people I invest out of state, it almost always elicits a strong reaction. People sit forward in their chairs, adjust their body position, and typically give me their full attention. They want to know how I manage all the tasks that are part of real estate investing. Do I fly out and look at each house? How do I find the contractors? How do I make sure they don't run off with my money? Do I use property management? If I turn the question back on them and ask why they *wouldn't* try out-of-state real estate investing, I'm typically met with a shoulder shrug followed by the response "I don't know, man. I just couldn't buy a house I've never seen."

Everyone says it, but very few of them really know why. Instead, it has just become a mindlessly accepted belief that you need to see a house before you buy it.

The whole thing just feels natural, doesn't it? You have to walk the halls, get a feel for the layout. You want to be excited and feel good about a purchase this big, right? How can you know what you're buying if you don't go look at it? It's just common sense to think that the risk gets bigger the farther away it is from you. The problem is, when I ask people why they believe that, or what they are basing this belief on, they usually can't come up with many objective facts to back it up.

The reality is, people *feel* uncomfortable buying a property they can't see in an area they don't live in, and fear has a lot to do with it. The thing is, you aren't buying a home; you are buying a small business—an investment. There aren't many reasons to feel so afraid if you're looking at things from an investor's perspective. Investors focus on numbers; consumers focus on feelings. Going beyond our gut feelings as real estate investors forces us to get serious about our guidelines.

If you want to get into real estate investing and think your feelings will be a good financial barometer, you are making a rookie mistake. It can be scary, but decisions that once terrified me are now on autopilot. It takes a different level of thinking.

When D.A.R.E., a program with police departments to keep kids off drugs, was popular when I was a student, officers would go to elementary schools and talk to kids about the dangers of drugs and alcohol. One of the more common things they would show us was how hard it is to trust your motor skills when impaired by alcohol. The officers would place a pair of "drunk goggles" on students and then ask them to walk in a straight line. The goggles were designed to filter the image coming through them in a way that confused the students' brains, much as alcohol would. We all laughed hysterically as student after student tried to walk in a straight line wearing the goggles but were unable to, despite their intense focus and effort.

When it came to my turn, I was able to walk the entire line straight from beginning to end without much difficulty because I thought about the solution at a different level. My peers and teachers were amazed and all thought I had some kind of superpower. The officer, however, just smirked and chuckled. He knew exactly what I had done to defeat the system and appear sober. All I had to do was close my eyes. The act of closing my eyes removed the stimulus that would have confused my brain and caused the senses I normally relied on to go haywire. By relying instead on my natural sense of balance controlled by the inner ear, not my eyes, I was able to appear unaffected. Simple, right?

Real estate investing should work this same way. Your emotions are the goggles, and your sense of balance is the numbers you use to evaluate properties. By learning to tune emotions out, you too can walk freely and easily in the world of real estate investing while those around you stumble and fall. It is the act of relying on a different set of parameters than those you are used to that will bring success in this business. It takes the act of faith of closing your eyes and blocking out the senses you have used to make decisions your whole life to reward you with the wealth you seek. If you are relying on the wrong advice, or the wrong senses, you can stumble and fall, setting you back years and erasing hundreds of hours of time and money. Don't fall because you're afraid to close your eyes.

Akira Mori, a wealthy Japanese real estate developer worth approximately $5 billion, has said, "In my experience, in the real estate business, past success stories are generally not applicable to new situations. We must continually reinvent ourselves, responding to changing times with innovative new business models."

The fact is, if simply doing things the same way they have always been done is all it takes to succeed, the same people would be the only ones succeeding. What makes business exciting are the new doors that are opened for those who anticipate changes to the market and get there first. This levels the playing field and lets the new guy have a chance to compete with those who have traditionally dominated the market.

DISRUPT THE NORM

For a long time, investing out of state was incredibly difficult to do. Before the Internet, real estate was run so differently. Real estate brokers wielded intense power because they were the sole gatekeepers to the information. If you wanted to know what was for sale, you had to go to a broker. If you wanted to know the price, pictures, or details of the listing, you needed to ask a broker. If that broker wanted you to buy one of his or her listings first, that's what you were shown. There was no way for people to know what was available to them because the information just wasn't available, and you had to trust the broker. Because brokers controlled the cards, they could very easily mislead clients.

When you asked whether a home was priced fairly, it was very difficult to determine unless you had intimate experience and knowledge of that market. You just had public records kept at the tax assessor's office you would have to go request in person and then read on your own! If you wanted to know what the school rating was like in a neighborhood, you had to actually *know* someone aware of the reputation of the school district.

The same was true for crime stats. If you were looking at a home in a new neighborhood you were unfamiliar with, how would you determine whether it was safe? Would your tenants want to live there? Would your tenants themselves likely be criminals? With no online crime stats to look up, you were more likely to be relying on the information provided to you by your real estate agent or broker.

When people don't have information, they rely on trust. When people rely solely on trust, the odds of being taken advantage of increase exponentially. Unfortunate situations like this led to out-of-state investors being easy targets and getting a bad name.

The whole thing was ripe with opportunity for fraud, and that's exactly what happened. Imagine people buying houses over fair market value because Wisconsin prices seemed cheap to a California buyer or buying homes that needed major repairs because the inspector collaborated with the agent to give less-than-accurate information. People bought in neighborhoods that locals were leaving and in known gang areas because they were shown pictures of beautiful front yards!

Investors had no other way of knowing whether the deal would work. Only those with an inside scoop, or an ally in the area, could really know what they were buying, where they were buying, or who would be living in it. The lack of information created an unfair advantage for anyone who could get accurate information. These were the industry leaders who monopolized the market places and gobbled up all the best deals for themselves. The whole system seemed rigged, and that's exactly why it was wise counsel to tell someone to stay far, far away from out-of-state investing. The Internet and smartphones have changed the game, but not everyone has realized this yet.

Zillow is a great example of this. It's a website that allows homeseekers to search the databases of local multiple listing services (MLSs) to see available properties, pictures, locations, statistical analyses, price estimates of homes for sale, and other pertinent information. Zillow's service is pretty dang simple, but it has revolutionized the way people buy real estate.

Home buyers are no longer captive to brokers who have all the information. Instead, the modern home buyer turns to Zillow and starts looking immediately at what's available to compare the houses in a neighborhood.

If you were a real estate agent who wasn't able to adapt to this new advance in technology, you likely lost a huge percentage of your market share. If you were someone who recognized how powerful and influential Zillow and its competitors became, you likely were at the very front of a huge land grab and made yourself quite a bit of money. The agents who adapted to the new model survived and thrived. The emergence of Zillow in the residential real estate sector changed the entire way business was done when it shifted the rules of the game away from the brokers and toward the clients.

Technology changes things, and using it well wields a weapon that the competition cannot compete with. Learn this. Remember this. Train your mind to look for ways to take advantage of it. We are going to talk a lot about how new technology can assist you in your goal of buying, rehabbing, and managing out-of-state rental property.

INVESTING IN YOUR OWN BACKYARD

"Investing in your own backyard" is another way of saying "investing where you know." It is good, sound advice that you are likely to do better investing in an area you inherently understand. Investing in an area where you live makes things much easier. It's easy to drive by a house, walk by it, and see how it looks. It's easier to feel comfortable with your decision when you know you can drive by every now and then to see that the tenants haven't burned the house to the ground.

There is a very powerful core truth wrapped up in the idea of investing in your own backyard, but the real wisdom is that *you understand the market where you're investing*. It doesn't matter that the area itself is near you; it just matters that you know it! You need to know what you are buying, and you need to know why you are buying it. Good investors understand this, and it is one of the reasons they have been so bearish about out-of-state investing over the years.

Know that different real estate markets behave differently, with their unique pros and cons, strengths and weaknesses, price points, sensitivities to market cycles, and opportunities for investors. It is the wide range of options different markets offer that makes real estate investing such an attractive vehicle for the average Joe. Nearly everyone can find a market that works for his or her situation! Once you realize you don't have to be limited by geography, you can see the true potential that real estate investing can bring to your life.

THE CROP ANALOGY

Think of different real estate markets as different fields to grow crops. Each field has different soil, sunlight, water access, and minerals that determine where which crops will grow best. If you are a farmer and plan to invest in growing a certain kind of crop, it's important to know which crop will grow in the field you own. It would be foolish to plant peas in a field where only corn grows well. "Knowing your own backyard" would serve you well in the sense that you would understand which crop to plant. This would result in a higher likelihood of a successful harvest and an increase in your wealth. Smart farmers know what they can plant and where. But the question is, What if the crops that grow where you live aren't the crops that are selling for much right now?

What if rather than insisting on growing crops only in your own field, you went and rented ground from another farmer in a different area? What if rather than only learning how to grow corn, the lifeblood of your own agricultural area, you studied the underlying fundamentals of farming and learned to plant peas, peach trees, grapes, and many other kinds of crops? What if you realized that the process of growing has similar patterns that emerge no matter what kind of crop you plant?

The wise farmer would surely understand that while different crops require different knowledge to grow, they all follow a similar pattern. They would be able to hire people anywhere, not just in his or her own hometown. A farmer dedicated to the study of agriculture would have full confidence that he or she could do this well. If you studied farming instead of just copying other farmers, you wouldn't hesitate to apply what you'd learned in the areas where it made the most sense to do so.

As real estate investors, we don't plant crops. But we do plant *seeds*, in a sense. Real estate investing is a get-rich-slow game. Each property I buy is purchased with the understanding that I am planting a seed that will someday grow into a large, powerful tree supplying me with more fruit than I'll ever need and giving me the opportunity to plant the seeds it produces. While I typically want to know that that property will be producing for me right out the gate, I don't expect the production to be much. The real value comes years later, when rents have risen, inflation has lifted my property's value, and I've created significant equity by paying down the loan balance. Just like a farmer, I don't plan to harvest my crops when they are young. I will wait for them to mature. Just like a farmer, I don't want to be pigeonholed into growing a specific type of crop because that's all people grow where I live. It's about knowing when and how to diversify.

Don't settle on one backyard. Investing in many backyards is a *great* idea, meant to help you grow wealth strategically. The best real estate investors will invest in areas where demand is growing, not just in what is geographically close. Understanding different areas, emerging markets, and price-to-rent ratios is a crucial aspect to real estate investing well!

I understand the fears, concerns, and worries you may have. I understand the stigma out-of-state investing has earned over the years. But it's different now. We have resources, content, and a brand-new system with which to buy real estate that we didn't have before. Keep an open mind as I walk you through exactly how I buy, rehab, and manage out-of-state investment property.

If you want to build wealth, buying real estate is the best way to do it. If you want to build that wealth faster than everyone else, combining different real estate investing strategies like flipping, buy-and-hold rentals, and anticipating/reacting to market changes will enable you to enjoy the best that each aspect has to offer while avoiding the worst. Don't be an investor who just plants a seed, walks away, and comes back thirty years later to see what the tree looks like. Be an investor who diligently studies what to grow, where to grow it, and how to hire field hands to do so.

It doesn't matter where you started. What matters is what you do and where it takes you. I'll show you how to put out-of-state teams together to work on the properties you buy to make a profit. I'll tell you how to use modern technology to make the entire process feel seamless and efficient, how to figure out where to buy, what strategies to use for different markets, and how to know when it's time to pack up and move on before the market changes. Once all of this is done, I'll give you some great tips on how to learn your market so you can maximize the value the area provides and help you get the very most out of the money you spend by doing so. By the time you finish this book, you will know how to buy, rehab, and manage out-of-state rentals and flipping opportunities.

I'll also teach you a lot about the different jobs you can hire, from the agent to the property manager to the contractor and everybody in between. You will understand how to keep them happy, how to manage them well, how to get the best workers, and how to keep them once you find them. As you progress through your career, you should be able to open this book, find help, advice, and guidance on whichever aspect of investing you are struggling with. It is my hope that once you realize how different real estate is from what it used to be, you will also realize how many opportunities are available to you that you never knew existed.

I started investing in out-of-state properties because I had no choice. Properties in my own backyard had appreciated to the point that they no longer cash-flowed positively. I had no idea what I was onto when I first began looking at out-of-state property, buying it, rehabbing it, and then renting it out.

What began as something I thought was a necessity became something I've become extremely excited about. It ended up making me a millionaire by the age of thirty, without my realizing it was happening! The potential to buy in different markets and enjoy the fruits of those markets' strengths opened up doors for me I never thought were possible. With that came exciting opportunity! I can now flip houses in one area and use the proceeds to buy high-cash-flowing properties in another. I can ride the cycles of the coastal markets, buying at the bottom and then selling at the top only to move my capital gains to a more stable market. I can take risks in buying property as appreciation plays out because I know I have strong cash-flowing properties to prop me up and mitigate the risk elsewhere. Once you understand the fundamentals of real estate investing, you'll learn to apply them anywhere.

When you invest in real estate, you build wealth in your sleep. You build it while you're working at creating other wealth. You build it while you're on vacation and when you're working out at the gym. Like many of you, I have worked nothing but blue-collar jobs and had no advantage, nobody to give me a hand out, and very few mentors during the process. When I bought my first rental property, I unknowingly backed into the most powerful wealth-building vehicle I would ever find and started a journey I would later come to love. In my opinion, it is the very best means of creating wealth for an average Joe like me.

I want to teach you how to do exactly what I did. While working a full-time job over ninety hours a week for several years, I was able to build a portfolio of over twenty-five rental properties with several millions of dollars in equity. During this process, I learned how to work as efficiently as possible, how to leverage technology to work for me, how to hire people to do things better than I could, and how to build a network of "team members" actively looking for deals and working on my behalf.

During this journey, I learned a lot of things the hard way and paid a price. Let me shorten that learning curve for you to achieve the same success I now have in much less time. Real estate is an incredibly powerful vehicle to build wealth, create passive income, and take control of your life. I know that not everyone lives in an ideal market to get started. Don't make excuses to not move forward—make progress toward your goal of financial freedom!

Landlords grow rich in their sleep without working, risking, or economizing.

—JOHN STUART MILL

CHAPTER 2

THE POWER OF THE INTERNET

Knowledge is of two kinds. We know a subject ourselves, or we know where we can find information on it.

—SAMUEL JOHNSON

The Internet is amazing. There was a time when we needed to know smart people, wise people, to gather valuable information. Now we just need Google. While experience is still the best teacher, Google isn't a bad substitute when investing in real estate presents a unique set of challenges. From finding deals to finding people to manage your deals, the Internet can help you do it all. If I want to reach out and talk to an expert, it can be as close as a Google search and an e-mail.

The Internet has also allowed the ability to buy and manage houses thousands of miles away from you. The fact that the Internet is growing so rapidly, apps are springing up left and right, and more and more businesses are being taken online is what makes out-of-state investing not only possible but also nearly identical in many aspects to traditional real estate investing in your own backyard. When it comes to new opportunities, the Internet has opened doors many people haven't realized. I'm hoping to open your eyes to just how manageable out-of-state investing can be, show you how I do it, and encourage you to do the same if it's right for you.

This allows you to systematically grow your wealth by investing in the markets that work best for your objectives—not the markets that are geographically close to you. We live in an amazing world, and it's time we started learning about and benefiting from all of it, not just the part we happened to be raised in!

FINDING HOMES THROUGH THE MLS

When searching for homes to buy, the most common and simplest method to use is a multiple listing service. Realtors and real estate agents use different regional MLSs to showcase their properties for sale. Putting a property for sale on the MLS allows all the other real estate agents to see it is available, what it looks like, and other pertinent information. These agents then forward these properties to their clients. This is how the majority of homes are sold in the United States.

The MLS is the largest, most convenient, and most commonly used method for buying properties by far. Popular websites like Zillow, Trulia, and Movoto get their information by pulling it from an MLS, regurgitating it, and displaying it in their unique format. This information is then disseminated through the Internet as home buyers search the popular sites for pictures, prices, and other information.

Believe it or not, there was a time when if you wanted to see what homes were for sale, you had to make an appointment with an agent who had access to the MLS and go look at a big book full of listings! Now we can see everything we need from the convenience of our living room, bed, car, or office. This means we have access to insane amounts of homes for sale that we can look at anytime, anywhere, in almost any way we prefer. Furthermore, technology like GPS recognition allows the mobile sites you're looking at on your phone to know exactly where you are and shows you homes for sale in your area. On vacation and want to know what the beachfront properties are going for? Pull out your phone and open an app. It's really that easy these days. Anywhere you go, at any time, you can see what homes are selling for and begin your process of getting a feel for the market.

If you're using a real estate agent (which most investors do), you can have a custom search for homes that meet your specific criteria sent directly to your e-mail inbox. The MLS is at your fingertips! Many searches can be set up so you, the client, receive an e-mail from your agent's MLS system the second a new property hits the market. It doesn't matter where you are or what you're doing; as long as your phone has reception, the MLS can find you.

FINDING PROPERTY TAX RECORDS

In addition to the MLS, you can also access property tax records directly from the Internet. Property taxes are one of the bigger expenses in real estate investing, and they really do matter. If you want to know what the property taxes were for any given property last year, you can usually find this information by plugging in a few numbers in a county's tax assessor's website. If this is too cumbersome for you, sites like Zillow will report a property's tax info right there on the page! Forget the time when you needed to know an expert in the field to look at a map and tell you what the property tax rates were for specific parts of town. The Internet makes it as readily accessible as finding a recipe or directions to a baseball game.

Property taxes are one of the easiest expenses to account for, yet they frequently get overlooked and miscalculated more often than any other predictable expense. Let me give you a real-life example of what I'm talking about:

The very first home I ever bought (you can hear my story on the BiggerPockets podcast number 169 for more info) had higher property taxes than I had anticipated. My agent didn't tell me about them, and I didn't know what to look for when signing the Housing and Urban Development (HUD) paperwork. This is not an excuse, but it did teach me a valuable lesson. When I did my initial "due diligence," I basically asked my dad what he paid in property taxes. Because this house was about the same size as his, I ignorantly assumed the taxes would be comparatively equal. What initially appeared to be really good cash flow turned out to just be marginally good after the extra costs were accounted for. At the time, I didn't know what I was getting into. I didn't know how much property taxes were or even that there was more than one kind! Imagine my surprise when the bank collecting my mortgage sent me a bill for almost $300 more than what I was anticipating!

Property taxes aren't all created the same. Different areas can attach different taxes to properties in their jurisdiction. You want to know what these are before you commit to buying to make sure your expenses are as low as you're expecting them to be. California passed a bill (commonly referred to as Proposition 13) that prevents the government from collecting more than 1 percent of a property's assessed value in taxes each year. Sounds good, right? In theory, it is. Knowing this, I budgeted to pay 1 percent of the price I paid for the property every year to cover my property taxes. It worked for my dad, right? The problem was, I didn't know what I didn't know, and nobody told me. Turns out the house I bought was built in a development where the home builder had borrowed money to build the infrastructure and that money had to be paid back over the years by the homeowners.

That's right. The builder borrowed money to build the roads, sidewalks, streetlights, sewers, and water lines. The money, collected as a bond, was paid back by the homeowners every year and collected along with the property taxes. Of course, this was disclosed to me when signing my closing paperwork, but in California, we sign a stack of papers thick enough to stop a bullet. I had missed it, nobody had bothered to tell me about it, and I felt like a moron.

To make sure I didn't make that mistake again, I learned how to use my county's tax assessor's website to check on the property taxes for a specific property I was considering. Goodbye, ignorance; hello, information! If you're using a real estate agent on a deal, he or she likely knows how to check this information out for you, but you still need to know to ask! When going to these websites, be prepared—they are the tech equivalent of a bran muffin—boring, dry, but full of fiber. You are going to find them a little redundant and not user friendly.

Don't let this stop you. Once you learn the unique vocabulary for the county you are looking at, it shouldn't be too difficult to navigate the site and find what you need.

Each state may do things a little differently, but a property's tax statement in California spells out what my 1 percent of the value of the property will be (split into two payments paid every six months) near the top. Below that, the individual "assessments" are spelled out. This is the section where you will find the different amounts you will need to pay for different public projects the government undertakes and then collects from homeowners to fund. Some of the more popular fees in my area are taxes to pay for schools that have been built, parks, roadways, levies for flood control, mosquito control, the bonds taken out by home builders I mentioned earlier, and special voter-approved taxes to pay for more firefighters, police, and other community services.

The moral of the story? Use this easy-access technology to find out exactly what kind of property taxes you'll be paying before you buy the house. Better yet, look them up before you even begin a search in a specific area! If you know from the get-go that a specific neighborhood pays a lot of extra taxes (bonus tip—most of these higher taxes are in new home developments, not the older areas of town), you can avoid searching for properties in these areas from the start. Target the areas with the lowest overall expenses, and see your cash flow increase and the demand for your property in the future rise faster than in the areas with higher taxes.

All these public records are now being made available on government websites, and you don't even have to spend your gas to drive to the city/county offices to look them up! You can literally save the website of the county you are interested in as a favorite on your web browser and be one click away from all the property tax info you need.

HOMEOWNER'S INSURANCE ONLINE

In addition to property taxes, you'll also want to know how to determine your homeowner's insurance. There are several ways to do this that don't take much time.

My favorite method is to fire off an e-mail to my insurance agent with the property address and my specific desires, like the largest deductible possible. With so much information available on the Internet these days, your agent can often get the answers to the questions off popular sites. If there is anything he or she can't answer, a quick phone call to you with a list of questions is usually all that's needed to get a quote. If you're just starting out, you may want to call several different insurance agencies to look for the most competitive quote.

In addition to speaking with an agent, there are several other methods you can use. If you're not a phone person, you can easily find sites that provide online quotes for insurance purposes. Simply entering "homeowner's insurance Atlanta" into a search engine will give you a full page of names and phone numbers for insurance agencies in the area. While that can actually be useful, I prefer a different route. If you scroll about halfway down the page, you'll likely find a blog or a website with reviews of the "best" insurance companies in that region, with comparisons and a lot of research done for you. If I Google "investor homeowner's insurance Atlanta," I am even more likely to find reviews or blog posts of insurance specifically tailored toward investors.

Read just one comparison review of five insurance companies, and call the ones that got the highest reviews! The Internet is making it almost too easy to find the pieces you'll need to put this puzzle together—even if you have no assistance from others or experience in finding these kinds of services.

WAYS TO DETERMINE AN AREA'S DESIRABILITY

Another huge factor you'll want to consider before buying something in an area you aren't as familiar with is the desirability of the property. Owning a rental property doesn't do you any good if people don't want to rent it. While the best information is always going to come from someone with intimate knowledge of the area (like a real estate agent or a property manager), sites like Zillow and Trulia can help you with determining walk scores, school district scores, and crime stats. While I never rely solely on this information, it is very helpful for fact-checking info provided to me by different property managers or agents.

SCHOOL RANKINGS

For instance, if I ask a property manager what the schools are like in an area, and he or she tells me they are top-notch, it would raise some red flags if Trulia shows the schools are ranked very low. The same would go for crime stats and public transportation availability. I don't want to buy in a high-crime area. I've found the juice just isn't worth the squeeze. However, agents looking for a quick deal might tell me something different. I don't want to buy in an area with low-ranking schools either. The worse a property's school rank, the less chance I'll have of seeing good long-term appreciation. Property managers desperate to lock up my business might focus on the one property that did well in an area known for high crime or bad schools versus the many that are problematic. Many times, it's just human nature to look for a way to justify something when you want it bad enough.

Lucky for me, one quick web search can give me more information than I need to verify whether the intel being given to me is accurate. And this, folks, is the beauty of how the Internet can help you get a good idea of an area's desirability. I don't rely on the information that popular websites provide as my main source, but it does come in very handy when trying to determine whether the information being provided by outside vendors is accurate.

WALK SCORE

Properties in big cities or major urban areas will often have a rental demand that is determined in large part by their walk score, though it won't apply to every property you buy. Walk scores are concepts that became very popular around 2013, when people started leaving suburban areas for smaller, more humble dwellings closer to city centers. As more people wanted to be closer to local businesses, restaurants, friends, and their jobs, the need for cars became significantly less. Often, it's difficult to find parking anyway, so these areas became known for the value they provided by reducing the need for private transportation. Bus routes, bike lanes, and public transit all became much more desired as people ditched the gas-guzzler and car insurance to save money by living in smaller properties in the inner city.

This opened the door for websites like WalkScore.com to provide data to help potential homeowners or tenants determine how friendly an area was for those without a personal vehicle. WalkScore will give you a number (with a perfect score being 100) that corresponds to how friendly the area is for walking, biking, or commuting. Simply typing in the address to the search bar at the top of the page will give you a quick-and-easy way to see what your tenants or future home buyers will be looking at when they research your place.

If you're considering buying a property in a large city or a densely populated area, I recommend using the Internet to search sites like WalkScore to help determine how friendly the area is for those without a car. You should be looking because your potential tenants most likely will be too.

CRIME STATS

Crime and investing do not mix, and it's a harsh reality that many investors have learned the hard way. This is especially true when you are investing out of state and will not have direct contact with the tenants or direct access to see who's going in and out of your property. Property managers will handle your property for you, but they won't be going by your place every week.

High crime leads to lots of problems in real estate investing. It's tough for your tenants to pay the rent when they are in jail. It's tougher still to pay the rent when your car has been stolen out of your driveway and you have no way to get to work. According to many police departments, high crime is often associated with drug use, and drug use provides a strong correlation between property crimes like auto thefts and home burglaries. Even if your tenants are hardworking, honest folks, it's too easy for them to get distracted by problems with their kids or family. In addition to the added headache of trying to be a landlord in this environment, you should also consider that there will be a much smaller pool of interested buyers when you decide to sell your property.

Lucky for you, many police departments are making crime data available to the public. Online real estate sites can mine this data and post the information on their websites—often in the form of crime ratings. Some sites will also provide a list of the actual calls for service that a police department receives. While you may think all crime is bad crime, I can tell you from firsthand experience that there is a big difference between the nuisance calls for things like barking dogs and disturbing the peace and the ones for more serious crimes like robbery and shots fired. By seeing an actual list of reported crimes, you can get a much better feel for the temperature of a neighborhood's crime patterns.

Another helpful tool is Trulia's crime Heat Maps, which put together a map to provide a quick visual portrayal of crime that is easy to interpret and universally understood (plus they're free). You can avoid the "hot" areas (areas portrayed in red and orange) and stick to the "cool" areas (green) to get a really good idea of what kind of neighborhood your property resides in.

For so long, out-of-state investing was tough to master because when you bought a house somewhere you were unfamiliar with, you had no idea what you were buying into. Technology is now improving to the point that you can be so informed, it's hard to be caught off guard. I'm not talking about expensive websites available only to licensed professionals or high-net-worth individuals or complicated web pages that only computer geeks and hackers can understand; it's stuff your grandma can use. These websites were made for people who don't know anything about technology. They offer efficient, simple, and impressive ways to acquire the information you need to put yourself at ease.

You can use this same technology to see maps of commute times, schools, and proximity to amenities like grocery stores and banks. Getting a good idea for the makeup of a potential neighborhood you'd like to invest in is great, but when you're looking for an area in which to buy rental property, there is another factor that makes a pretty big difference in your overall success—the rents!

DETERMINING RENTAL RATES

In addition to using the Internet to help you determine what a property will cost to own, use it to calculate rent. While property managers will typically be your most accurate source of information, I find they are often overly optimistic in order to secure your business or not aggressive enough if they want to make their job easier and don't think you know any better. The same can be true for agents, wholesalers, and anyone else with skin in the game when it comes to encouraging you to buy something. You want to trust the experts, but you also want to make sure those experts aren't selling you a false bill of goods.

Rentometer.com has become my go-to tool when it comes to getting a rough idea of what I can expect for rent on any property I'm evaluating. Rentometer compiles large amounts of information on what other renters are paying for their properties in relation to the number of bedrooms and puts that information together for you to access. By plugging in my property's address and number of bedrooms, I can get a quick rundown of the average rent, median rent, and a map of surrounding properties. Sometimes this map even provides the full address of the comparable properties, and I can use that address to see pictures of the houses that are owned by my competition. If the property I'm looking at is in better condition and in a comparable area, I can usually assume I will get at least the same rent that those houses do. Think Zillow's Zestimates but for rent.

Once I've checked out Rentometer, my next stop is Craigslist.org. By searching for homes for rent in an area similar to your subject property's, you can get an even better idea of what others are paying for rent and what types of properties are available. Curious about the vacancy periods for a two-bedroom unit in an area? E-mail some of the people with homes listed for rent and ask them how long the properties have been vacant. Want to know how many renters are actively searching for somewhere to live? Ask how much activity their rental is getting. If you find out the people with houses for rent are struggling to get them rented, that's your first clue not to buy in the area. If you keep checking and never see the same property available for more than a week, that's a good sign that the neighborhood is experiencing a lot of demand and units are going fast. While Rentometer is the fastest,

Craigslist is the most detailed. By combining these two resources, I can usually get a really good idea of what to expect. This helps in determining whether I want to pursue opportunities in this area, but it also helps to determine whether the numbers I'm being provided are accurate and trustworthy.

If you're partial to Zillow, you can also find quick-and-easy rent estimates there. You'll find the rent estimate right between the Zestimate and the Zestimate forecast. Just by following the examples I've given you so far, you can get a clear picture of what the market is like in a city you're considering investing in. What's more, everything I've talked about can be done from practically anywhere. This due diligence is made very easy by way of the Internet, which has opened doors that investors would have never dreamed were possible fifteen years ago.

I will add a disclaimer that the best information comes from people, not websites. I'm going to show you exactly how to find those people and pick their brains to get the intel you need to buy the properties you want throughout this book. However, when some of this information is available so easily, don't waste the opportunity to fact-check what the "experts" tell you. There's no excuse to blindly follow advice, especially when it's so easy to see for yourself.

FINDING PAST PERMITS

When buying rental property, you're often looking at older homes that haven't held up well, need work, or aren't as desirable as the bright shiny new homes being built across town. This is the reality of our situation, and it's not a bad thing. Finding homes in some sort of distress is what enables us to buy them below market value and add equity to them through quality rehab work.

The problem is, you don't always know what's been done to the house, how the work was handled, or when it was completed. A beautiful new roof could have been installed the previous year, but the homeowners didn't have it inspected by the county—leaving you with a ticking time bomb. The bottom line is that you want to know what was done to the house and whether it was done professionally. The Internet can help with that too.

Many counties keep a website with a public record of permits that were pulled, just as with property taxes. Take Florida, for example. I want to check how old the roof is because of the heavy rain season that causes roofs to wear out faster. I can look up the permits for that property in the North Florida county website. This problem isn't unique to Florida either. Other issues to look for: problems with snow sitting on roofs or plumbing freezing in the cold temperatures on the East Coast and HVAC problems in hot Arizona. When these problematic areas haven't been updated, you can rest assured it's only a matter of time before you, the new owner, will be replacing them.

Still worried about buying because the property isn't in your backyard? This may change your perspective. If a house is right down the street, you may fall prey to the temptation to drive by the house just to see it. People love the emotional comfort that comes from being able to drive past a house and see that it is indeed still standing. I prefer the comfort that comes from research and objective facts uncovered by using websites to confirm what was done.

Think about how much wiser it is to research what work was done rather than walking a house with an untrained mind and giving it the "eye test." Sure, those roof beams look solid. But can you really testify that you are trained and skilled in the art of visually determining the structural stability of roof beams? Or do you just feel better because the wood doesn't look too old? In my opinion, it's a much better system to research the work previously done to a property through city/county archives and see what work was done by a licensed professional and what was done by a self-proclaimed handyman before you buy the property.

If we are being honest, what excuse do we have to not consider this stuff when it's so readily accessible? You don't need to know a contractor anymore to go by the house and tell you whether the work appears permitted. All you need to do is check the county website with public records of permits and see for yourself whether the seller is shooting straight with you or blowing smoke.

THE INTERNET CHEAT SHEET
1. Use popular websites like Zillow and Trulia to get a basic idea of what home and rent prices are like in an area that interests you.
2. Use popular websites and county tax assessor websites to get detailed information on what to expect for property taxes, one of your biggest expenses.
3. Use online quotes and e-mails with insurance agents to quickly determine homeowner's insurance rates.
4. Use popular websites to fact-check information provided from property managers on crime rates, walkability, school district scores, and more.
5. Use websites like Rentometer and Zillow to help you get a general idea of what rental rates are like.

USING YOUR SMARTPHONE TO MANAGE YOUR BUSINESS

It's hard to believe now, but there was actually a time when if you wanted to talk to someone on the phone, you had to make an appointment so you could both be ready and waiting near a landline to have the conversation. Can you imagine how inefficient that must have been? Today, it's all different with the smartphone. I'm often waiting at an open house for clients to walk in while talking on the phone with another agent about an offer he or she wants to make and simultaneously firing off text messages with questions about a rehab project, reading e-mails about construction bids, and watching a video of the interior of a house a wholesaler wants me to buy. It probably sounds as if I'm exaggerating. I'm not.

Real estate is a fast-paced environment, and the best deals always go quickly. Most people vastly underestimate the value of their smartphone, how much money it can make for them, and the ability it allows them to multitask. In the last section, we talked about how increasing your confidence through knowledge increases your success. In this section, I'm going to show you how to use your phone to increase productivity.

USING TECHNOLOGY TO BUY PROPERTY SIGHT UNSEEN

In investing, what is comfortable is rarely profitable.

—ROBERT ARNOTT

I have never seen in person most of the houses I have bought. A common question I'm asked is how I know whether the property really exists or how I feel comfortable buying something I can't drive by or touch. While the truth is I know it exists because my agent, contractor, property manager, and lender all verify it does, the quick answer I usually give people is I know it exists because I have seen videos of it. Humans are emotional creatures. Like it or not, that's how it works. A popular maxim I've learned in real estate is "Information makes people think; emotion makes them act."

There is something about seeing a picture or a video that puts people at ease. How a house looks from a visual perspective theoretically doesn't matter. If the house doesn't look nice, you're probably going to fix that through the rehab. If it does, it still doesn't matter because someone else will be living there. Your physically seeing that property does nothing to make it more profitable, make your numbers look better, or make your investment safer. That doesn't stop you from wanting to see it, though. You'll just feel better when you do.

I've accepted this fact, and now I'm 100 percent comfortable with buying a property I've never seen in person. What I've learned is that pictures, and specifically video, from a smartphone are a more-than-sufficient substitute for my physically being there. I'm constantly hounding contractors to take more pictures and video because I know that other than for my personal comfort, there are many purposes they will serve. Below are some of the common ways you can use video taken of your rehab project to benefit your business.

THE BIG PICTURE

The main benefit of video is to get an idea of what a property looks like to help me determine the repairs or upgrades I want to make. While looking at the property can help me come up with ideas, there's no reason I need to physically be there to do it. A walk-through video supplemented with individual pictures of specific areas does just fine. Another reason a video of the house is of benefit to me is to serve as proof the contractor did the work I paid for. The contractor won't mind taking thirty seconds to show off his or her handiwork. Plus, my contractor is already taking pictures to show other clients how great the work is. If your contractor won't send you pictures or videos, there is something fishy going on.

Another benefit video can serve in your project is to document each step of the process. By showing several videos highlighting each step of the rehab process, you have a technological timeline to show prospective buyers or tenants just how the project came along. This technological trail can serve as powerful marketing material to show prospective tenants or buyers what their property looked like before and after it was upgraded. It provides history, and everyone likes that.

In addition to documenting the rehab project, I also have my agent, wholesaler, or deal finder send me a video of the property he or she is presenting. The process is simple. I just ask my rep to start on the sidewalk in front of the property, start the video, and walk the exterior of the home before entering. As my agent or wholesaler walks the house while recording it with a smartphone, I have him or her audibly point out the features of the home I should take notice of, the areas I may miss, and the problem areas I will want to note for later. Take a second to think about how much information this presents:

1. The "flow" of the home. This showcases areas where space may

not be utilized most effectively, features that may turn off tenants or future home buyers, or extra walls that don't serve a useful purpose.

2. Areas of the house that are connected to one another. While still pictures highlight individual areas, they don't show the relationship between areas and what walls or spaces they share. Knowing you can turn a den into a bedroom is nice. Seeing the video that shows the den abuts to a guest bathroom really helps determine the viability of strategic rehab planning.

3. The overall impression of the home. The way the home strikes me will be the same way it will strike the people walking in to buy or rent it once it's finished.

4. The areas that need to be fixed and where they are located in the house so that info can be passed on to the contractor.

5. The ability to forward the video in a matter of seconds to the property manager, contractor, and anyone else who is involved in the process. Now they instantly have all the same information listed above. Think about how much faster and more effective that is than trying to describe in a phone call what the agent told you about the place.

BATTLING THE BUGS

Bottom line: Video is powerful. As investors, we gather information, run that information through our specific criteria, and make a yes-or-no decision based on the outcome of that evaluation. However, while video is powerful, it's not perfect, and there can be bugs. A common one is when your phone struggles with memory issues or displaying certain video files. When that happens, ask the sender to post the video on YouTube and send you the link instead. Another irritation is when your phone won't let you send an entire video because the size is too large. When this happens, you can choose to send the video in several parts or use the same YouTube trick. Learn to let technology do the heavy lifting for you. You won't regret it.

USING YOUR SMARTPHONE

Are you one of those people who don't have enough time to put the work or due diligence into investing wisely? I've spent the past three years averaging ninety-plus hours a week working. I had to in order to get my investing business off the ground. While it's true I don't have kids to take up my time and attention, it's also true that many of you reading this aren't as busy as you believe.

I found a way to take very small chunks of time, communicate with the people I needed to, and then check in later when I had another small chunk of free time. You may prefer speaking on the phone and trying to hash out as much as possible at one time, but that isn't the most effective way to communicate. If you were to break down each phone call you were on, you would find a pattern they all tend to follow.

First, there is the obligatory greeting where you say hello and ask totally unrelated questions to the purpose of the phone call: "How are you?" and "What's been new?" and "Did you hear about ...?" are all totally unnecessary, waste-of-time statements that we all make so we don't appear rude. These take up a significant amount of time in each phone call but offer very little value toward accomplishing your purpose.

Then you look for a transition into the topic you called about. Sometimes this doesn't come easy. Once you've done that, you can finally ask the question you needed the answer to. When you've obtained that information, you now need to look for a non-awkward way to get off the phone without appearing rude or as if you just used someone. All this time adds up, especially considering you'll be making several calls a day trying to get the information you need to make wise, informed decisions.

Sound familiar? While I'm portraying this in a somewhat harsh manner, the fact is, at certain points in the day, you just do not have time for the culturally acceptable phone call, and you need to obtain or convey information in a fast, efficient way that requires minimal attention. This is where text messaging comes in handy. It is a far more effective means of communication to quickly get the information you need without the conversational greetings that a phone call might require.

SMARTPHONE APPS IN YOUR BUSINESS

Smartphone apps can be powerful little widgets when you know which ones you need and how to use them. In addition to the calculator app, there are several others I use on a daily or weekly basis to help me accomplish various tasks necessary for real estate investing.

One of my all-time favorite apps is called Mortgage Calculator Plus. This app allows me to enter a mortgage amount, interest rate, and amortization and quickly see exactly what my mortgage will be. I help clients calculate the payment for a house they want to buy in a snap. I compare different interest rates for financing options in a matter of seconds to determine how much of a difference that half a percent will make. With a few taps on my screen, I can have whatever I need to fill in the mortgage portion of a spreadsheet analyzer.

You can also see the full amortization schedule over the life of your loan so you know just how much of your payment goes to principal and how much goes to interest (this matters, trust me). I can also find out how quickly I'll pay off a loan if I add an extra amount to the payments, how much total interest I'll pay over the life of a loan, and how my payments will be affected if I make them weekly, biweekly, monthly, quarterly, or yearly.

Another app I love is called JotNot Pro, and it makes my life so much easier for just a few dollars. JotNot allows me to take pictures of paper files and converts them to other various formats, like PDFs. Once the file has been converted, I have the option of e-mailing it, printing it, faxing it, opening it with an app, or saving it to my cloud.

Imagine how easy this makes filling out all the forms you need to sign in real estate. I am frequently e-mailed by real estate agents and told I need to sign a form and get it back to them, sometimes immediately. With JotNot, I never need to go running for a fax machine. If a "wet signature" is needed, I can print out the document, sign it, and then take a picture with JotNot and convert it to a PDF. Once it's converted, I can e-mail it to anyone I want.

I also have an app for DocuSign on my phone. With DocuSign, I can open a form (from either my e-mail or photos on my smartphone), add an electronic signature/date/initials, and then send that form back to whoever needs it. As an agent, I can use this same app to send documents to my clients for signatures. When I'm told I need a wet signature, I use JotNot. When I don't, I use DocuSign. These two apps alone can handle pretty much any signature I need to give.

At some point, you'll find there are some signatures you need a notary to view, and the official documents need to be mailed. Fear not, technology can help here too. Some mobile notaries now use Skype to watch you sign the document without having to be there personally. While the specific laws and requirements of each area vary, there are often ways you can leverage technology to save you time and increase value to your business.

To keep track of all my properties, I use an app called Numbers (if you aren't a Mac user, Google Sheets or Excel works in a similar way). Numbers is a spreadsheet maker that can assist you in all kinds of ways. Prefer to use spreadsheets instead of the napkin method to calculate the potential returns on your properties? Numbers allows you to create a spreadsheet in five minutes that you can use to plug in your mortgage, tax, insurance, property manager's fees, homeowner's association (HOA) fees, vacancy, repairs, and whatever other expenses you have. Once you've saved the spreadsheet with the necessary formulas, it's as simple as plugging in the numbers and seeing what the return on investment (ROI) spits out.

But wait, there's more! Numbers isn't good for just calculating returns; I also use it to keep track of every single property I own. I've created a Numbers spreadsheet with spaces for every single expense on every single property. At a glance, I can open the app, look at a specific property, and know exactly what my property taxes, insurance, or water bill is. I use this same spreadsheet to calculate each property's ROI, as well as the return on equity (ROE) (we'll talk more about that later—you'll love it). I can also update the app with my property's current value and how much I owe on each loan. This allows me to program a slot to have each property's equity available at a glance. With one look after opening this app, I can see:

- What the total equity is in all real estate owned
- Which properties are performing best
- What was paid for each property
- How much has been paid on each property
- What the ROI is for each property
- How much extra is paid toward the principal for each property
- The current value of each property

Another app I love is a voice recording app called Rev. It allows you to record messages and label them to listen to later. One thing new investors never take into consideration is how many properties they will be looking at and evaluating, as well as how hard it can be to remember which info went with each property. I use Rev to make a recording of everything I'm thinking about when evaluating a property. Once I've made the recording, I save it with the address of the property as the name. This makes it super-easy to connect each property with the notes I've made about it in my mind. The less you have in your brain, the less stressed you'll feel while trying to remember everything. You'll come to value this when things pick up.

I also use my free Keller Williams home search app to find the price of nearby homes or search for homes available in specific areas I'm interested in.

When you combine just these apps I've mentioned, you have nearly everything you need to make it happen in real estate from the seat of your car.

THE CLOUD

An awesome and powerful feature of smartphones is their ability to connect to other devices through cloud technology. While the name sounds cool and modern, all it really means is information storage for the Internet. Cloud technology allows your smartphone to share information with other devices like your desktop computer, laptop, and tablet. The effortless sharing of information means you need to enter info only one time and can then view it from any device connected to the cloud. This technology makes your job organized, informed, and much easier.

If you use an iPhone, your apps will update on your Apple computer or iPad as well. It's very nice having all your info available to you anytime, anywhere. I would be completely lost without this technology to keep track of all my properties and help me determine which ones are performing best. In a matter of seconds, I can confirm what rent I'm getting for a property, compare it with the rent that Rentometer. com shows I should be getting, send a text to my property manager to ask whether we can raise the rent on the next lease, and then sign a lease for the new rent through DocuSign and e-mail it back to the manager. This entire process uses five different sources of technology, all available on my smartphone, and can be completed in about a minute through the cloud. Smartphones have truly opened doors the past generation would have killed for. If you're not getting the most out of your phone, you are leaving precious time on the table. Time is money, so step it up.

Never before in history has innovation offered promise of so much to so many in so short a time.

—BILL GATES

CHAPTER 3

RULES AND RELATIONSHIPS

If you don't have a competitive advantage,
don't compete.

—JACK WELCH

While it is obviously important to know that the area you are planning to invest in has a healthy economy, increasing housing demand, appeal to tenants, and likelihood to grow, it is even more important to have a competitive advantage in the market you choose. Real estate investing is about finding deals, plain and simple. You make your money when you buy. It has always been this way, and it won't change. The entire investing process should be viewed from the perspective of trying to lose as little equity as possible from when you purchased the property. Think of it this way: When you purchase a property at a great price, you fill up a bucket with water (your equity). This water is your reward for doing the work of finding a great property and having the means with which to purchase it. This water is the whole point. You should be protecting this water with everything you've got! The process of making your investment "rent ready" should be done by trying to spill as little of this water in the bucket as possible throughout the rehab process. The water you have left over in the bucket when you're finished is the equity you have left in the property itself. The more water you're left with, the better you've done. The more properties you buy, and buckets you fill, the larger your portfolio will grow, and the greater your wealth will become. If you think about it, the most efficient investors are those who have learned how to:

- Find properties below market value
- Prepare those properties to be rented or sold by adding the most value for the least money

When taking that into consideration, it's crucial you have a competitive advantage in your business.

As an investor, you're the captain of your team, and your main goal should be finding quality efficiently. Perfect the process of investing and developing a system to allow you to replicate this process with speed and ease. That starts with having people in place who can find you great deals, rehab for great prices, offer great financing terms, and manage efficiently and wisely. Paying full price in a great area won't build wealth as fast as getting a great deal in a good area. Those who excel at this process have the opportunity to find success! Compare this to those who simply pay the asking price for a standard home in an area they love. The latter group will typically have to wait much longer to see their wealth grow.

As you grow in influence, skill, and knowledge, you will get better at anticipating which areas are likely to grow and be the next big thing. While it's an incredible benefit to know how to determine which areas you want to be buying in before the crowd figures it out, it really does you no good if you don't know how to put a team in place to capitalize on these opportunities. If you can learn how to build an out-of-state team, which you will learn how to do in this book, you can confidently pursue opportunities anywhere and know your investment will likely pay off.

It's exciting to realize how this machine can sustain itself and build wealth without much attention once it's been put in place. I've come to a point in my business where I've learned there is really a small portion of the entire system that I need to master and perform myself. The rest can be leveraged to others who will do a better job than I would, which lets me focus on my areas of strength and avoid my areas of weakness. This chapter is intended to help your own learning curve be far less steep than mine was.

Take it from me—you *will* quit if you make things too hard on yourself. Everybody has a breaking point. Willpower is great, but it will take you only so far. As a word of caution, I would also advise you that most people believe their own willpower is much greater than it really is, especially in the beginning, before they are experiencing the negative emotions that tempt them to quit. Don't let that be you. Use these next steps to start your own team, learn the first basic rules, and be on your way to building wealth one property at a time.

PRICE-TO-RENT RATIOS

Buy not on optimism but on arithmetic.

—WARREN BUFFETT

In addition to looking for people you already know and trust, you will save yourself a lot of time by determining whether the state or area you want to invest in will work for your goals. Assuming your goals are to buy rental property to hold long term, the price-to-rent ratio is one of the most important metrics you'll need. Price-to-rent ratios are very quick and simple units of measurement that indicate how much a property costs to buy versus how much rent it is likely to produce. The stronger this metric is, the easier it will be for you to buy properties that will cash-flow positively.

The whole reason I began investing out of state is because the prices in California rose too high to provide a reasonable ROI. While rents generally rise with prices (both increase with demand), there comes a point in the price-to-rent ratio when rents cannot keep up with rising prices. As prices continue to increase, rents become somewhat stabilized, and more expensive homes have higher mortgages. This becomes a problem if your goal is to find properties that will cash-flow positively. Without increasing rents to offset this cost, you can quickly find your odds of locating cash-flowing properties significantly reduced. In markets like this, buy-and-hold models end up getting paced out until prices drop again.

If the market you're considering has this problem and you are a buy-and-hold investor, you probably want to do yourself a favor and look for another market, unless you're primarily considering flipping houses out of state. If that's the case, you can still make money in these markets because, while the skill set and knowledge base is similar for flipping houses as it is for buying rentals, the criteria for the two strategies are different. With buy-and-hold rental property, you are primarily looking for properties for which the rent is higher than the expenses associated with the property. With house flipping, you are primarily looking for properties that will sell for significantly more than the expenses associated with acquiring and rehabbing the property. You run your numbers the same way, but the numbers you are running are different.

If you're still skeptical about this, take a minute and think about all the investors you've heard of who own very large portfolios of buy-and-hold rental property. I'm willing to bet that almost every single one of them owns their portfolio in an area with a strong, healthy, investor-friendly price-to-rent ratio. It's just the way it works. The more podcasts I listen to, and the more successful investors I meet, the more it becomes clear that they accumulated these portfolios in areas like the South or Midwest, which are notoriously popular for having strong price-to-rent ratios and the existing infrastructure (property management companies, investor-friendly lenders, and so on) that goes with that. You won't find very many people with large portfolios in California, New York, and other high-priced areas because, unless you're buying in a down market, it's just extremely difficult to find properties that cash-flow well. Don't go against the grain just because you're personally more comfortable with those areas. Go where the deals are. Find an area where you're more likely to find something that makes sense to buy and hold, then become an expert in that area. This is how you'll build an amazing portfolio and how you'll build passive income. Eventually, you'll be active enough to build the relationships that allow you to scale up your business to find big success.

DETERMINE AN AREA'S PRICE-TO-RENT RATIO

This may all sound well and good, but what if you don't know what a good price-to-rent ratio is? While these numbers may sound complicated at first, the more familiar you become with them, the better you'll be at rapidly deciphering whether the price of a home is worth considering based on its anticipated rent. Real estate investors spend a lot of time crunching numbers and evaluating properties. People have been doing this for a long, long time, so you don't have to reinvent the wheel. To state it simply, your goal when buying income property is to buy a property that will make you more money each month than it costs to own. To determine whether the property will be profitable, you'll simply add up all the different costs associated with owning the property and subtract them from the rent. If the number you are left with is greater than zero, that's how much money you can expect to make each month. If it's less than zero, then that is how much money you can expect to lose.

With enough practice, you can begin to anticipate patterns and trends to save yourself time. We refer to these patterns as rules of thumb. These rules of thumb are not hard-and-fast but rather more general observations that are helpful in quickly determining whether a property will make sense to buy or not. When you consider how many properties are available for sale, it makes sense that you want some good, solid rules of thumb to help save you time and effort on your search.

THE 1 PERCENT RULE

One of the most common rules is referred to as the 1 percent rule. The 1 percent rule states that if a property can rent for 1 percent of the purchase price each month, it is highly likely to be profitable and cash-flow positively. An example of this would be a house that rents for $1,000 a month with a purchase price of $100,000 or a house that rents for $1,750 a month with a purchase price of $175,000. Investors have learned to pay attention to metrics like this because it saves time from analyzing properties that clearly will not make sense. This rule is an easy one to calculate quickly in your head, saving you the time of even having to punch in numbers on a calculator before determining whether the price-to-rent ratio makes sense.

Start by working backward with it. If an agent sends me a list of houses that have been sitting on the market for a long time, I'm likely to do a quick search of what rents I can expect in the area. If I find I'm likely to rent the house for approximately $1,150 a month, I will look further into the likelihood that we can buy the property somewhere around $115,000 (assuming there are no major repairs needed, of course). If my agent tells me the lowest the seller will consider is $190,000, I know right away this property will not work as a rental. My next task would be to determine what the house would be worth if I fixed it up and tried to resell it, evaluating it as a flip, not a buy-and-hold opportunity.

The 1 percent rule is the one I most commonly use for a few reasons:

1. You can readily find properties that are cash-flowing positively.
2. Tenants are accustomed to paying more for rent than it would cost to own and have accepted this fact.
3. The properties are not in such dangerous, hazardous, or poor condition/areas that owning them could create a huge headache or result in conditions contrary to successful buy-and-hold investing (these are typically 2 percent rule properties).

What does this mean for you? Well, first, we've already discussed how important it is to choose areas that increase our likelihood for success to save us time, money, and discouragement. The 1 percent rule helps ensure to this. Second, you don't want to be in an area where tenants are resentful that they are paying more for rent than they would be paying to own a home. In certain areas of the United States, the inventory of available, affordable homes has decreased while the need for housing has remained the same or increased. This has led to many folks unable to find a home to buy that meets their needs and has turned them instead into reluctant tenants. In some areas, the presence of active real estate investors has contributed to this lack of inventory. For those who would rather own their home than rent, it can become increasingly difficult to establish a long-term occupancy.

Tenants who don't want to be renting will look for opportunities to buy and leave your property vacant. As a landlord, vacancy is an enemy because it equates to loss of rent, loss of advertising costs, and make-ready repairs that can become very expensive.

If possible, you want to own properties that people are more than willing to rent. Some people prefer the freedom and lack of surprises that renting offers in comparison with the rigidity and risk associated with homeownership. If you can find an area where the tenants are fine renting and have no plans to change, you can reduce your costs associated with vacancy. You will also be much more likely to find tenants who treat the property as their own—saving you money in the process.

Third, properties that appear to be even more profitable than those adhering to the 1 percent rule are often in areas where I don't want to invest. These areas, often referred to as war zones, are associated with high crime, headaches, high vacancy, and expensive repairs because of tenants who are not taking pride in the home. This is an example where more is not always more.

THE 70 PERCENT RULE

The 70 percent rule is more of an equation than a rule of thumb. Used for quickly determining a price to pay for a potential flip property, the 70 percent rule states that if you multiply the after-repair value (ARV)—the price a home is expected to sell for once it's ready to hit the market—by 0.70 and then subtract your estimated repair costs, you can come up with a conservative number to offer for the property.

(ARV x 0.70) – rehab costs

So for a home with an ARV of $100,000 and a rehab cost of $10,000, you would be looking at a formula that would be:

($100,000 x 0.70) – $10,000

This would end up as $70,000 – $10,000 = $60,000. With this number ($60,000), you could confidently make an initial offer on the property and feel good that you would still make money after holding costs, quiet costs, unexpected expenses, permits, commissions, and taxes were paid for.

While this is a "quick, fast, and dirty" way to make an initial offer, please keep in mind that most people who make their initial offers this way fully expect to renegotiate their price once they have inspected the property in more depth. Like the other rules of thumb, the 70 percent rule represents a starting point, not the finished product.

As I mentioned early, when an agent brings me a property he or she says is a good deal, the first thing I do is run it through the 1 percent rule to determine whether it satisfies my standard for that metric. If it doesn't, I apply the 70 percent rule to determine whether it will work as a flip. If the property cannot be purchased in a way that complies with either of these metrics, I tell my agent no thank you and move on.

This entire process can take less than thirty seconds and be done with the calculator app on your phone if you aren't good with math. What's more, you can teach your agent to run the property by these numbers before even sending it to you and save yourself even more time.

THE 2 PERCENT RULE

Another common rule of thumb is the 2 percent rule. As the name suggests, these are properties that rent for approximately 2 percent a month of the purchase price. While many investors (usually new ones) begin salivating at the ROI that is possible at this price-to-rent ratio, I would strongly caution you to ask *why* the properties are selling for so low compared with the rent because it might be too good to be true.

If you find yourself analyzing a property that fits this rule, you are looking at either a screaming deal that few have ever seen or a property in a neighborhood you do not want to own in long term. Successful long-term investors tend to avoid properties that meet this criterion—and for good reason. Too many people have lost their shirts trying to strike gold in these swamps. Typically entered into by the naive, novice, or "theoretical" investor, these properties can be more like buying a job than buying an investment property. Though the numbers can look like spreadsheet magic, keep in mind that properties like this tend to be high maintenance and high risk.

While I would caution most investors to stay away from these types of properties, there *is* a specific investment niche that caters to them and does so successfully. Property managers who are highly knowledgeable, good at reading people and building relationships, and willing to take a much more hands-on approach will thrive in these areas. If you're just starting out, don't tackle a 2 percenter unless you have help from someone else who has had success—things can get out of hand very fast.

Like the sirens that called out to sailors and then dragged them down to their doom in the old stories, the appeal of these properties has led many a promising, future investment career to a premature end. Don't make that same mistake, and leave these properties for the experts! There is plenty to go around, and you don't need to chase properties like this to successfully build your portfolio.

THE 50 PERCENT RULE

In addition to the 1 percent and 2 percent rules, many investors like the 50 percent rule (no, the 50 percent rule does not mean a property rents for 50 percent of the purchase price each month—you wish!). The 50 percent rule states that you can count on 50 percent of the income that the property generates to go toward repairs and holding costs other than those associated with debt or the mortgage. Though many investors really like this rule, I am not a fan because it's too general.

The main benefits of this rule of thumb are that it is very conservative and very fast. Erring on the side of caution is always better than miscalculating your numbers, and investors who like this rule are usually more comfortable working with worst-case-scenario-type figures.

To use this rule of thumb, simply take the expected rent (in this case, $1,000), cut it in half ($500), and then subtract your mortgage payment. If you're expecting to borrow $50,000 at 4 percent interest on a thirty-year loan to buy a property, you know your mortgage payment will be $238.71 monthly (easy to calculate with your new Mortgage Calculator Plus app).

By subtracting this $238.71 from the $500 you have left, you can quickly determine that the property will cash-flow around $261.29. This would let you know it would be worth spending more time analyzing and considering the property. This is how rules of thumb are meant to work. You would never want to buy a property based solely on whether it meets these criteria, but you can quickly determine which properties are worth more of your time and which are not. When you're trying to determine where to start putting an out-of-state operation together, consider using the 1 percent and 2 percent rules as measuring sticks to help save you time.

ALTERNATIVE STRATEGIES TO BUY-AND-HOLD

Now that you understand how the 1 percent and 2 percent rules work, you should be able to quickly rule out areas with prices that aren't suited for long-term buy-and-hold investing. But what if you feel as though you have a competitive advantage in an area that doesn't make sense to own rental property? This is where you learn about the power of options and how important they are both to hedge risk and to make money.

While some areas are specifically suited only to a certain investing model, others can work for several. These "hybrid" areas are the most ideal to begin your process. If you find yourself with a competitive advantage in an area where rentals don't make sense, don't give up! Start asking yourself what you *can* do with the deals you find.

The obvious answer is to buy properties that are great deals, fix them up, and sell them again for a profit. I've found that the process for buying, rehabbing, and managing investment property isn't much different from the process for buying, rehabbing, and selling flipped property because you make the money when you buy. Your profit comes when you either rent the property out (slow, consistent profit) or sell the property to a home buyer (fast, bigger profit).

In both investing strategies, your goal is to create as much equity as possible, and you do so by leveraging the talents of other skilled professionals. The only differences are found in what you do with the finished product (rent or sell) and what type of materials you use during the rehab. Typically, rental property will be rehabbed with cheaper materials, and house flips will use more expensive ones. Often there isn't much of a difference in the price of the materials at all. While you can lose money, flipping properties in areas where you do not live is absolutely possible. I do it, and I am going to teach you the process for acquiring the properties, managing the projects remotely, and exiting safely. Just as with investment property, the key is in having the right people working for you and making sure you have accurate numbers. Don't assume that all real estate investing activity needs to be buy-and-hold rental property. Opportunity is opportunity and comes in from many places. When you stop looking at what could go wrong or thinking about how scary it feels not to see a property, your mind can be opened to all the ways that flipping out of state is just like flipping at home.

Up to this point, I have primarily focused on owning traditional rental property or flipping houses. The truth is, there are many, many different ways you can invest in real estate. Some people like the "slow flip" model, in which they buy a home under market value, live in it for a year or two, and then sell it and realize the profit later. This can be a great way to make money in areas that aren't prone to heavy cyclical market trends. It also makes sense if you don't want to take out an expensive hard-money loan, if you enjoy working on the house yourself but don't want to be rushed, or if you are looking to avoid paying expensive capital gains taxes. If you live in a property for any two years of a five-year period, you are likely eligible to sell the property for a profit without having to declare it to the IRS for taxes. Consult with your accountant first, but this is a strategy used by many investors to grow their wealth without feeling rushed, stressed, or anxious.

Other common strategies include lease-to-own, selling a property "turnkey" style, assigning the contract to another buyer, and selling off a property while holding on to the note as passive income. Real estate provides the opportunity to create wealth in many different ways. Remember, options are your friend! While there are many ways to exit a property, by far the most commonly used strategies are to hold the property as a rental or flip it to another buyer.

VACATION RENTALS

A new, less common but rapidly growing strategy is to consider renting the property out as a vacation rental. Vacation rentals are also becoming increasingly profitable. Think of vacation rentals in terms of how hotels are run. Tenants will rent your property out on a nightly or weekly, as opposed to monthly, basis. The benefit is that they will pay more per night to stay in the property, but the drawback is that the property will likely be vacant more often, require more work to keep rented, more time spent preparing for the next guest, and could expose you to more legal liability.

This model has become increasingly popular in areas with high corporate rental demand. Large cities, downtown areas, and vacation locales have been awesome places to own vacation rental property, often bringing in returns that dwarf traditional ROI. Investors are learning they can double or triple their returns by renting out properties vacation-rental style. Platforms like Airbnb, Craigslist, and VRBO assist with this process and have become a hotel replacement in many places.

Keep in mind this is a hot-button topic in many areas and is still widely considered controversial because county and state governments are creating more rules and regulations for these types of rentals. There is no guarantee the areas you're buying in will always allow vacation rental access, and you may find yourself in a tough spot if you buy and plan to rent out on a nightly basis and find the city passes a measure prohibiting this. But don't make this your sole investment because this is just one option of many.

Information is power, particularly when the competition ignores the opportunity to do the same.

—MARK CUBAN

Maybe you were raised somewhere, or went to college there, and the rental opportunities are phenomenal. Maybe you used to work somewhere and remembered how hard it was finding somewhere to stay near the company's headquarters. Perhaps you stayed in touch with the dean in charge of your college housing and can find out exactly what people are paying for rent and what the demand is like. This is ideal! Having intimate knowledge of an area where price-to-rent ratios make sense is a *huge* upper hand when it comes to investing out of state. In addition to knowing the neighborhoods, streets, freeways, and property values, there is also a very good chance you have contacts in this area who can help you break ground and get started. Don't underestimate your own knowledge of an area when considering where you want to start investing. If you know the area, it may as well be your own backyard. Use this to your competitive advantage anywhere you can. A perfect way to pick an area out of state to start investing in, is to look for ways to create a competitive advantage for yourself in areas you have existing knowledge of.

HOW TO LEVERAGE RELATIONSHIPS

The older I get, the more I realize that relationships drive success. The person who is successful at building relationships always seems to do better than the person who is naturally brilliant. Knowing someone who can teach you what you don't know is one hundred times easier than having to teach yourself. I'm sure you can see the point. Relationships make things happen. They get stuff done. In fact, you're building a relationship with me, through this book, that is enabling you to learn how to invest out of state and see all the doors it can open.

When you're looking to start investing in an area where you don't live, one of the first things you should ask yourself is "Do I know someone who lives there?" Of all the people crucial to your business, the most important member of your team will be the person finding you the deals. Period. Deals are the lifeblood of this business, and without them, you're just spinning your wheels. You may have an all-star team in place, capable of preventing even a drop of water from spilling out of your bucket, but it's useless if you don't have a way to fill that bucket with water in the first place. Since you make your money when you buy, your deal finder is the person who will make sure you're filling your water bucket to the brim. Your deal finder could be your uncle in Phoenix who works in the mortgage industry, your high school friend in Fort Lauderdale who works in construction, or a wholesaler you know through a mutual friend.

Take a minute to sit and think about people you know related to real estate or investing in some way in the area you're interested in. Write their names down on a piece of paper. When you can't think of anyone else, start looking them up on Facebook and seeing where they live now. If you find some who are in areas in which you want to invest, you've just found your first leads toward breaking ground and planting your flag of success in a new and possibly unfamiliar area.

As I've grown as an investor, I've stopped looking for deals and I've started looking for the people who have them. Of the homes I'm buying now, I chose the area primarily because I know a wholesaler who gives me first crack at every deal she comes across. This wholesaler was able to put me in touch with a lender who gave me the best terms I've ever seen. Once I realized I had these two crucial elements in place, I determined I would find a way to get the pieces I was missing. It was ten times easier than having to build it from the ground up.

I know this may sound odd. Conventional wisdom tells you to do your research, find the area you expect to boom next, and try to get in before the next guy. This is a great strategy if investing were easy, but this method actually makes it extremely difficult. A large part of real estate investing success is how you've created your infrastructure. Sometimes you have to stick with what works, not necessarily with what the ideal situation is.

When I started buying in Florida, I realized I had a competitive advantage over other investors because I had a wholesaler who was bringing deals to me first and a lender providing me financing I was never going to beat anywhere else. I decided to make the effort to find the pieces I didn't have by leveraging the ones I did. After having gone through this experience, I now know this is the way to do it. Leveraging relationships and building on a foundation already laid is much more efficient than trying to start from scratch. Building these relationships takes time and effort, and not every one will be a home run. We all know somebody, and that somebody knows other somebodies who might be helpful for us in reaching our goals.

> *The richest people in the world look for and build networks; everyone else looks for work. Marinate on that for a minute.*
>
> —ROBERT KIYOSAKI

CHAPTER 4

THE FIRST MEMBERS OF YOUR TEAM

Everyone enjoys doing the kind of work for which he is best suited.

—NAPOLEON HILL

Leveraging the talents, skills, and abilities of others to make you money—that's the name of the game when it comes to any business. Real estate is no exception. While it can often be tempting to think you need to do it all yourself, the truth is, for the overwhelming majority of us, we do much better when we hire a specialist to do a job. As an investor, you should make it your goal to find jobs for these people. When you hire people to do something they love, you help them build their own wealth, and you build your own from their gain.

Up to this point, we have discussed why out-of-state investing is a viable option, how technology has changed the landscape of investing to even make this possible, and how to determine where you want to invest. While these are all important topics, they've basically served as a foundation for what the *real* value of this book is. You may believe that you can find a place in which you'd like to invest, but when I tell people I invest out of state, the number one most commonly asked question is "How do I do everything that needs to be done from miles away?" The answer is "Pretty much the same way you do it when the house is next-door."

Your first inclination may be to doubt, and I understand that. I went through all those same emotional objections when I first started, and all I could see was what could go wrong. But over time, with consistent practice, I've grown confident I can find the right people to manage every aspect of my business from thousands of miles away.

Now, in all fairness, this is not a unique concept to real estate investing. Businesses everywhere have been outsourcing work for years, and most big businesses follow a model that consists of (1) automating the business—making you go through the process of speaking to a computer before a person—and (2) when you finally do speak to a human being, it's from a call center in another country that has lower costs than what it would take to hire someone local.

The automation process (as annoying as it is) helps solve commonly encountered problems and saves money. This means businesses can hire fewer workers to do the same job and money is saved. Much like Henry Ford's assembly line, automation means hiring specialists to do specific tasks often. And it's not only big companies. More and more entrepreneurs and individual investors are hiring "virtual assistants" to help perform some of the tasks involved in the daily process of their business. This frees up more time for the individual to do what *really* matters, depending on what that means for him or her. As long as the projects are being completed in a satisfactory manner, it's better to hire someone else to do them.

Your real estate investing is a business. Run it like one. Find the right people to create your team. By virtue of trial and error, consistency, and wisdom, you'll eventually find people who are really, really good at those tasks. You'll save money, have more time, and reduce your anxiety. Here are the people you should be looking for.

THE DEAL FINDER

Without a doubt, in my system, the absolute most crucial, important, and foundational piece of your business is your deal finder. Traditionally, this has been a real estate agent. As investing has evolved, the effectiveness of wholesalers has emerged as a viable and sometimes even superior alternative. While I'll likely refer to the deal finder as an agent, please keep in mind it could be anyone (wholesaler, Realtor, probate attorney, turnkey provider, and so on).

Since most investors will find their out-of-state properties through the traditional means of using a real estate agent, that's where I'm going to focus the bulk of my attention. Good real estate agents are worth their weight in gold because they are surrounded by the people who are likely to find properties that investors want. They are trained in the process and (hopefully) experienced in finding properties *and* managing the transaction.

When you think about why people use real estate agents, it's not just because they can find homes their clients will like. There are so many moving pieces, so many hiccups, so many terms people do not understand, and deadlines that must be met. Most people who buy or sell a house have very little idea how much work is being done or how exposed to risk they are.

When you're buying investment property, and especially buying property out of state, I highly recommend using an agent as opposed to a wholesaler or other means, at least in the beginning. Agents know the laws in their specific area, and those may vary from what you're used to. If you are a very experienced investor with a good accountant, good counsel, and a knack for understanding paperwork, you might want to try buying in a new area without representation. If you're anyone else, don't.

As a buyer, you need to understand you aren't paying your agent anything. The seller of the property is. While it's true that in some circumstances you can get a "better" deal by helping the seller avoid paying a commission and therefore get a lower price, that rarely occurs. Investors look for deals, and deals do not often come up without some work on behalf of the investor or his or her agent.

As an investor, you are almost always targeting situations that indicate some form of distress. People do not sell their home under market value unless there is some compelling reason for them to do so. This means the seller isn't motivated purely by money to sell. "Saving the seller money" by not using a buyer's agent isn't always a necessary or even useful practice. In my experience, motivated sellers will sell if you can offer terms and a price that make sense to their situation. Saving them money is often just icing on the cake and not always a deciding factor.

With this in mind, I think it's a really good idea to use a real estate agent whenever possible. The drawbacks are small and the benefits are large when you're starting out or investing in an area you haven't before.

FIND HIGH-PRODUCING AGENTS

At this point, you know you want to start looking for properties, and you know you want an agent to help you, but you don't know anyone in the area to ask for a referral. This is where you usually get stuck and stop, right? While a personal referral is ideal, online reviews are essentially referrals from a bunch of strangers you haven't met yet.

Online reviews are becoming one of the most powerful ways business owners find leads and drive business. Reviews can lead to its success or failure. When it comes to real estate, few websites or programs can compete with Zillow, the easiest, most convenient, and most useful way to kick-start this process. Zillow allows you to search for agents and see who is doing the most business in an area and what others are saying about them. While I don't often use Zillow just to find a new agent, I will often use it to do a little background research on an agent someone has recommended to me. When you think about who is most likely to come across the best deals, it makes sense to consider that it is often going to be the person with the most contacts and influence in an area. If you want to find who that is, look first to see who's doing the most business.

Zillow reviews will provide you with enough information to get a decent idea of what an agent's reputation is and how popular he or she is with past clients. While number of sales is definitely not the most important factor to consider when looking for an agent, it is usually a great indicator that the agent works well with others. It also indicates the agent is less likely to waste your time and is more likely to have resources you will need later. Agents who do a lot of business meet a lot of people. Just by virtue of sheer volume, they are much more likely to have other clients doing the same type of thing you are. These clients will need the same things you do. Your agent can help you find them too. Contractors, investor-friendly lenders, handymen ... the list goes on.

You don't want to gamble on your future. You don't want to take risks with your own motivation or drive. Starting your search with top-producing agents will give you a higher likelihood of getting a great list of agents to interview. It will also give you a much better chance of finding a deal. Real estate is a relationship-oriented business, and top-producing agents get recommended more.

Ready to see just how easy it can be to use Zillow to find the best agent? Just go to Zillow.com/agent-finder. Zillow provides us a list of the high-producing agents in the area with all the things I would want to see if I were looking for an agent there. These agents show great reviews and many houses sold. By using Zillow to search for top agents, I can be comfortably assured I'm finding agents who know what they are doing and have had a lot of past success.

Earlier I mentioned it's a good thing to find an agent who runs his or her own team. Agents with teams typically had so much success, they needed to hire others to help them manage the volume of clients they were receiving. Agents with teams also have the luxury of being picky about whom they choose to hire to be on their team and can cherry-pick the best and brightest agents available. Once you understand how to leverage the resources of these super-successful agents, you'll find you're one step closer to finding that same success yourself.

AGENTS WITH A TEAM

If you've been around the block a time or two, you may be ready to object: "But David, top-producing agents are busy. I am going to be writing multiple offers and will require a lot of time. They aren't going to want to work with an investor." Now, I actually agree with this statement. Many top-producing agents just do not have the time to put into working with a needy investor (and make no bones about it—we are needy). I've already given you many of the advantages that using a high-producing agent brings. If you are looking for someone to help plug you into the local pipeline, this is the easiest way to get in. There are many reasons why these agents will benefit your business. There is also one big disadvantage: They are stinking busy.

To sell a lot of real estate, it takes a lot of time. The better you are at doing it, the more your time is worth. Good agents' time is worth a lot. They know how to get things done. They know how to avoid problems. They know what works and what doesn't. Most important, they know all the people you need to know. They hold the cards, and this makes them worth a lot. I used to get frustrated by this. It was very difficult having someone with all the resources I needed to help my business but who was too busy to return my calls.

A popular model used by many high-producing agents is to build a team. They hire others to help handle the influx of business they receive and pay those employees a percentage of the commission. Because I am now also a real estate agent, I've seen firsthand how this works. I've also seen firsthand why so many agents want to be part of a great team with lots of business. It's more steady income for the agents on the team via a constant stream of new leads. In addition to a steady income, the newer agents on the team get to learn from the best. This works great for agents joining the team because they get to work with and learn from the top dog in the industry. It works for the best agents because they can leverage the time, abilities, and skill sets (that pesky concept coming back again) of their team members to make them money.

I haven't heard any other investor talking about using teams in this way yet. I myself have used it with good results, and I think it's a no-brainer method to find a great agent and use him or her to your advantage. When searching for top-producing agents, consider narrowing your search even further to those who run a team, like the "David Greene Team." When you find an agent who runs a team, put that name on the list you are compiling of agents you want to interview. You'll want to keep this list of names, phone numbers, and e-mails handy for later.

When you contact the agents via e-mail or phone, they are going to get an idea of what you are looking for and quickly determine whether it's something they can help you with. If it is, they will refer you to their "buyer's agent," who will most likely be your point of contact from that point forward. While this agent is still highly likely to be a good one since he or she is working for a top producer, there is an even better benefit to this technique. In addition to finding a talented agent, you *also* get access to the top-producing agent's time and resources through a team member.

When you want to leverage the contacts the agent has accumulated over the years, your "assigned" agent will be able to facilitate that. As a member of a top-producing team, the agent you are working with will have support from the top down. When you need that contractor recommendation, the agent you've been referred to is going to have access to the same contacts the top producer does. By getting your foot in the door with a team member of a high-producing agent, you can usually secure an audience with the big dog himself or herself. Boom, all the benefits of working with a top producer without the drawback of not having his or her time.

In addition to having access to the team's best, your agent will also be able to leverage the knowledge of the other team members, who are likely to have come across some of these same valuable contacts. So you are working with one very talented, hand-selected agent. This agent has access to one of the very best and most talented agents in the area you're looking at, *and* you will have access to all the other team members in this group who are also highly talented and handpicked. What are the odds with circumstances like this that you might start finding some good deals?

I used this same concept a few years ago in Arizona. While doing research to find agents near Phoenix, I came upon an agent named Joshua Smith. Joshua had a web page (more about that soon) I found on Google. Today, Joshua has blown up to become one of the most well known agents in the country. His success has reached such a level that you now can't even pay him to coach you anymore. He is so busy, you can't contact him directly. Lucky for me, at the time, he had not become quite so unreachable, and he responded to my e-mails.

I reached out to Joshua, told him exactly what I was looking for, and let him know how great I thought his business was. I also told Joshua if he was too busy to be taking on new clients, I would love if he could refer me to someone he trusted. I knew there wasn't a good chance he would give me the time I was going to need if I wasn't buying million-dollar homes. I was honest about the fact that I was an investor, that I was looking to buy several homes a year, and that I knew it would be a time-intensive process to help me find what I was looking for.

It worked. After a few back-and-forth e-mails, Joshua put me in touch with one of the buyer's agents on his team who matched the profile of what I had said I was looking for. This buyer's agent ended up being a total rock star, and I have no doubt that in a few years, he will be just as impossible for new clients to reach. He's that good.

Not only did I form a relationship with Joshua Smith, but I also cemented a relationship for years to come with his buyer's agent—one of the very best agents I've come across in my life. Through this team, I've been able to find a great contractor in a different location, an awesome property manager that took the place of the one I was using before, and an entire team of agents looking to find me deals. Later in the book, I'll explain just how I leveraged the rest of Joshua's team to assist in finding me houses to flip.

AGENTS WITH WEBSITES

I hope by now you understand that not all agents are created the same. Better agents have more to offer, more to teach you, and make the process much smoother. Once you've done a little research to compile a list of the top-producing agents in your area of interest, you want to do a quick Google search of the agents' names for their websites.

Most agents will have some form of their own website to introduce themselves to new clients, explain a little about their own business, and provide their contact information. I like to look up client testimonials posted on the sites and see whether I can find a name that is also on their Yelp site. Sometimes these reviews and testimonials will even share specific details of what agents did that was different from what others provided or that made them stand apart from the crowd. I like to look for anything on the site that specifically mentions work they have done with investors because we have a unique niche and set of needs. If agents are publically welcoming investors to contact them, there is a good chance they have an existing system in place to service investors and keep them happy.

While Zillow may be the big dog on the block when it comes to Internet real estate websites, it's not the only one. Several other websites are growing in popularity and functionality and can also be of benefit to you when looking for agents or cross-checking names you've acquired. Consistency is important. You'll want to check the reviews in one location against those in another to make sure the consensus is the same across several different mediums.

Now, if you *are* a fan of online real estate sites, I hope you have already heard of BiggerPockets.com. It's a real estate investors' paradise because it has the best online blog I've ever seen, for any topic. It also has top-rated podcasts that are my all-time favorites to listen to. If you are looking to increase your knowledge of real estate investing, there simply is no better place to start.

As much as BiggerPockets has to offer in the way of free information and educational value, that's not all you can use it for. BiggerPockets has also become the number one platform for networking with real estate investors and those catering to their needs. Many agents, lenders, and handymen all flood to BiggerPockets to offer their services to those likely to need them. If you are looking for an investor-friendly agent, you stand a very good chance of finding one there.

WAYS TO SAVE TIME ON YOUR SEARCH

> *Efficiency is intelligent laziness.*
>
> —DAVID DUNHAM

If you've been following along so far, you should have a nice, neat list of top-producing agents you've found online. Make sure to include any referrals you've received from other trusted sources. Once your list is complete, you're ready to step into the next phase. It's time to start reaching out to these agents and finding the one with the personality, experience, and skill set that's of most use to you.

As with everything else in real estate investing, your time is important. Trying to personally call all the agents and follow up with them is likely to take the better part of a day, or several days if you have other things to do. Use e-mail instead.

E-mail works for several reasons. For one, agents are trained to check their e-mails. Some high-producing agents have secretaries who answer them on their behalf. Second, there is a good chance that if you call busy agents from a number they don't recognize, they aren't going to answer the phone. This becomes even more likely if you are calling from an out-of-state phone number or an area code they don't recognize, which is why e-mail works much better. Keeping this in mind, I recommend sending an e-mail to the agents on your list to reach out and make your initial introductions. E-mails allow you to include more information than a text message and are considered more considerate and more professional. They also have one other really big advantage—they can be copied and pasted.

WHY SEND AN INITIAL E-MAIL?

The point of the initial e-mail is to give the agent an idea of who you are, what you are looking for, and how you will be of benefit to the agent. Top agents are skilled in recognizing who is worth their time and who is just going to waste it, and they will be evaluating you just as they do everyone else. It's important that your initial e-mail makes the right impression and conveys enough information to engage the agent while still portraying you as a competent professional. One e-mail copied and pasted to each agent will be all you need to start the process of finding the right one for you.

When it comes to what to put in your e-mail, there are a few main topics you need to cover. The most important things to include are:
- That you are an investor who understands real estate
- What specifically you are looking for
- How you intend to purchase (loan, cash, and so on)
- How you heard about the agent

If you include this specific information, it should be enough for the agent to realize you are serious and that you are less likely to waste his or her time. This is an important point to convey when dealing with high-performing producers. When you want access to the best, they always expect the best from you.

An example of an e-mail would look like this:

To: _____

CC: _____

Subject: Researching rentals

From: David — david@realestateinvesting

Hello,

My name is David. I'm a real estate investor in CA, and I've been doing research to determine the best place for me to start buying rentals to hold long term for cash flow. My research led me to [*your town*], and I've found you are the top-producing agent in the area. I'd love to speak with you sometime and see whether you can help me out.

I'm looking for single-family homes with three bedrooms and at least one and a half bathrooms. My goal is to buy them with conventional financing, repair them to be rent ready, and hire a property manager to rent them out. I plan to buy two to three homes this year and have experience managing rental property already. My goal is to find properties that need work or are owned by motivated sellers that I can purchase for 80 cents on the dollar if possible.

Please let me know if you would be interested in taking me on as a client. If you have a preferred lender, I would like to get preapproved with him or her. If you or anyone you know has a property manager you can recommend, I would love to reach out and get in touch with that individual as well.

I see your reputation is stellar, and you seem to be the best of the best. I hope we can develop a very strong relationship that is profitable for us both!

Looking forward to speaking more in depth.

—David

For those who aren't intimately familiar with how the real estate industry works these days, please allow me to share an important fact: It is highly, highly automated. Homes are searched for on electronic databases, contracts are drawn up, signed, and submitted electronically. Communication is done through e-mail, text, or phone conversations. Pictures are posted online. Reviews are given online. Your real estate agent will be used to strangers e-mailing with introductory messages like this. The agent will also be familiar with the questions you're asking and know how to respond. If you're considering investing out of state, you should take a lot of comfort in the fact that even if you were investing locally, the process would be almost identical. Technology has made things so much easier for so many different tasks. Real estate is one of those industries that have benefited greatly from this. It's time you took advantage and started using some of this to better leverage your own success.

ASK THE RIGHT QUESTIONS TO FIND THE RIGHT AGENT

If you've done everything correctly, you should be getting replies from some, if not all, of the agents you e-mailed. Once you get the replies, it will be much easier to know how to proceed. The agents who respond will likely express appreciation at your reaching out to them and have a list of questions they have for you. This is a normal next step in the process of getting to know each other and trying to determine whether the two of you will be a good fit for each other. While you should be sure to answer all the agent's questions, there will be some of your own I'm going to teach you to ask. It's important the agent feels comfortable that you will keep your word and not waste his or her time. It's also important you feel comfortable that your agent has the time, knowledge, and skills to help you accomplish *your* goals.

The first thing you want to make sure you address is whether the agent has experience working with investors. While it isn't an absolute deal breaker if the agent hasn't, it is likely to slow things down for you a bit. If you find the right agent, it's possible it would be a good investment to teach him or her how to find what you're looking for. The right drive, skills, and attitude are tough to teach, and if your agent already has them, that's a good asset to have on your side. In general, it is much more favorable to have an agent who has experience working with investors and even better if the agent is an investor himself or herself.

An agent who has experienced these emotions will be much more likely to have already looked for answers to any inherent problems, and this is a good thing for you. For many of us who have done this for a while, we remember the initial temptation to buy in less-than-reputable neighborhoods because the deal just looked so good. An agent who has also already made this mistake won't be as likely to advise you to buy these properties. For any investor who has bought a rental property already occupied by so-called "good" tenants, it's not a great feeling when the tenants are late on their second payment to you and have to be evicted after a few short months. An agent who has already undergone this experience will be much more likely to negotiate that a property be delivered vacant to help you avoid this scenario and save you quite a bit in legal fees.

There is no substitute for experience, so don't be afraid to ask whether the agent has ever owned any rental properties or currently owns any. If he or she has or does, ask where they are and what kind of returns the agent is experiencing. Ask how the agent found the properties, what kind of analysis was used, and what drew him or her toward buying them in the first place. If the agents tells you someone said it was a good deal and he or she just had some extra money lying around and thought it would be a good idea to invest, take note of that. This is not the process of someone with a plan, systematically growing a portfolio and building net worth. If the agent tells you he or she searched for months to find a property that met his or her criteria and then moved on it instantly once it was found, take note of that too. This is an agent who understands the unique challenges of real estate investing and is much more likely to know how to find you what you're looking for—and help ensure you get it when he or she does.

Another important question to ask an agent is what kind of support he or she can provide. You want to know whom your agent knows. As I've already explained, good real estate investors have teams of support they lean on to do the jobs they cannot. Since most of your business will be done by other people, they are pretty important to your success. As your deal finder, your agent will be the foundational piece of your business and the most influential in pointing you toward the right people to hire as support staff.

In real estate, we know our success will be largely dependent on the numbers. Not only do we need to understand how to analyze properties, but we also need to be willing to analyze large numbers of them. If we consider that each deal brought our way is a "lead," we can quickly see the difference in value between a "hot lead" and a "cold lead." Hot leads are those that are much more likely to fit our criteria. Usually accompanied by some form of distress or a motivated seller, hot leads are worth much, much more than cold leads. Good investors eventually get to the point where all they are looking at are hot leads. *Great* investors get to the point where they don't even look for hot leads—the hot leads are brought to them.

If a hot lead is a lead that is much more likely to fit your criteria because it has already been vetted by someone else who approves of it, you can think of a "personal referral" the same way. By looking for support from "cold" databases like online reviews or different forms of advertising, you are giving yourself an opportunity to find the right person but not necessarily a great chance of doing so. It will take more work, more time, and more effort to find the right fit for you as you go through each name or lead you've developed. This is just like filtering through cold leads to find a house that fits your investing criteria. When you skip this filter process and deal directly with referrals from a trusted agent who is putting his or her own reputation on the line, you significantly reduce the odds that the referral won't be a good fit. This is why you want to ask about what kind of support the agent can provide and whom he or she can recommend for doing different jobs.

When people choose me to be their real estate agent, they don't get just my knowledge and skills, they also get access to my network. When clients of mine buy a home in California, they get to use my contractors and my handymen to fix the place up. Think of the options this opens for them. While the rest of the market is fighting over the same attractive, move-in-ready homes (and offering top dollar for them), my clients can pay much less for outdated homes getting much less attention. They instantly add equity when they fix the houses up. While I can offer a value in explaining how this process works for those unaware, I can also add value by letting them use people I already use or people whom investor/agent colleagues of mine have referred to me. This cuts down on the odds of my clients' having a bad experience and leaves them happy and comfortable trusting me.

When people approach me to help them find investment or personal property out of state, they benefit from the same concepts. They don't just get to pick my brain and come up with strategies for buying in new areas; they also get to know they will be working with a top-notch agent I have referred them to. The odds for their success skyrocket once you consider they are being put in touch with the best and brightest. This is significantly different from asking friends in the area whether they know an agent and just hoping the agent is good. Can you see how this systematic approach to mitigating risk starts to pay off in the long run? By doing things in a way that increases your odds at every turn, small victories will start to add up to major accomplishments and eventually life-changing wealth. The very best investors have perfected this process and have replicated it many times over. Once they have mastered it, it appears effortless and natural. Wouldn't you like to be able to say that's how your own experience is? It's a far cry from anxious, terrified, and full of white-knuckled prayers that you aren't making a mistake. Learn this system and learn to enjoy investing much, much more. The longer you stick with it, the more money you'll start to make.

Lastly, you'll want to ask your agent how he or she plans to find you potential properties. If your agent doesn't have a response to that, you may be in trouble. Agents who think they will find properties that match the specific and often rare parameters an investor demands are in for a surprise if they don't have a plan. It's better to find out this information up front rather than taking time to establish a relationship only to be confronted with the fact your agent doesn't know how to find you deals that will work for you. While you shouldn't be surprised if your agent needs a little guidance from you regarding where to start, you should also expect the agent to have some ideas of his or her own. Agents who know they can search in REO (real estate owned) databases, who can find short sales on the MLS and properties listed for long periods of time, and who network with other investors are much more likely to be able to find what you're looking for than agents who do not. Make sure you ask what your agent's game plan is and how he or she is going to approach it.

Once you've determined how your agent is going to find you properties, the only thing left to work out is what kinds of properties he or she will show you. As an investor, you will be going through a lot of different options. In the beginning especially, it will take a significant amount of your time to do so. You *don't* want to be looking at automated searches full of properties that will never work and waste your precious time in the process. Be sure to communicate with your agent and make it clear that you want to see only certain properties that meet your specific criteria, and then ask your agent not to send you anything that doesn't. The more specific you can be and the more detailed you are, the less likely you will be to get properties that waste your time.

AN AGENT AND AN INVESTOR—MY ADVICE TO YOU

> *The most important single, central fact about a free market is that no exchange takes place unless both parties benefit.*
>
> —MILTON FRIEDMAN

My journey started off with my getting into real estate as an investor. For six years, I approached real estate through the eyes of someone buying properties under market value, making any needed repairs, and then renting them out. I was trying to do this part-time, in states that were very far away from me, and without a mentor to teach me. While I was slowly building my portfolio, I was working more than ninety hours a week, often sleeping in my car or on friends' couches. I was always tired, always dragging my butt, and rarely at my best. It felt as if I was constantly operating at half my mental capability. Imagine a car working on half of its cylinders, and you'll get a good feel for my mental state. It was tough, and my road was slow and gradual.

If I had the faith to pour more of my time and effort into real estate instead of working as a police officer, I think I would have had much more success and it would have come much sooner. However, that being the case, I still found a way to make this work. Since I did not have the time to run a direct-mail campaign, I was unable to find my own deals. Because I was unable to network with others, I was unable to get access to quick and easy deals through wholesalers. Because I could not drive for dollars, attend real estate investor association (REIA) meetings, or make phone calls, I was completely dependent on someone else to bring me my deals. This someone was my agent, or rather, agents.

It became very clear, very quickly that if I wanted to continue buying homes out of state, I needed to make sure it was worth my agent's while to keep working with me. If I passed on a deal that clearly met my criteria or assumed expectations that were clearly unrealistic, it wouldn't be long before my agent was sending that deal to someone else. This isn't unfair; this is just the way the world works. If I am honest with myself, I must admit that what is unfair is allowing my agent to spend time and effort working on my behalf without ever compensating him or her for it.

And this, my friends, is an important lesson for us all to learn. In business, it may seem as though the ones who are the most successful or make the most money are always the ones who "win." Those who dominate their competition, spend as little as possible, and always come out on top are the ones who usually create the reputation as the wealthiest. I've found that often this just isn't the case. The ones who win are the ones who are skilled in creating win-win scenarios that meet *everybody's* goals, not just their own. If I wanted my agent to make me money, I needed to make sure my agent was also making money. If I wanted my agent to protect my time and send me only deals that met my criteria, I needed to make sure I was protecting my agent's time and purchase the deals he or she brought that made sense.

It may be tempting at times to cut your agent out of the deal and try to save on the commission. It may also be tempting to call or text your agent every time you have a question even if you have no intention of buying from him or her. It is always tempting to be selfish, but it is rarely fruitful to do so. The most successful businesses have the most contacts for two reasons:

1. They are well liked by people and draw successful people to them.
2. They have been doing this consistently for a long time.

You want to be one of these successful people. You want to be in business for long enough to benefit from this. When you first start off in real estate, it is all about hunting for deals. Once you master that, you'll find that a lot of the deals start coming to you. Investing becomes a lot more fun when you aren't doing so much work to find each property. If you want to get to this point, you need to be around for a while. If you want to be the one to whom people, including agents, are bringing the deals, you need to make sure you are treating them well.

Fast-forward seven years from when I bought my first rental property, doubling as a real estate agent. As an agent, I have been exposed to this whole real estate thing from a completely different perspective. I have seen how many people out there are perfectly fine with wasting my time with no intentions to buy anything. I have seen how they are fine working around me, even as I have been working for them, if they think it will benefit them in the short term. I see much more clearly why certain agents behaved in a way that made me feel as if they didn't value my business. If I look back at those times now, I can see exactly why they did. I wasn't valuing them!

My advice to you is to make sure you are just as good to them as they are to you. I am not speaking from the perspective of an investor. I am speaking from the perspective of someone who understands the full picture of how buying and selling real estate works and has learned that for the unique relationship between client and agent to work, it needs to be treated like a real relationship. There needs to be mutual consideration and trust. There needs to be a need that each side provides for the other and an understanding of the stresses, challenges, and concerns that the other side has.

Those who do best in business are those who bring the most value to others. Don't assume that because you are the client, it means you have no value to bring to the other party. Putting money in an agent's pocket is a great way to strengthen a relationship with that person. Doing so for a good, top-producing agent is a really good way to increase your odds of getting the best deals before anyone else does. When you consider the value this will bring you and then multiply it over your investing career, it really makes sense to take the initiative in proving your value to the agent—even if your pride prefers that your agent prove his or her value to you first.

THE LENDER

As I mentioned previously, the deal finder is *the* most important member on your team. The one finding the deals is where it all begins, and everyone else is basically support staff who will make you go far to accomplish your goals. When it comes to real estate, a lender is a vital piece of your team. Unless you have access to private money or all-cash capabilities, you will need a lender to help you buy the property. If you have the cash available to buy without financing, there will still likely come a point when you will want to take out a loan to leverage your returns. In just about every situation, you're going to want a good lender working for you. Period.

This makes your lender another important member of your team and one of the first pieces you'll want in place before you get started, and a good lender can be much more difficult to find. Knowing this, I usually start trying to find a lender before I bother doing anything else. If I can't find the financing, there is no point in putting the time into finding anything else.

Lending is set up differently. There are a lot of different lenders you can use, but the odds of finding wildly different rates, terms, or products among them are low. Furthermore, it takes much less time to determine whether the lender you're talking to is someone who can help you than it takes with an agent. Lending is a much, much more standardized process in this country, and that makes your job of finding a lender much easier.

LENDING STANDARDS

When lenders review your file to see whether you are eligible for a loan, there are a few specific metrics they use that are universal among just about every financial institution. As an investor, it behooves you to understand these metrics. By knowing what banks look at, you can make sure not only that you are conforming to them but also that you can stay that way to ensure you get multiple loans.

While I'm not going to go into detail about everything a lender looks at to qualify your eligibility, I am going to share with you the main things. Once I learned how important these metrics were, I adjusted my personal financial life to conform to them. I really want to be a good investor, and that means I need to make myself as attractive a candidate as possible for banks to make loans to. Doing so gives me a competitive advantage and makes sure I don't sabotage my own success. Once you learn what banks look at, the process of appearing more attractive becomes very simple.

DTI

The first and biggest metric a lender will look at is your debt-to-income (DTI) ratio. DTI is a simple equation that compares how much money you are obligated to spend every month to cover your debts with how much money you are bringing in. The lower the number is, the more attractive you become as an option to lend to. This isn't rocket science. If a bank is going to give you a loan, the first thing it wants to know is whether you can pay the money back. Your DTI is the quickest thing it can look at to determine how likely you will be to do so.

When you apply for a loan, the bank will ask you for all your debt. It wants to know your mortgage payment, your car note, any child support you pay, and any other financial liabilities. The bank will add this monthly debt up and come up with a number that represents your total debt obligations.

Most banks don't want a DTI higher than 3–6 percent. While debt itself makes up only half of your DTI, it's still important to work to keep your debt obligations as low as possible. Paying off credit card debt is usually the fastest and simplest way to improve the debt side of your DTI, as it typically carries the highest interest rate and can be paid off the easiest. In most cases, it is easier for people to pay off existing debt than it is to earn more income if they need to improve their DTI. For that reason, I always encourage people to start there.

The income side of your DTI works similar to calculating the debt. The lender will look at the income you are bringing in every month and ensure this income is consistent. Ever wonder why the lender is always asking for bank stubs and recent paychecks? It's because the bank needs those to confirm the amount of money you have declared you make. It's also important to note that not all income is considered equal. Some loans will allow you to declare your overtime, bonuses, commissions, profit sharing, and so on, while others will not. Sometimes you need to show these additional revenue streams as consistent for a period of time before the bank will allow you to use them. In general, more income is good and will help improve your DTI.

LTV

The next metric a lender will be concerned about is your loan-to-value (LTV). While DTI is a measurement of how likely you will be to make your payments and pay back the loan, the LTV is a measure used to ensure the bank can recover the money it lends you if you stop making those payments. From a bank's perspective, the lower an LTV is, the safer the investment will be. Interest rates are often based on a direct relationship to the LTV. The lower the LTV, the lower the rate, because it's a lower risk for the bank. This is important to understand because later in the book, we will be discussing strategies to improve your ROI and manipulating the numbers so your LTV is higher. If you don't understand how this works, you won't be able to work the situation for your own advantage.

To calculate an LTV, the bank simply takes the amount of the loan and compares it with the value of the asset. Simple, right? If you take the amount of money you will be borrowing and compare it with what the bank determines the asset to be worth, you can quickly see what the LTV will be. To find the value of the asset, most banks will use an appraisal. An appraisal is a written report and recommendation conducted and engineered by a trained professional who evaluates the property and delivers his or her opinion. While an appraisal is how most banks determine the value of real estate, you should know that in some cases (usually cash-out refinances), banks will just use the purchase price of the property. Sometimes they will allow you to take the purchase price of the property and add the cost of any repairs that increased the value of the property.

In a nutshell, a bank wants as low an LTV as possible. This protects the bank because if it must take the asset back as collateral for the loan it gave you (most commonly through a foreclosure), the bank is more likely to get the majority of its investment back if the asset is worth more than the loan was for. In fact, if the LTV is low enough, the lender could theoretically make even more than the principal amount of its investment through the sale of the asset.

For you as an investor, a low LTV is typically considered worse because you have less of the value of the asset available to you as cash. If you're looking for a bank to finance your investment properties, you're more than likely planning on taking out a loan and putting in a down payment to purchase them. Most of us are used to hearing loans referred to by their down payment as "20 percent down" or "10 percent down." While the people borrowing the money often refer to loans this way, a bank would be looking at it from the reverse perspective. To a bank, a 20 percent down payment really means nothing more than an 80 percent LTV. When you put money "down" on a loan, you aren't giving the money to the lender. You are giving it to the seller so the lender doesn't have to.

CREDIT SCORES

Credit scores are pretty self-explanatory. Your credit score is a metric that lenders look at to determine your likelihood to pay. Credit scores are determined by complicated algorithms created by three main companies—Equifax, Experian, and TransUnion. The longer you have been faithfully making payments on your debt, the higher your credit score will theoretically grow to be. The higher your credit score is, the more likely you are to be seen as a trustworthy applicant. This means you will typically receive better interest rates and have to pay less money in points, and more loan options will be available to you.

For the most part, your credit scores aren't as important as you may think. I've heard many people brag about credit scores in the 800s. This is mostly a useless, vanity number. In all the loans I've applied for, nothing over 720 will make a difference. Depending on how many properties you have, a credit score in the mid-600s will usually still get you a good rate. Banks have minimum credit scores they'll accept for different loans or interest rates, so making sure yours is in good shape is a pretty crucial part to ensuring your own desirability for lenders.

The bank typically checks all three scores and then picks the middle one. Knowing this, it's extra important to have at least two healthy credit scores at all times. While some lenders may use only one specific credit bureau (more commonly found in credit unions and savings and loan institutions), the majority tends to stick to the middle credit score.

LOANS FOR INVESTORS

When a bank gives you a loan, it is not very likely to collect the loan payments from you the whole time you are making them. Most loans originated in this country are sold to other banks or packaged up as mortgage-backed securities (MBSs) and sold through the stock market or other means. While I'm not going to go into a lot of detail about this (because it doesn't really matter for us on the investing side), I do want to point it out because this factor indirectly affects your ability to qualify for mortgages.

In America, the majority of loans are insured by the government. When the government insures a loan, it gives banks more confidence to make more loans with less fear of losing money. This in turn encourages more loans to be made, which pushes more money into circulation and theoretically helps the economy. The two biggest government-sponsored enterprises (GSEs) responsible for insuring these loans and helping to repackage them as MBSs are the Federal National Mortgage Association (FNMA, a.k.a. Fannie Mae) and the Federal Home Loan Mortgage Corporation (FHLMC, a.k.a. Freddy Mac). These GSEs set lending standards for loans before they will insure them. These lending standards are a big factor in determining what those annoying banks demand from you or the hoops they make you jump through.

The main thing I want to point out is that many lenders will do only loans that conform to Fannie Mae and Freddy Mac standards. These standards are pretty much the same for the first four financed properties you own. Once you pass four, the terms become stricter. You need better personal numbers to qualify for any loan over four. Once you've reached ten financed properties, you no longer qualify for loans insured by Fannie Mae and Freddy Mac. This is where your job at finding lending becomes much more difficult.

It's important to note that for some reason, our federal government in its infinite wisdom has determined that it's only the number of financed properties you own that matters. Not the amount of money held in those mortgages, not the overall LTV, not your individual DTI, or your personal net worth or income even. Really, none of the things that professional banks look at to determine your creditworthiness seem to matter at all. For this reason, it hurts you more to have ten loans for $50,000 each than it does to have one loan for $500,000—even if the $500,000 loan is on a property that is underwater and bleeding money every month. Smart, right?

The point is, you'll find it's relatively easy to get your first four standard loans and not too difficult to get the next six, as long as you maintain a healthy DTI and keep your credit scores up (As of 2017 for loans six through ten, you need to be above 660). It's once you reach ten that the real challenge begins. At this point, you will start hearing people refer you to portfolio lenders.

A portfolio lender is a slang term used by investors but not always used by banks. It refers to a specific loan that a bank or financial institution will keep on its own book—collecting the monthly payment and not selling to anyone else. These loans become very important to investors once they have over ten financed properties for a very specific reason. *Once you have ten financed properties, banks cannot sell your loans to be packaged as mortgaged backed securities.* Not with the Fannie Mae seal of approval, that is. This makes your loan less valuable to a bank, as it has fewer options with which to dispose of it. Remember how I've mentioned that options build wealth? Well, banks know this too. Would you pay the same for a house that had rent control associated with it? Or that you were prohibited from selling until years went by after buying it? Those restrictions make the deal less enticing and therefore worth less to you. It works the same with the banks.

The goal of a good house flipper is to get in, get it sold, and get out. The goal of a good buy-and-hold investor is to get a great house for a great price and collect small payments for a long time. Think of banks as using the same strategies. Most banks want to get you the loan, make their money, and then sell the loan to someone else and recover their capital for the next loan. This is like flipping a loan. Some banks want to hold the loan long term and continue to collect the payments from you. This is like owning a buy-and-hold property.

If a bank is going to give you a loan it holds on its own books, it's not going to offer you the same stellar terms we can currently get on Fannie/Freddy loans. Since early 2017, my clients are routinely able to secure 3.5 percent interest rates on thirty-year fixed rate loans. This is incredibly low from a historical perspective. A lender would be foolish to offer a rate this low for thirty years, as it is very likely interest rates will rise significantly in the future before that thirty years is up. That is the purpose Fannie and Freddy serve. If you take away that option from the bank, you can surely expect the terms to get much less desirable.

You wouldn't be very excited to buy a rental property if you knew you couldn't raise the rent for the next thirty years. That is like what a bank is agreeing to when it gives you a fixed, low rate for a long period of time. As investors, we expect to retain the right to raise or lower our rents as the leases expire. A bank wants this same right as well. When a bank retains the right to raise or lower its interest rate on the loan, this is referred to as an adjustable rate mortgage (ARM). From a bank's perspective, an ARM is more desirable when rates are relatively low. If a lender intends to hold a loan long term, expect it to insist on an ARM.

Once you understand that fact, it gets easier to understand why portfolio loans aren't quite as sweet as the standard we have become accustomed to. Most of the portfolio loans I have found are ARMs with rates about one point higher than Fanny/Freddie loan rates. This means you can expect your rate to start off a little higher than average loans and stay that way for a specified period of time (often five or seven years). Once that specified period is up, the interest rate can go up if the prime rate set by the Feds goes up. This protects the bank from losing money on its loan to you should rates increase before you've paid the bank back. Portfolio loans are also considered riskier by banks and therefore typically have lower maximum LTVs.

What does this all mean for you? It means once you get to the point where you need portfolio loans, two things are going to happen.

1. Your terms and rate are going to most likely get less favorable.
2. You are going to have to start working a whole lot harder to find financing.

Thought this chapter was going to be an unnecessary one you could skip because lending is so easy to find, right? Well, think again, partner. Once you get to the point when you need a portfolio lender, especially if you live out of state, you are going to find it gets much, much more difficult to finance your properties. Lucky for you, I've already been through this finance disaster, and I can share with you what I've found.

HOW TO FIND A LENDER

While I have been previously referring to lenders synonymously as banks, it's important to note they are not the same thing. Lenders come in many forms. Some banks do originate loans that they keep on their own books or sell to other financial institutions. Most of us are familiar with these banks and assume they are the main source of finding a loan. Institutions like Chase, Wells Fargo, and U.S. Bank are very well known and have strong brand recognition, but it's also for that reason that they don't always offer the best rates or terms.

There are other lending options available to you, starting with a mortgage broker. Mortgage brokers find out what your need is, collect your personal info, and then shop for an institution offering a product that will work for your individual need. While you don't pay the broker directly, you'll often find the loans that these brokers bring you have extra costs tacked on to help pay their commission. This results in your paying a higher rate and/or more points up front. Mortgage brokers are typically not the best option if you're looking to save money, but they can be a *great* option if you need someone to go to work on your behalf to find you a loan. Mortgage brokers often have access to several different loan packages and can find the right one for your needs, especially if those needs are challenging or unconventional. Depending on your situation, a mortgage broker might be a good option to help you find a lender that will lend to someone in your situation.

In addition to mortgage brokers, there are also credit unions and savings and loan institutions. I have found these to be *extremely* useful institutions when it comes to working with investors like myself. Credit unions are more likely to keep their loans on their own books, so they won't have as many overlays or requirements as national banks. Because they are often smaller, community oriented, and individually managed, I've found they have so much more flexibility than large corporate banks.

When you apply for a loan at a credit union or a savings and loan institution, you are going to be considered individually more so than checked to see whether you meet a rigid set of standards. If you've set your finances up in such a way that you are a responsible and safe lending option, you stand a much higher chance of getting a loan from these places. Expect a high-touch relationship with these institutions, with in-person meetings and phone conversations.

If you know these places are primarily interested in developing a relationship with you, you should immediately begin thinking about what *you* can do to strengthen this relationship. Remember how I told you wealth is built on relationships? Well, here is your chance to find out just how this works. These institutions are used to people coming to them and asking for loans. In essence, this adds up to a lot of people showing up and saying, "You have something I want. Give it to me." Does this sound like a healthy way to form and strengthen a relationship? Now, what if you—the smarter, cooler, wiser, better investor—shows up asking about a loan but takes things one step further? What if you tell the institution that if it is willing to work with you on giving you the loan you need, you are willing to put a large amount of money on deposit with it? What if you furthermore say that once it gives you that loan, you will then take that money and put it right back on deposit with the institution until you need it for the next property?

What if your doing this just solved both sides of the problem at the exact same time...

This is a great way to prove your worth to these lenders and take big strides to strengthen your relationship. By applying for a loan, you are giving them business. By putting money on deposit with them, you are enabling them to continue giving loans. You are showing that you are not just about yourself and your own needs; you are also about theirs. Now, when you're walking into a large corporate bank, this isn't likely to help you. You aren't going to be dealing directly with a person making the decision to lend to you or not. You'll be dealing with an automated process, a computer basically, making that decision.

Credit unions can work for investors where banks cannot because of this unique flexibility. When a human being is making the decision on whether to lend to you or not, you have the opportunity to influence that decision in your own favor. If you want to have a positive influence on another human being, *look for ways to bring value to that person first*. Just like the top-producing agent you are trying to impress before asking for his or her time, you can take the same initiative with the lender.

This technique is a great way to do that. I use this technique often, but it's not the only one. Remember how I mentioned these institutions make money by giving loans? Make it a win-win for the lender by referring it to others, and conduct an introduction yourself. Your referral gets to do business with an entity you have vouched for, and you have explained what to expect. The bank gets to make more money *and* recognize you are the direct reason for that.

Looking at business from this perspective opens doors that you *need* opened for you if you're going to have a long-term career in real estate investing. Not only can it open doors, but it can also lead to your getting better terms than you otherwise would have. When you're investing out of state, a certain mystique comes with that. The bank or credit union doesn't know anything about you—it just knows you seem to be very helpful and have a limitless supply of referrals. Use this mystique to benefit you and your business by starting things off on a great foot and never looking back. It's much more attainable than you think.

HOW TO REACH OUT TO LENDERS

I hope you are seeing so far how my system is easily replicated and works with just a few tweaks for many different purposes. Honestly, the fact that it is so easily adaptable is the only reason I've been able to do this for as long as I have with the success I have had. If I can do this, there is no reason you can't!

The e-mail we sent out to top-producing real estate agents works because it spells out exactly what you are looking for right away. The agent doesn't need to spend much time talking to you to figure out whether he or she can help you. The agent knows right away whether what you want is something he or she can provide. With lenders, it's even easier. In most cases, lenders will just need to collect some information from you to run through a system that will tell them whether you are eligible or not, and they collect it through the boring old loan application. Now, let me tell you, lenders love these things. Their answer for almost any question you ask will inevitably be followed with "Just fill out my loan app." It's inescapable.

Now, why do they love the app so much, you ask? It saves them time. They do not need to ask you many questions when they can just pull it off the loan application. In fact, many of them use systems that take the answers to these loan applications and automatically populate them into the program that is used to determine your eligibility. If something is missing, or if something doesn't work out, the computer program will tell them exactly what needs to be changed, from a higher credit score to less debt. Loan apps are great tools for lenders but terrible for investors.

They take time, time that you could be spending on much more productive things than entering in bank accounts, spelling out all your other real estate owned on a schedule, or looking up old leases to attach. If we can, we want to avoid this process. Take it from me, the guy who thinks he has filled out more of these and wasted more time doing so than any human being alive. *You do not want to keep filling these out.* Now, how do you avoid this burdensome requirement? Is such a thing even possible, you wonder? The answer to that is: sometimes.

When reaching out to different banks, credit unions, and mortgage brokers, you want to spell out very specifically what your situation is, what unique challenges you possess, and what kind of loan you are expecting. If you do this right, you can get a yes or a no before ever filling out the loan app. If you get a yes, congrats! You'll likely be directed to fill out that darn loan app. Hopefully this bitter pill is chased with the excitement of knowing you might get approved for a loan and might be able to use it to buy that awesome property you want. If you get a no, well, that is a bummer, but at least you saved the time of punching in mindless data into an online loan application.

With this goal in mind, your e-mail to the lender should look something like this:

To: _____

CC: _____

Subject: Researching rentals _____

From: David — david@realestateinvesting _____

Hello,

My name is David. I am a California investor looking to invest in Tennessee rental property. I currently own four financed investment properties in Oregon, and I'm looking to start buying in your state, as the returns seem much better. I'm looking for a thirty-year fixed loan with an interest rate below 5 percent. I can put 20 percent down and do not want to pay more than one point for my rate. The following is a list of some of my information. Please take a look and tell me whether you have a program I would qualify for.

- I live out of state.
- My middle credit score is 680.
- My DTI is at about 30 percent.
- I'll have $25,000 in reserves after making the down payment.
- I have six months of reserves for each financed property.
- I have claimed the income from my rentals on my tax returns.

As you may already know, FNMA standards are stricter once someone owns more than four financed properties. If you do not have a loan package I would be eligible for, can I ask whether your institution makes portfolio loans to real estate investors?

I plan on keeping a savings account open with your institution and keeping a sizable deposit should we be able to work something out.

Thank you for your time, and please let me know whether you have done loans like this before if possible.

—David

Now, this isn't likely to answer every question that every bank is going to have, but it *is* enough information for many lenders to know whether you automatically disqualify. Hearing that no is what is going to save you time, and when you consider how many lenders you will need to be checking with, that time starts to add up. Just as with agents, I recommend copying and pasting this narrative into the body of different e-mails and just changing the investment location and the address of the person you're sending it to.

When searching for different places to apply, you will need to look for institutions that are more likely to have a product that will work for you. If this is loan one to four for you, you don't need to be that picky. Most of them will offer similar products. If it's loan ten, you might want to conduct a Google search like "investor-friendly banks in Nashville" or something like that to narrow it down. Some more popular searches that will yield you more specific results for your needs are:

- Investor-friendly banks (*county you are looking in*)
- Credit union (*county you are looking in*)
- Savings and loan institution (*county you are looking in*)
- Portfolio lender (*county you are looking in*)

Always remember that most of the time, you are going to be told no. It's OK if you are told no. Your follow-up response should *always* be "Thank you for looking into it. Do you know of or have you heard of any other lender making a loan like what I need?"

I rarely ever find success on my initial e-mail, but asking this follow-up question will often lead me to another lender who might know of a third lender who used to work at a different bank, and this fourth lender is offering the product I need. Always, always, always be asking who might be doing what you need done. This is just another way to ask for referrals that takes very little time but can yield hugely productive results.

ALTERNATIVE LENDING OPTIONS

If you have exhausted all reasonable options when it comes to finding a lender and are still striking out because of your unusual circumstances (poor personal credit, too many financed properties, and so on), there are other, more specialized lenders who offer real estate loans for people in your situation. Many of these lenders know their target audience is very specific and therefore advertise on mediums, sites, and groups where they feel investors are likely to be. This is a great reason why you should belong to a local REIA or other investment group.

If you want to find these lenders, refer to BiggerPockets. While listening to the BiggerPockets podcast, I have heard of companies like B2R Finance and RealtyShares advertising their products. It's not very likely they are going to offer something as competitive as what you'll find at other, more conventional locations, but sometimes beggars can't be choosers. I've had success finding these companies by googling something as generic as "real estate loan" and seeing whom the top paid ads are from. If you still don't have luck after this, go to the BiggerPockets marketplace and see who is advertising their products.

In what should be coming as no surprise, another really easy way to find investor-friendly lenders is by asking other investors. As I've stated before, referrals are the single most efficient way to find a good, trustworthy, qualified team member to add to the out-of-state crew you are assembling. The simple fact is if your agent is working with investors, he or she is going to either know which lender you should speak with or which investor to ask about it. Agents don't make money unless deals close, and most deals aren't going to close without financing. "Wealth has gravity." It pulls in other wealthy people, but wealth is about more than just money.

Skilled workers want to be associated with other skilled workers. Good people want to work with good people. People with honesty, integrity, and talent want to be around other like-minded folks. Take advantage of this fact in your business. Offer value to the very best at what they do, and earn their trust and favor. Reap the benefits of this as they slowly pull you into their circle and introduce you to other highly skilled and trustworthy folks. If you prove yourself worthy to every person you meet, eventually you are going to gain the trust of the right ones. This is how you network correctly. It's not about passing out business cards to everyone you meet or tagging them all on Facebook. It's about winning them over and being rewarded with access to the people who can really make your business thrive.

Leveraging your existing relationships is the fastest, easiest, most efficient way to find whom or what you need. Start there before you look anywhere else. Cultivate these relationships like a farmer in his field. Weed them of negative emotions or selfish actions, water them with mutual respect, and then harvest the benefit of having the tools you need to accomplish your job.

THE EASE OF ELECTRONIC PAYMENTS

I think so far you can agree that advances in technology have made it easier than ever to invest in real estate. A large part of our success is determined by how well we can use it and how effectively it works for us. If you aren't actively looking for ways to find good tech to make your job easier, you are slowing yourself down unnecessarily. Don't be that person! Let technology do its job of helping you be the best investor you can be. So far, I've talked about ways it can help us find what we want. Now I'd like to share with you some ways it can help us manage what we already have.

Once your financing is sorted and your agent finds you the perfect property, it's only a matter of time before you're closing on the deal and having an out-of-state rental property to call your own. While this alone is a significant accomplishment, there are still other important team members you need to put in place. Before we continue with that, I want to take a minute to spell out one more important way technology can assist you in creating an easier system to manage rental property anywhere.

I was just asked the other day how I manage making the payments on eighteen properties. Eighteen properties with payments that need to be received from tenants and then made to the lender can sound daunting and intimidating. Again, I've outsourced it through automatic electronic payments. Every loan payment I am responsible for making is automatically electronically deducted from an online account, the same checking account in which my property manager is depositing the rent checks received. The only work I need to do is setting up the information in the very beginning to ensure the lender knows where to pull the money from. Money comes in, money goes out, and you don't have much to worry about. If you do this cleanly, you won't even need to wonder how well your properties are cash-flowing. All you need to do is check the account balance!

If you include the property taxes and homeowner's insurance in an impound account (where the lender collects those on your behalf with your payments and pays them off for you when they are due), you'll have two fewer things to worry about. Banks get their money, you get your expenses paid, and you don't spend any time or energy trying to remember whether you made that payment or not.

SUPERCHARGING YOUR EQUITY GROWTH, THE EASY WAY

If you want to create wealth faster, you can use this system to help you do so. Many people are unaware how amortization schedules work for loans. While it's slightly complicated to explain, the gist of the system is that the lion's share of the loan payment goes toward the interest in the beginning. As each subsequent payment is made, more and more starts to go toward the principal. This is important to understand because every dollar that goes to the interest is a dollar lost. Your goal is to get as much of that payment going toward paying down the principal as possible. This grows your equity, and therefore your wealth, faster.

When extra payments are made toward the principal, it changes the formula that determines how much of the next payment goes toward interest and how much toward principal. If you continuously make extra payments toward the principal of the loan, you not only pay the principal down faster through the extra payments, but you also ensure a larger percentage of your next payment goes toward the principal. If you consistently make these extra payments, you can pay thirty-year loans down much, much quicker than thirty years. This can save you quite a bit of money you would have lost by giving back to the bank in the form of interest.

One common way people take advantage of this phenomena is by making half of their monthly payment every two weeks as opposed to one payment a month. At first glance, this might seem silly, as it appears to be the same amount. Let me tell you, it's not. Making a payment every two weeks is the same as making one full month every twenty-eight days. Because most months have more than twenty-eight days in them, this leads to your paying more per month. Let me explain further: There are fifty-two weeks in a year. If you make one half payment every two weeks, that is the equivalent of making one half payment every twenty-six weeks. This would be the same as making thirteen full payments in the year.

This is not magic—it's math. Knowing this math can help save you a lot of money wasted on paying interest. On a thirty-year loan with a 5 percent interest rate and a balance of $250,000, you can expect to pay $233,139.46 in interest over the life of the loan if you make just the standard monthly payment with nothing going toward the principal. If you take that same loan with the same terms, but you make one half of the mortgage payment every two weeks, you end up spending $190,193.73—a savings of $42,945.73 from making the equivalent of just one extra payment a year.

Not interested in doing the biweekly thing? There is another, easier way. To speed up the early payoff of the loan (as well as save on the interest you'll by paying), you can simply increase the amount you pay each month and have the difference go toward the principal on the loan. In the example I've given, the monthly mortgage payment would be $1,422.94. If you round this up to $1,500 a month, this reduces the total interest you pay to $201,999.02 ($31,140.44 less) and reduces the loan from 360 payments to only 319 (just under three and a half years). Not a bad return for $77.06 a month, right?

If you want to supercharge this technique, consider making one half payment every two weeks *and* adding a set amount to the principal payment every month. This can really speed up the rate at which you pay off the loan. I use this method myself and typically round the biweekly payment up to a round number. This gives me the advantages of making an extra payment a year as well as the advantages of making extra payments toward the principal. While the argument against this is that it reduces your cash flow, I would argue that the exponential benefits you gain by paying a loan down faster can be worth more to many investors than extra cash flow.

ELECTRONIC RENT DEPOSITS

As I've previously mentioned, it's in your best interest to look for as many ways as possible to leverage technology to make your job of managing rental properties easier. This is especially important as your portfolio grows over time. The system of electronic payments works just as smoothly when it comes to making deposits as well. In most cases, it's pretty easy to find a property manager (or to teach your tenants if you manage them yourselves) who can electronically deposit your rent for you. If you're going to be drawing from the account to make the payments, it would only make sense to add to the same account to keep the balance up, right?

Whenever I'm considering choosing a new property manager, I always ask whether he or she is willing to make electronic deposits into my checking account. For a long time, property managers just mailed checks to their clients. This is why passive investment came to be known as mailbox money. While it may sound trivial, during my stages of working large amounts of overtime, I often didn't have time to go to the bank. This became especially true when I was sleeping during banker's hours. As a result, I would get rent checks I was unable to deposit piling up in my drawer. This became a bit of a problem. Eventually I began carrying the checks around in my wallet and hoping I would get some free time when I was near my bank. That never happened, but what did happen is my checks became too worn out that the reader at the bank wouldn't accept them and I needed to have my property manager issue new ones. When the new ones came, they went right into the drawer again, and the cycle continued.

The solution ended up being pretty simple. I had to get the property manager to deposit the checks in my account for me. Some of the property managers I had hired didn't mind, as they lived near a local branch and would just stop in to deposit it, then text me when it was done. Others refused to do so and stuck to the old check system. I ended up having to arrange for my property managers to contact their own banks and have them transfer the funds to my account through an electronic check or automated clearinghouse transfer. It took some time to get this accomplished, and I wasn't so happy with the amount of effort it required on my behalf.

My advice to you is to ask your property manager whether this is an option before hiring him or her. If the manager refuses to do so, it might be worth looking somewhere else. If your property manager hasn't learned it is in his or her own best interest to use electronic means for funds transfer, it would make me wonder how efficiently this property manager runs his or her business at all. But what if you find a property manager you just love, and the only problem is he or she insists on old-school snail mail checking writing? Well that can be OK, but only because we now have online banking apps for our cell phones that allow us to work around this problem. Thank goodness for that! Most decent-sized banks (like Wells Fargo) have recognized the need to provide flexibility for their customers and have created apps that allow them to perform many basic banking tasks with their smartphone, including mobile check deposits. Enroll in mobile banking, and the app will guide you through a step-by-step process on taking photos of the check from your phone for the deposit, and you can see the money in your bank just as if you had gone to a branch.

If you want to take advantage of the electronic transfer perks, but your property manager just doesn't want to take the time to handle this for you, there are still other options—PayPal and Venmo. PayPal is a very well known service that makes it easy to pay for things with your checking account without writing a physical check. Think of it as wire transfers with few to no fees, but more secure. Because of its popularity online, there is a good chance your property manager already has a PayPal account and can use it to transfer your funds. Many times, someone who is hesitant to set up online banking transfers won't mind using PayPal to transfer funds.

Venmo works very similar to PayPal in this way (fun fact: PayPal owns Venmo), and it's the most popular for smartphones. Like PayPal, Venmo links to your bank account and can be used as a third-party service to move funds to and from your account. What makes Venmo attractive is its growing popularity and ease of use. I have used this to pay contractors, requested payment from agents, pay assistants for gifts delivered on my behalf, and more. If your property manager will download the app and enter his or her bank's routing number and account info, your manager can instantly be connected to you and able to transfer money.

As you may have already guessed, this doesn't work for just property managers. Many of you managing your own rentals can use this system to collect rent from your tenants. Tenants can easily transfer the funds from their account to yours, and you'll get an instant notification advising you it's been done. Have a tenant who "forgets" to pay the rent every month? In a matter of seconds, you can request the rent from him or her and wait to receive it. You can also send a reminder after you've sent the request, and the tenant will get a notification on his or her phone. The only downside is that you'll need to transfer the balance from both PayPal and Venmo to your account physically. It's not hard, but it does take a few seconds. You'll see the "Transfer Funds" option on both apps to put the money into your bank account. The future of money transfers is moving in this direction, and it won't be long before nearly everyone with a smartphone is using services like this to transfer money easily, directly, and conveniently. While I can't give you any legal advice on how safe or secure these methods are, I can tell you that a very large group of people use them without concern, and they make it much, much easier to pay and request money.

LEVERAGING FINANCING

One of the best perks of real estate investing is the fact that you can borrow money from one source at a lower rate than you can make investing it in another. This fact, referred to as leverage, is what enables the common man to grow his wealth at rates typically enjoyed only by the wealthy. It's amazing how easy it is to obtain so much money with so few qualifications if you really think about it. What other opportunity does the average Joe stand to borrow $400,000 from a complete stranger at an interest rate below 4 percent? It is the fact lenders that consider a loan secured by real estate to be so safe and manageable that they are willing to do so—and do so this often. While it can become easy to take this ability for granted, I promise you that if you lose it, you'll miss what you had. The opportunity to borrow money to invest is one of the most powerful driving factors in the process of growing wealth through real estate.

Credit enables people to grow (or lose) wealth at a rapid rate. Credit offered at interest rates this low is even better. With real estate, you don't need to save $400,000 to buy something worth that amount. If you're using a Veteran's Affairs or U.S. Department of Agriculture loan, you might not need to save anything at all. Other people's money (OPM), when used correctly, can vault you into great amounts of wealth when consistently and wisely applied over time. Losing the ability to use OPM will greatly disrupt your opportunities to do so. You want to make sure this doesn't happen. It's for this reason I've broken down the foundation of how lenders view your creditworthiness. I want you to understand how they look at you to make sure you are *always* considered creditworthy. Too many investors don't plan for this, and it comes back to haunt them.

When you are new, the money comes easily. As the loans start to pile up over time, however, the process begins to become less and less straightforward. If you're not careful, you'll hit a ceiling and before you know it be unable to obtain more financing. Watching sweet deals pass you by because you can't borrow money is heartbreaking. Having a powerful skill set you've developed that enables you to acquire below-market-value properties and managing them well are things you'll take a lot of time to develop. It's hard work, but eventually you'll find yourself progressing through the ranks until you become a black belt investor. Getting there, then being unable to use those skills, can be extremely discouraging. Don't let this happen to you as it did to me at one time.

Once I learned how lending worked, I found it was completely in my control to ensure I always qualified for it. This empowered me to continue progressing in my investing career, continue acquiring new properties, and continue growing my wealth and passive income. It can do the same for you. With a few small tweaks to your life and spending habits, you can make sure you always qualify for loans until you get to the point that lenders are coming after you trying to sell you their loans.

DEBT-TO-INCOME (DTI) RATIO

The number one thing you can do in your financial life to help make sure you can always get financing is to maintain a very healthy DTI ratio. You want to make sure you *always* have a significant amount of income rather than money going out. While this is the best way to make yourself look appealing to potential lenders, it is also beneficial in growing your own financial health. Why wouldn't you want a significant amount of income that is more than your expenses? That's the goal after all, isn't it? Too many times we see that we have made a few good moves and allow ourselves the luxury of buying things we don't need or spending money unnecessarily. Don't make that mistake. You worked too hard to build up your passive income to throw it away on expenses.

Keeping a healthy eye on your DTI ratio is a great way to make sure you don't get swept up in believing you have more money than you really do and erasing all your hard work with a couple of new car loans that you really don't need. I make sure that for any new expense I take on, I have much, much more extra income to make up for it. I recommend you do too. A healthy DTI is a great indication that you are living a healthy financial life. Think of it like your body fat percentage. If you get into fantastic shape, you want to keep an eye on it to make sure you don't lose it, right? Finances are a lot like weight. If you take on more debt (calories) than you bring in income (burning calories), you'll end up in bad shape. Your DTI ratio is the first thing you want to look at to ensure a healthy financial life and the ability to obtain financing throughout it.

PORTFOLIO LTV

The next thing you should watch closely is the LTV of your real estate investment portfolio. When I first introduced this concept, it was purely regarding an individual property. This is where the LTV ratio starts and where a lender looks when determining whether to give you your first loan on the property. It stands to reason that if this metric matters on one property, it will also matter on many. Once you've got an entire portfolio of properties, you will want to make sure that the LTV ratio is at a healthy level. A 70 percent LTV would be a good goal to aim for.

As you refinance property loans and take money out, it would be wise to keep track of the balance of the portfolio as a whole and not look at them as individual pieces unrelated to the others. A lender wants to know that if you fall on hard times, you'll be able to liquidate some of these properties to continue making payments on the others. The more equity you have in your portfolio, the easier it will be to manage it if something goes wrong, like the market turning around or unexpected expenses taking you by surprise.

Another perk of maintaining a healthy DTI is that if you ever need to take out a blanket mortgage that covers the entire portfolio, it won't be too difficult to do so. When you apply for a blanket mortgage, you are essentially applying for one loan that is secured by multiple properties. When a lender takes an application for a loan on one property, that lender checks the LTV to ensure it is an investment with a risk factor it is willing to take on. The same thing happens with a blanket mortgage. When you apply, the lender will either order appraisals or perform its own due diligence to make sure the value of the properties are within an acceptable range compared with the debt you are requesting to take on. Most blanket mortgages come with terms that are closer to commercial loans than residential ones, and the standard LTV ratios are much lower.

When you're applying for a residential loan, the lender will be primarily concerned with your ability to repay the loan and secondarily concerned with the equity in the property (the LTV). Your ability to repay the loan is determined by your DTI ratio and your personal credit history. If you yourself appear like a good candidate and have enough for the down payment, you are very likely to get the loan.

When you are applying for a commercial loan, the lender is still concerned primarily with your ability to repay the loan and secondarily with the equity in the property (the LTV ratio). The difference is, commercial lenders care much less about your personal DTI and about the DTI of the property itself. The lender wants to see how much income the property produces versus how many expenses it is responsible for. Are you seeing the pattern here? Lenders use these same standards, applied in different methods to different subjects, to get their information on the creditworthiness of an applicant. Learning these patterns is how you make sure you will also be a good candidate.

On a blanket mortgage, the lender will use more of the commercial method than the residential one. The lender will want to see how profitable the portfolio is. If the portfolio is profitable, you'll just need to make sure the LTV ratio is also favorable. Closely watching the LTV ratio of your portfolio and making sure you don't refinance existing properties too often or with too much debt is a great way to make sure you keep the possibility of a blanket refinance in your future.

ACCURATELY REPORTING RENTAL INCOME

This topic is a fun one. There are three schools of thought on this. One says if you can avoid paying taxes, you should (when legal, of course). Those who fall into this camp believe you are not only saving money when you don't pay it in taxes, but you are also increasing the amount of money you need to invest in new properties and therefore grow your wealth faster. Investors who fall into this category are always pushing the limits of what they can get away with to avoid showing a profit on their taxes. They use strategies like cost segregation to increase depreciation on their taxes and avoid having to report as much income. They make improvements to the property that may not be absolutely necessary to have more write-offs and look for every little thing they can do to ensure they pay as little in taxes as possible.

Investors in the second school report their income fully and want to make sure their properties are run as profitably as possible—even if that means they pay more in taxes. These investors are looking for ways to increase rent in their multifamily complexes and make improvements that are only absolutely necessary unless they are going to increase the rent. They are less likely to speed up the depreciation on their properties and instead focus on buying in areas where they think they will get the most returns. These investors are often more likely to be concerned with the ROI on their money than they are with the amount of money they have left at the end of the year from their investment. They don't spend as much on accounting, and they are much less likely to get audited.

A third and much smaller group believes your money is your money and you shouldn't have to pay taxes on it regardless of what the law says. These investors manage their own properties to make sure the property manager isn't reporting the income to the IRS (managers are required to do so). They are less likely to raise rents on their tenants in hopes that the tenants stay in the property and just keep paying their rent in cash. They don't hire bookkeepers, so they save on that expense as well. These investors are actually sabotaging their own success in many ways and are at extreme risk of being audited as well as being convicted of tax evasion. This is not how things should be done, so don't be that person.

So which side is right? Like most age-old debates, this one has such staying power because the sides arguing over it haven't bothered to define what the goal is. The right question is: Which way is right for you? Determine that by understanding the strengths and weaknesses of each position. Luckily for us, these are really easy to determine. One way saves you more money now but looks worse on paper. The other way looks better on paper but takes away from your income. In my opinion, the way to determine which road to take depends on where you are in your investing career and how badly you need the cash. Let me explain.

If you are looking for every possible way to save on how much income you report to the IRS, this may look like the obvious better choice at first. What you need to realize is that lenders don't take your word regarding how much a property makes a year. They look at what you told the IRS. This is why lenders request copies of your taxes when you request a loan. They know it's very unlikely that an applicant is going to pay extra in taxes by fraudulently reporting a property is more profitable than it is just so they can look better for a loan application. They also know if it really came down to it, they could reconcile your bank statements with the amounts you claimed on your taxes to see if you're on the up-and-up.

The short of it is, if you are looking to scrimp, save, and keep every penny, it could hurt you when you go to apply for new loans on new properties. Nobody really talks about this, and I've seen it hurt some of my very good friends when they apply for financing in the future. If your primary goal is to build your portfolio for *future cash flow*, it is better to show your properties as more profitable on your taxes so it's easier for you to get more properties in the future. The future benefits of exponential growth will dwarf any benefits of experiencing more cash in your pocket now.

Conversely, if your primary goal is to live off or enjoy *present cash flow*, it makes sense to avoid showing profits and write off as much of your properties' expenses as possible. Obviously if you're at a stage where growth isn't important, it doesn't make sense to give up tax breaks or lawful write-offs. This is the best way to determine which direction you should take when it comes to reporting your income to the IRS. As far as those who illegally do not present their income to the government, can you imagine how difficult it will be for them if they ever want to apply for a loan? Pretty rough karma.

Keep in mind that all this advice is coming from the perspective of someone who is *not* making money hand over fist at his W2 job. You may be in a position where you are making so much money (good for you!) that you don't need to worry about what your rental income on your taxes shows. If this is the case, you should be saving as much as possible and taking every allowance available to decrease your taxable income. Just remember that some loans, or some lenders, won't even look at what you make yourself. If they are using commercial standards for the loan, they will be looking at what the properties themselves bring in. Knowing what kinds of loans you will be applying for, and how lenders look at them, will help you determine which road to take.

Once you understand this, it really makes you question the wisdom in quitting your job as soon as you have a couple of thousand dollars coming in every month in rental income. Why not reinvest that income into new properties? Pay down your loans faster, refinance them, and then reinvest that chunk of tax-free income into a new multifamily property or several single-family properties?

This is why it's so important you make sure you are always eligible to obtain more financing. You can become a millionaire several times over in under ten years of solid, consistent, and prudent investing if you have access to other people's money, a solid deal flow, and understanding of the fundamentals of investing. It's powerful, it's magical, it's life changing, and it's real. The price you pay to develop the personal discipline to maintain a strong financial level of health is well worth what you'll get back for it in return. Know the rules, play by the rules, and win the game. When it comes to finding lenders, it's as simple as that.

CHAPTER 5

THE REST OF YOUR TEAM

If I have seen further, it is by standing on the shoulders of giants.

—ISAAC NEWTON

So far, we've talked about the deal finder who will help find you properties to buy and the lender who will help you pay for them. Once you've got those in place, you're going to want to find the next crucial member to your team—the property manager.

Now, obviously, your property manager will manage your properties for you while you go about your business. You want to hire property managers when you're dealing with properties that are thousands of miles away, in areas where you may not be familiar with the landlord laws, and have different expectations regarding rental amenities than what you may be used to. Property managers will advertise your unit for rent, find you a tenant, perform background checks on them, coordinate moving them in, collect the monthly rent, and help take care of any issues that arise. This can include maintenance, repairs, neighborhood disputes, code violations, and late or missing rent payments.

They say if you ride a motorcycle, it's not a matter of whether you will go down; it's a matter of when. The same can be said of rental property. If you are a landlord, it's not a matter of whether you'll have an eviction; it's a matter of when. Even if you look for properties in the very best areas you can afford, vet your tenants the very best way you can, and set expectations as perfectly as possible, you are still going to end up with an eviction at some point. Things just go wrong. People lose jobs, get divorced, have unexpected medical bills pop up, wreck cars, or have other life-changing events happen to them. Your tenants are going to fall on hard times, just like you could.

As a landlord, one of your biggest expenses is going to be vacancy and the repairs that accompany it to make your unit rent ready for someone else. Having good property management in place to prevent this is an excellent way to reduce these costs. In my experience, good property management will pay for itself.

In my opinion, property management isn't a luxury. It's a requirement. If you are actively managing your own properties, you may be saving a little bit of money, but you aren't investing anymore. Now you are working. If I bought a franchise, I wouldn't do it with the expectation that I would be working at the cash register to save the wage of one worker. That's not buying an investment—that's buying a job.

Property management is a rough and frustrating job, and most important, it really doesn't pay well. I pay my property managers an average of 7 percent. On a house with a rent of $1,000 a month, they make $70. That's about three to four hours of overtime for most people working a blue-collar job, and I'm being generous with those numbers. Property managers can do this successfully on such slim margins because they have systems in place that allow them to manage things smoothly and efficiently. This allows them to take on large volumes of work and carve out a profit while still handling the large amount of busy work that is associated with property management. It's the economies of scale that make it all possible for them.

I, on the other hand, do not have these systems in place to make it efficient for me to manage my own properties. The time it would take to put them in place is not worth the loss of productivity it would incur on my business. Taking all of this into consideration, it just doesn't make much business sense to try to manage my own properties. And this is only for the properties I own near where I live. When you allow for the fact you will be purchasing other properties, thousands of miles away, the need for property management becomes even more apparent.

I will go into greater depth regarding the value that property management can bring when investing out of state later in the book. Once you hear all the different ways I use my property managers, you'll understand exactly why I'm such a big advocate for them. For now, I'm going to show you some great ways to find ones that will work for you and train them in the ways you want their help. Much like the ways we found the other team members, the methods will look familiar when we dig into how you find a property manager to add to the team. As I mentioned earlier, the fundamentals of real estate are very similar, and patterns begin to emerge when you commit yourself to mastering them. The way you find team members, regardless of the role they will play, is one of those patterns.

FINDING REFERRALS

While there are important questions to ask your property manager once you get a list narrowed down (and we will talk more about those in a bit), the first thing you should do is start asking around to see who has a good property manager they can recommend. Much like a mechanic, you want your property manager to be trustworthy, skilled, and available. Also much like a mechanic, once you find a good one, you don't want to let him or her go. It's very hard to find people who are good at what they do and still willing to work in property management. The margins are just too slim, and the headaches are just too great. If you think about it, these are the people who'll take the late-night phone calls, deal with the angry tenants, and maneuver the huge array of lies and excuses tenants will have for you. Finding someone who is good at this can sometimes feel like finding a needle in a haystack—but trust me, they are out there!

BIGGERPOCKETS

If you want to find the best referrals for a property manager, the first place to look to is other investors. There is no greater resource you can find than another investor who has used the property managers for a significant period of time and knows exactly what the experience has been like. I'll tell you, just as in many relationships, your initial experience with your property manager is likely to be all sunshine and rainbows. In an effort to start things off on the right foot, he or she will usually be good about returning your phone calls, responding to your e-mails, and explaining everything in great depth. This honeymoon period is usually sufficient to win you over and satisfy your fears about what the experience will be like.

Once you're past that stage, you will usually go back into the spin cycle of daily e-mails they get that many of them cannot respond to in a timely fashion. After enough time goes by when you feel as if you're just not a priority, you will feel dissatisfied and unhappy, eventually starting a new search all over again for a different, better property manager who wants your business more and can satisfy your needs. When you find one, you'll let him or her manage your next property and hope it goes better than the first. While trial and error is one way to try to find a good property manager, it is far from ideal. Investors have leverage to negotiate better prices and better services based on the size of their portfolio. The more properties you bring them, and the more total revenue they are managing, the more money they will make. This, in turn, makes them much more likely to make you the priority you always wanted to be. It can also mean you negotiate lower prices! When you spread your property out among several different property managers, you are weakening your own position to save money and get better service.

We want to avoid this. If you can lock down good property managers in the beginning stages, you can save yourself a lot of time by giving them each additional property you purchase. You'll also save the time spent on having to save everyone's e-mails, phone numbers, passwords for their software, procedures, and names. Each company works differently, and it is always a bit of a headache in the beginning trying to learn how to dance with them.

BiggerPockets doesn't really cater to anyone other than current and aspiring real estate investors. You aren't going to be dealing with many people who are in a different situation from yours. Because the site is so large and basically dominates the market share for its category, pretty much every major market center is going to have members on the site. Whether you're buying in Columbus, Ohio, or Los Angeles, California, there is likely going to be somebody else who also owns and manages rental property in those areas. Since there isn't much incentive for investors to hide their property manager from you (as you might find they do with a contractor or a handyman), you'll find that almost everyone is more than willing to help.

When using the BiggerPockets.com website, there are a few different ways to tap the networking features it can offer. The most basic way is by posting in the forums. People go to the forums to ask questions, solicit advice, introduce themselves to the site, or just participate in the community. The next way is by using the search bar at the top of the page and typing in "property manager [*name of city you are looking for*]." One of my favorite ways to use this site is to do a search like this, click on the person's icon who made the request, and send a message asking whether he or she found a property manager and, if so, how the person is liking the experience. This will literally let you jump to the front of the line and piggyback off someone else who has already likely vetted several property managers and found one he or she likes.

The search bar will show you more than just the forums, however. You can also see just how many times the words *property manager [your city]* have appeared in the different sections of the site. Talk about useful! With one glance, I can immediately see how many people are associated with those words, how many blog articles were written about them, how many times they were mentioned in the "Marketplace" section, and, most important, how many companies are advertising on the site. Many times, you can click on the "Companies" tab in the search results bar, and it will take you to a screen with several different companies all advertising themselves on BiggerPockets. By clicking on their profiles, reading their bios, and watching their videos, you can get an idea of whether you would like to look into them further. If you do, you can send them a message right from that screen. Want to know even more about them? Search their specific name in the same search box you looked for property managers in. Once you get your results from that, click on the "People" tab to see who has used these property managers and what they had to say about them. Investors love sharing their experiences, good and bad, with others.

Find someone who has used them and see what they liked, what they didn't like, and what they recommend you do.

The search bar on the BiggerPockets website is being vastly under-appreciated here. It is 100 percent possible this is all you would need to do to find a good property manager and be done with your search within fifteen to twenty minutes if you are in a big enough market. While it's likely, there are always situations in which you don't find someone who is a good fit for what you're looking for. In those cases, BiggerPockets can still help you out.

Another way to use the site is by hovering your cursor over the "Education" tab, selecting "Blog Topics," and then choosing "Property Management." Talk about a cornucopia of ideas relevant to your task of finding a good property manager. If you weren't sure what questions to ask, what traits to look for, or what terms to expect, you are pretty much guaranteed to find answers to those questions here. The BiggerPockets community is huge, and there are a lot of people who have been here before you and found the same answers you are looking for.

REAL ESTATE AGENTS

In addition to helping you find a house, real estate agents can be awesome resources for finding property managers as well. The nature of a good agent's job means understanding everyone else's job as well. This makes agents a great go-to resource, even for property management.

Depending on where you want to invest, there are many states where property managers are required to also have their real estate license. This means they are by nature real estate agents! Make sure to find out whether this is the case in the state where you will be investing. In states like these, property managers have to understand the job of a real estate agent and vice versa. Based on their licensing requirements, they must be cross-trained. When the walls are broken down like this, the odds are pretty high that your real estate agent can refer you to a good property manager.

Even if this is not the case where you are investing, there is still a good chance a top-producing real estate agent is going to know who the best property manager in town is. Many real estate brokers form relationships with property managers—often to the point where the property managers share office space with the agents. The real estate industry, just like many other industries, is based on reputation. Agents don't want to give a referral to their clients and not have it go well. This reflects negatively on them, their reputation, and eventually their business. To avoid a swing and a miss, agents are likely to go for the safe bet and refer you to a property manager who has a long-standing reputation as a solid service provider and resource.

If there is one company that is growing faster than all the others, managing more doors than all the others, and taking over market share faster than all the others, there is a good chance it's for a good reason. This company is most likely doing things right, treating people right, and seeing the fruit of that labor. If you ask your real estate agent for a property management referral and he or she tells you about the biggest name in town, that's a great place to start your interview process.

OTHER INVESTORS

As you may have guessed, other investors can be a key resource when it comes to finding good property management. Many people are afraid to ask other investors for recommendations out of fear the other investors won't want to share their secrets. In my experience, property managers experiencing growth only makes them better. They get better resources, can hire more people, and streamline their processes. Other investors may be hesitant to share resources such as a contractor or a handyman that are hard to replace or have limited time, but this isn't the case with property management and lenders.

So where do you go to find people to ask? Well, we've already mentioned BiggerPockets. Another resource are REIAs, real estate investment associations. They are local organizations where other investors meet up to talk shop. These can be amazing resources to network with other individuals. You may have a hard time finding deals at meetings like this (they are full of other investors who also want deals), but you likely *won't* have a hard time finding the little pieces you need to add to make your team stronger.

Attending these meetings and getting in good with the other investors is a terrific way to earn their trust and make them much more likely to help you. If you're looking for a great handyman who can handle everything and doesn't charge much, this is the best way to find one. If you're looking for something else, like a property manager who is trusted, competent, and experienced, this is the place you're going to find the biggest group of concentrated investors for you to ask. REIA meetings are gold when it comes to getting good resources from other investors.

To find a local REIA in your area, it can be as easy as googling the name of your city followed by "REIA." There is usually one person in charge of them, and that is the person whose contact information will show up in your Google search. If you want to get the best results, don't just e-mail the leader and ask for a property manager referral. You want to find out when the next meeting will be and ask whether you can attend. While showing up at these meetings can have multiple advantages for your businesses, one of them is the ability to ask other investors in your area (who likely own several units of their own) who the very best property manager is in the area.

One thing about real estate investors you need to understand is we love to talk about our business. I don't know why, but the majority of investors have a soft spot in their heart for people in their shoes when they were first getting started and will talk with anyone who rubs them the right way. Meetings like these are the perfect place to find these kinds of mentors. By showing up, introducing yourself, and making your needs known, there is a good chance you can meet someone who will help you with much more than just recommending a good property manager. REIAs are great places to learn new strategies, pick up new ways to find properties, and find blueprints of other investors who have gone before you. If you're looking to step up your game in all areas, not just one or two, this is where you want to be.

WHAT TO ASK BEFORE HIRING A PROPERTY MANAGER

In my opinion, the single most important factor to consider when hiring a property manager is his or her reputation. The job the manager has done for all the people before you is a better indication of what kind of service you can expect than anything else. It is true that a leopard can't change its spots, and this is no exception. If a property manager has a bad reputation, it really doesn't matter what he or she tells you in the interview. If you hire someone known for less-than-stellar performance, you are a fool if you think you will get anything different.

Despite this, you still need to know what to ask when interviewing potential property managers. When it comes to this issue, all I can share is what I've learned in my own experience. The most crucial topic that will determine the profitability of my rentals is the maintenance issues.

This may come as a surprise. For most people new to the business, the first thing they want to know is what percentage they will be paying in rent. While this is usually the most striking number, it is rarely the most important. New investors don't realize how much money gets poured into properties for things other than property management fees. Understanding where your big hits are going to come from is a big part of minimizing your operating costs and increasing your profit.

When I interview property managers, I like to get a feel for how they run their company. I want to ask them basic questions like what experience they have managing rentals personally, how many doors their company manages, how long they have been in business, and what they feel their company's strengths are. I also want to ask them how they collect rent, how they enforce late fees, what systems they have in place to make things efficient, and how long they have worked for their current company. These are all basic questions you want to ask any team member you are considering working with, and the way they answer these questions will either help you feel more comfortable or leave you with more questions than answers.

Once I have a good idea for the basic way the company is run, I start asking more about the specifics. The main questions I'll want answers for are:

1. What is the monthly percentage of rent they'll take?
2. What other fees are assessed to owners? (Half of first month's rent for new tenants, advertising fees, yearly walk-through fees, callout fees, and so on.)
3. How often will the property be inspected each year?
4. How will maintenance/repair calls be handled?
5. How will evictions be handled?
6. What is your average turnaround time for vacancies?

While I could surely go on for pages detailing all the questions you can ask a property manager, these are likely to be the most important. Asking these six questions will give you a good idea of what kind of experience you can expect in having this company manage your property and what kinds of headaches you are likely to receive. The best property managers can handle most issues that arise (cleanings between tenants, legal paperwork for evictions, coordinating plumbers, electricians, and repairmen for problems, and so on) without taking too much of your time. The very best ones can do this in a cost-efficient and timely manner. The elite ones can do this with minimal input from you.

When asking these questions, I'm looking for them to answer in a way that helps me feel confident they have seen everything before. If a property management company has been in business for any significant period of time, it shouldn't be taken off guard by any of these questions I am asking. Each of these companies should have dealt with these questions multiple times. If it is also a good company, the property manager will not only perform these duties but will perform them quickly and cheaply. If it is a great company, the manager will tell me of ways the company is actively looking to save its landlords money. Let me explain:

Let's say I ask the property management company the most important question—number four. I want to know how it will handle a maintenance request from a tenant. I usually pose this question with an example like a tenant who has called in to complain about the hot water not working in the shower.

Now, what I'm looking for in the answer is for the company to show me some form of initiative to save me money. You'll find that property managers, when they manage enough properties, become bombarded with maintenance calls like this from tenants. Most tenants either do not know how to or do not care to fix these issues themselves and don't hesitate to request that someone come out to fix the issue. In all fairness, it would be easiest for the property manager to simply call a plumber, ask when he or she can go check out the shower, and be done with the issue. The problem is, plumbers are licensed professionals and not cheap to hire. A plumber is going to charge a lot of money just to come look at the problem and a lot more money if it requires work. The trick is, there are some problems that can be solved by skilled individuals who are *not* licensed. These are the people I want my property manager to be looking to first.

What I'm hoping to hear this property manager tell me is he or she would first ask the tenant to check the pilot light on the water heater in the garage. I will start feeling really good about this manager if the he or she is shrewd enough to recognize this problem might have a simple fix, and skilled enough through experience to walk the tenant through the process of relighting a pilot light. This would be the ideal solution and would solve the problem in the fastest way, costing me the least amount of money and training the tenant to start solving these kinds of problems on his or her own.

The next-best answer I could receive would be the property manager's telling me he or she would send the handyman to the house to see if he can fix the issue. Paying a handyman $15 an hour is much, much more appealing than paying a plumber $150 an hour, and a skilled handyman would be able to resolve this issue by checking the water heater to see whether it is operating properly, then checking the plumbing for other parts of the house to see whether they are operating properly as well. A skilled property manager will have been actively looking for skilled handymen like this one to save a client's money.

If the answer I get is the easy, noncreative, easiest-for-the-property-manager-but-most-expensive-for-me type, I am going to look for a way to end the interview and move on. The thing I want you to understand is, I don't care that the property management company will work for 5 percent of the rent when everyone else wants 8 percent. I don't care that the company will do the yearly inspections for free. I don't care that the manager won't charge me for advertising. If the property manager isn't looking for ways to actively save you money, you don't want to hire that company.

Any companies that are willing to work for so much less than their competition are probably desperate for business and just trying to scale up in volume to a point where they have a chance to be profitable. If they aren't already profitable, you run a much higher risk of being ripped off by them when they need to pay the bills and the ends don't meet. If they are willing to do quarterly inspections for free, there is a good chance they won't be doing them at all when that time comes and they are busy with the other aspects of their business. If they are willing to avoid charging me for advertising, it may be because there is a good chance they won't be doing any. You'd be amazed at how many property managers have "marketing plans" that consist of taking some pictures with their phone, putting them on Craigslist and Zillow, and waiting for the phone to ring. This is not how you should be running a business.

Please understand that in the business of real estate, whether it is lenders who want to do your loan, agents who want to secure your business, or property managers who want to be put in charge of managing your rental, they are all going to tell you what you want to hear. These people won't make money unless you choose them, and that can make it easy to sell themselves pretty hard. Asking questions as I do is intended to find out how skilled they are. It is also intended to let me know what their mind-set is. I want to hire and surround myself with people who want to be really good at their job—who are passionate about their jobs.

Another important question I ask all property managers is what they are going to do about properties in less-than-desirable areas. This may seem like an odd question, as one would assume the job of a property manager is to manage a property regardless of where it is. I've come to find this is not the case, and you should be reluctant of any property managers who tell you they will.

The phrase "beggars can't be choosers" begins to apply here. War zone properties are horrible experiences for everyone involved. If I ask property managers what they would do if I brought them a property in a well-known war zone, I am looking for them to find a respectful way to answer that they are not the right company for me. Whether they tell me they do not specialize in these areas or flat out refuse to take the deal, I'm looking for them to turn me down. Why? Because if property managers are willing to take on a war zone property, they are likely not doing very well financially and are desperate for business.

Just like the agents who have to work with the nightmare clients because they have no choice if they want to get paid, the property managers who take on war zone houses are doing something no reasonable person would ever want to do because they likely have no choice. Just like top agents, the best property managers can pick and choose their clients as well. If I'm being totally honest, the answer I'd *really* like to receive from the property manager is that I shouldn't buy the house at all. War zones rarely ever work out financially. The evictions, damage, and other various rules of the lease being broken make them more trouble than they are worth. If a property manager has the guts to tell me a war zone property is something I shouldn't buy and he or she will not manage, I am much, much more likely to trust that manager's opinion later in the process. This is very important and something I'm going to spell out in more detail later in the chapter. Better are the wounds of a friend than the kisses of an enemy.

HOW TO NEGOTIATE BETTER TERMS

The question every investor wants to know the answer to! How to get more favorable terms from your property manager. When people ask me about my property management, the first thing they want to know is what percent I pay. This "vanity" number seems to dominate conversations when it comes to property management fees. Wise property managers know this and work in creative ways to make money so they can keep their "rent percentage" number low. Your job as the investor is to find all the ways property management will generate revenue for you, look at the big picture, and find out how you can save the most money. This means there is more than just telling property mangers you will pay them 9 percent instead of the 10 percent they are asking for.

Once you have determined the other ways they will make money, and you see the big picture, it's easy to know where you can trim some fat and negotiate better terms. If you try to skip the process of learning all the ways they will generate revenue, you will just end up in a classic "rob Peter to pay Paul" scenario—saving money in one area just to have them get it back from you in another. Seeing the whole situation from a solid vantage point where you have a good view of the whole playing field is the first necessary step to negotiating better terms.

The next step may sound contradictory to good business negotiating, but it is actually very crucial. During this phase, you need to look at *your own* playing field, including your expectations, demands, and requests, and ask yourself where you can offer something to the other side. This may sound wrong, but it's not. This is an underappreciated aspect of negotiating. The key to good negotiating, good businesses, and good relationships is to overcome your first instinct and think of the needs of others first. If you want to negotiate well, put yourself in the other person's shoes. If you want to influence others to help your business, you need to set the tone in that direction from the very beginning. If you want to negotiate better terms, think first about what you can offer. Odds are, what you are offering might not cost you anything anyway.

> *A barber lathers a man before he shaves him.*
>
> —DALE CARNEGIE

LEVERAGING YOUR PROPERTY MANAGER'S KNOWLEDGE

One way to get started right with a property manager is by appealing to his or her pride by asking whether it was OK to have him or her approve any properties you are considering. This is a strategic question and a huge part of running a successful out-of-state investing campaign. If you are buying in somebody else's backyard, you had better make sure you have some advisers on the ground who can tell you which areas are the best for you. The numbers may look good when you evaluate a property from afar, but the locals are much more likely to know whether that area suffers from problems you might not see.

This is where your property managers come in. They are like hired hands who spend all their time helping investors succeed. They see what is working, what isn't working, and why. They know which areas work best for which types of properties, and they know the best way to manage them. They know the area, and you want access to that knowledge.

When it comes to real estate, location is king. A property on one block can be *vastly* different from the same house just two blocks away. I've found this to be particularly true when investing in areas rich in buy-and-hold real estate prospects. For whatever reason, there often isn't a lot of consistency in the neighborhoods. If I had to speculate, I would assume it is because many houses in these areas aren't built as track homes. The lots are purchased and the homes are built individually, at different times and by different people. There is much less uniformity, lesser odds of convents, conditions, and restrictions being implemented to maintain the neighborhood, and a greater diversity in quality.

Knowing this, you really want an expert who knows the ins and outs of the neighborhoods and can make sure you're not buying on the wrong side of the tracks, so to speak. It makes sense that this expert would be your property manager. After all, this is all he or she does. Your property manager spends significant time managing tenants in different houses. Your manager also spends time helping prospective tenants find properties for rent, and he or she knows which tenants are drawn to which houses. If you don't think that's some valuable information, you haven't been a landlord very long.

Different tenants lead to vastly different experiences when you're a landlord. Some tenants make real estate investing feel like the best thing in the world, while others make you hate the idea so much, you are willing to sell at a loss just to get out. When it comes to your business, you want the very best tenants in your properties. Property managers know which properties the very best tenants want. They know which school districts they want. They know which size of a house, the age of a house, and which streets these tenants want to live on. More important, they know all the same information for the tenants you want to avoid.

If you're investing out of state, it is crucial you have an expert in the area checking out your houses for you. While your real estate agent should be proficient in this, as well, it definitely helps to have a second opinion to compare your agent's advice against. People ask me all the time why I use property management when I can manage properties myself. They remind me that I could make $500 a month instead of $425 if I would only cut out the middleman. In addition to the fact that I just don't think $75 a month is worth my time, the main reason is *I want the market knowledge specific to the area I'm investing in that belongs to boots-on-the-ground property management.*

This is so important to out-of-state investing. You don't want to be throwing darts on a map and hoping the house you buy is in a good area. This kind of strategy is what people used to follow before the Internet, and it is how out-of-state investing got its bad reputation in the first place. A good property manager very familiar with the area is an excellent way to obtain reliable information to use in your decision making. I would absolutely, hands down, no way around it, never do this if I didn't have local property management not only managing my rentals but also advising me on which properties to buy as well.

> *Plans fail for lack of counsel, but with many advisers they succeed.*
>
> —PROVERBS 15:22

THE CONTRACTOR

When it comes to successful real estate investing, I don't think many people would tell you the contractor is the most important person on your team. Several things need to be put in place and functioning well before you ever get to the point where you have a need for a contractor. While this team member may not be the most important, I think most people would agree this one is definitely the most difficult piece to add. Good contractors are very rare and very elusive and a secret that is very well kept by others. A good contractor is a treasure other investors are loathe to share, and for good reason. Contractors can make or break your deal, and their skill set is unique and difficult to develop. If you want to find a good one, it's going to take some work.

The first trick you need to know when managing an out-of-state rehab is to ask for the scope of work to be itemized. If you don't ask for an itemized list of repairs from your contractor, it's very difficult to know what you are paying for. If you leave it up to your contractor, you will likely get one lump sum for what the job costs. In addition to not knowing whether you are overpaying for the work when the invoice is presented this way, you also have to wonder whether everything that needs to get done is actually getting done. It doesn't do you much good if you have your contractor finish the project, pay him or her the last draw, and then realize several things that needed to be fixed or upgraded never got done. Having a partially finished rental is pretty much the same as having no rental. Both will provide you with zero income, and that's no good. You need to make sure the job gets done in its entirety before you let the contractor off the hook by paying him or her.

Another important thing to keep in mind when hiring a contractor: You are very likely going to go through several of them. The odds of your finding a great contractor to grow with on your very first try aren't very high. In general, it's wise to expect others to overpromise and under-deliver until they have proved otherwise, and contractors definitely fit this mold.

If you consider the amount of regulation when it comes to contractors and compare it with that of other professions like agents and lenders, you'll soon see why. Agents and lenders are strictly supervised and held to specific and detailed regulations. The risk of lawsuit is great, and the ways they can get in trouble are very objective and easy to prove in court. With contractors, it's different. There is much less regulation and much less supervision, and the standards with which you could claim you were harmed are much more subjective. This makes them more difficult to prove in court, and therefore more contractors don't worry about this happening. There are more bad contractors running around out there than any other team member you'll need to hire, and you should expect the search to find one you are comfortable with to take some serious effort.

WHERE TO FIND CONTRACTORS?

If it's clear you are going to spend some time looking for a contractor, the next question will inevitably be "Where can I find one?" If you're looking for a good contractor, you really do need to rely on word of mouth. Whether it comes from online reviews, other investors, or trusted team members, if you don't have someone you trust vouching for a contractor, you stand a good chance of being disappointed. We want to find ways to avoid that whenever possible.

The absolute best way to find a good contractor is by finding one through another investor you trust. Someone who has used the contractor and can vouch for his or her work and agrees with the prices is the surest form of referral you can find. While this is the most accurate way to find a good contractor, it is also probably the most difficult. Fact is, other investors don't want to lose the contractors they have. It's hard work finding one, and they have only so much time to go around.

If you want to get other investors to recommend their best contacts to you, you should recognize this is going to cost them something. If a contractor's team is working for you, that's less time the team is available for the other investor. If the contractor is going back to fix things that turned up on your job, he or she is being pulled away from that investor's project to do it. This is how real estate works when you get involved on a competitive level. There are limited resources, and we are all fighting over them. Whether it's where we end up on a wholesaler's chain (the front, where the best deals are, or the back, where the leftovers are), who is getting the best deals, or whom the best contractors are working for, everyone is fighting to be first.

Just as with what we learned in the property manager scenario, if you want people to give you their best (in this case, share their best resources), you need to have something to offer them. If you want to get that from other investors, you need to be willing and able to form solid relationships with them before they are even going to consider it. Relationships thrive on give-and-take. This give-and-take takes many forms. Before you get others to "give" you what they have, you likely need to have been giving to them long before you even ask. This is why networking works. This is why going to REIA meetings works. This is why getting out and meeting people works. Human beings like to help people they like. They don't like to help people they don't know if it's going to cost them something. This means you need to learn to be likable and have something to offer. This means you need to form relationships before you ask for things of value like contractor referrals.

So where's the best place to form relationships with other investors? Well, I'd have to say the usual suspects like REIAs and Bigger-Pockets will be your best bets. I recommend using the search bar at BiggerPockets.com to find a contractor the same way you did to find a property manager. While there is a good chance you can find someone who has done work in your area and see what reviews the other BiggerPockets members have given that contractor, you still run into the issue that finding a stranger on BiggerPockets isn't going to be an easy way to form a relationship with that person to get the best advice possible.

A much better way is to obtain a pool of names from different people in the area you want to invest in whom you already have a relationship with. This is exactly why I've listed the contractor as the last person you'll be adding to your team. Your odds are best if you can work over the relationships you have created with real estate agents, property managers, and lenders to see who can recommend a good contractor.

The first step I recommend is to contact each of these team members, tell them what your plans are, and ask whether they can recommend any contractors or handymen for the job. If your agent doesn't yet know any good contractors to recommend, you can bet that *somebody* in his or her office does. Property managers are also excellent resources for this. Keep in mind that there is a good chance you won't want the same contractor for a flip job as you may want for a rental rehab. Some contractors have become experts in keeping costs low and finding ways to save you money. There are guys who know how to paint cabinets, find and install the cheapest but best-looking laminate flooring, and have day laborers who can perform skill tasks like painting and dry rot repair for low hourly wages.

On the other side of the coin you have the contractors who do better with flips. These are the people with their fingers on the pulse of what is popular and contacts at the stores that have the items you will be wanting to purchase. These contractors have done many other house flips and know who is who and where you want to be buying your granite, quartz, new cabinets, tile flooring, and upgraded appliances. Upper-end finishes can get very expensive if you aren't careful. Watching your budget blow up before you even know what hit you can make an exciting flip project turn negative very fast. If you want a good contractor for a flip, make sure you specify that when asking for referrals. Communicating this clearly makes a big difference in the type of bid you are going to get when you send the contractors to the house to take a look.

This may sound simple. That's because it is. Nearly every single property I've bought out of state that needed work done (which is almost all of them) was done following this method. I'm so confident in this method now that I make offers and buy properties in states I don't have teams in because I know that somebody, somewhere, knows the contractor I need to talk to, and using the method I've just described is going to find me that person. When you do right by the people in this process and make sure they make money, too, you will find they are more than happy to do right by you and make sure you save money by finding you the pieces to the puzzle you may be lacking.

THE BIDDING PROCESS

Once you're at the point where you have a list of names, it's time to start whittling it down. Your goal at this stage is to find the person who impresses you the most, gives you the best prices, communicates with you best, and shows he or she wants to earn your business more than anyone else. There are several things that are going to stand out during this phase. I've found it to be very indicative of the way contractors think and run their businesses.

1. Your contractors will communicate very differently with you depending on how busy they are or how badly they are looking for new work.
2. Your contractors will likely be used to working with very little input from others or oversight and will likely be annoyed if you ask them to do something different from their "way," even if these requests are logical.
3. Your contractors will either understand your concerns and know how to ease them or will blow you off and ignore you.
4. Different contractors have wildly different ideas of what a fair price is, how strict the schedule of work needs to be maintained, and what liberties they are allowed to take.
5. Some contractors understand that what they tell you is something they should stand behind, and others believe it is more of a "guideline" with which they can vary from if circumstances dictate so.

While we would all love to learn just what to expect from our rehab crew during this initial "tryout" phase, the reality is you discover some things but you are not very likely to get the full picture. This is a stage where the best you can realistically hope for are clues that indicate what type of experience you are going to have. Things like promptness in their replies, thoroughness and attention to detail in their job descriptions, and proactive, forward thinking regarding ways to save you money and to solve problems are all things you should be keeping an eye out for. A contractor who sees a potential problem and reacts with "What would you like me to do about it?" is not as attractive as one who says, "This popped up. We can do A, B, or C. A will be cheapest, C will be the most expensive and thorough, and B will be a healthy combination of the two."

The second response is much, much more indicative of the type of person you want to work with on your projects. I can tell you from experience, a contractor who is actively looking for ways to save you money, understands the neighborhood of the house you are buying and what materials are appropriate for it, and isn't afraid to tell you when you are making a possible mistake is *exactly* the type of person you want to hire for this job. If you want to see which of your candidates excels the most in this area, make sure you very clearly communicate you would love to hear an opinion on what he or she would do differently or how the contractor would handle this project if given complete control. The contractors who reply with ways to blow up your budget and go all out without being able to justify why that adds more value are the ones you want to throw out right away. The ones who can show you how they can add more value for less money are the ones you want to dedicate more of your time to working with.

With all of this in mind, your first step will be to contact the contractor via e-mail or by phone and explain the plans you have for the property. Whether you have something under contract or plan on doing that later, the conversation is largely the same. You are going to explain to the contractor what types of properties you are looking for, what level of rehab you would like done, and what types of materials you would like to use. You should also explain how he or she will be paid and what your expectations are regarding the level of communication you expect and the way you would like the work to be proved to be done (pictures, video, apps you'll use, and so on). If your contractor balks during this stage of the conversation, you'll likely want to scratch that one off the list before you waste any more of either of your time. You need to feel comfortable with this person, and not everyone will be a good match.

If you already have a property under contract, ask the contractors to go look at the property and write you up a bid for the work they think should be done. I do this, as opposed to telling them what I want done, for several reasons:

1. If I have already explained to them what my goal for the property is (bare-bones rehab, HUD-approved tenant ready, all major issues repaired and the property brought up to modern-level expectations, and so on), they should be looking to do their analysis based on my needs, not on what will make them the most money or allow them to be done the fastest. I want them to prove they are listening to me and looking at this from my perspective.

2. I can tell how competent they are. If I've told them it will be a rental property that will rent for about $1,000, and they recommend crown molding, I know they are in over their head or are plain dishonest.

3. If they point out things I had missed, I learn from that, and it is better for my own education.

Odds are you have already anticipated what work needs to be done and may have even had a rough idea of what it would cost. By having them look at it and write you up a bid for what they think, you benefit from their experience and understanding of rehab work. This is a great way to improve your own education while also seeing how honest they are going to be with you. If your contractor recommends granite or quartz countertops in a Section 8 rental, there is a good chance you can cross that name off your list.

Once they have finished their walk-through (and you should have sent every single contractor you felt comfortable with from your list to do one), you should ask them to itemize precisely each task they would do and how much they would charge for it. That makes it easy to look over their bid and see exactly where your money is going and how much of it is going for what. While this makes a lot of sense for us as an investor, you are going to find that many contractors will just flat out refuse to do it. It's usually at this stage that you can cross a lot more names off the list. Most contractors are used to being in control.

They like to come back to you with a lump sum and say, "This job is going to be $40,000. We will do your kitchen, bathrooms, flooring, and paint." And they leave it at that. It's easier for them because only they know how much they are paying in labor to do this, how much the materials cost, and what their profit percentage is. Their job is to be as general as possible. Your job is to make this as specific as possible.

If your contractors refuse to provide an itemized list, ask them why. It may be an honest reason like they do not have time to do it. If that's the case, ask them to give you a list (when they have time) of all the things they plan to do on the rehab. If they refuse to provide these numbers, that is a bad sign. You don't want to hire someone who is not transparent. Either they do not want you to know how much they are making, or they do not know themselves. Both are bad.

Contractors like this may do stellar work, have honest reputations, and be great people. I would say to you that while this may be the case, they are still not ideal for working with investors. Leave these types for the remodals without a budget they need to meet or numbers they must stick to. Investors are unique businesspeople, and we need unique vendors to help us accomplish our goals. Be sure to keep in mind that you need an investor-friendly contractor through this process.

If you are to compare apples to apples, you need an itemized list with which to do so. Remember, you are likely to have received several bids at this stage in the process. If you allowed the contractors to give you the amount of work they recommended to be done, you need to keep in mind they aren't going to all deliver the exact same bid. Some will include roof repairs, while others will not. Some will include new appliances or new cabinets, while others will leave those out. If you simply look for the lowest price, you are surely going to miss the real question—who provides the most value? Trying to compare bids is impossible if they are not itemized in a way that makes sense for you to understand and compare them.

Once you have the list of itemized bids, it is now your job to go over them, look at each recommendation given to you by each professional, and choose the work you would like to be included on your project. Don't get too caught up in the price for that work just yet if you believe it is reasonable. What's important is we are trying to make these bids as similar as possible. Consider all the input you have received from all the contractors regarding why you believe the scope of work they provided is appropriate, and choose the one you agree with.

When this is finished, you should have one list you have made for yourself of each item in the scope of work you want completed. This "Frankenstein" method of taking bits and pieces from each contractor's submission is a great way to make sure you pick and choose the best advice from many different opinions. It is also one more way you are bringing value to your project through following the system as it's being laid out to you here. I've often found that things I would have completely missed showed up in the bids of contractors I ended up not hiring. While there may have been something I didn't like about the contractor, such as his or her pricing or business philosophy, I still benefited from our interaction. This is a great way to grow in knowledge and experience as an investor while putting your deals together.

Once you've got a list of all the items you want included in the rehab of your property, it's time to send this list back out to the contractors remaining on your list. Each contractor should get the list and instructions to please fill out a price for each of the items on it. When it comes to including the price of the materials in their bid, there are two ways to go about that. The easier way for you is to have them give you a bid that includes both labor and materials. This prevents you from having to do the work of ordering the materials yourself and arranging for them to be dropped off at the job site. Like most things in life, what you enjoy in convenience will usually cost you somewhere else. This is no exception.

The downside to having your contractors include the price of the materials in their bid is that you can't be sure they are charging you fairly for them. It's very easy for a contractor to inflate the price of the materials to make more profit out of the deal or make up for agreeing to lower labor prices to get the contract with you. This is one of those situations in which there is no easy answer. Some investors ask for their contractor to provide receipts of what was bought. This definitely doesn't hurt, but it doesn't prevent a shifty contractor from buying more materials than are needed and then taking them back to get a refund later—or keeping them for the next job.

My solution has been to pay for the materials myself outside the bid the contractor provides until I feel comfortable with the contractor and have used him or her several times. In the beginning, I want to be able to compare the prices on my itemized bid from one contractor against another's as evenly as possible. If one contractor overestimates the price of materials against one who underestimates it, it wouldn't be fair for me hold it against him or her for trying to be conservative, as I would want the contractor to be. For now, just be aware you need to make a decision and communicate this to the contractors submitting bids so there is uniformity when comparing them.

RESEARCHING THE CONTRACTORS

Once you've eliminated the contractors you don't feel comfortable with, crossed off the names who refused to submit their bid in a manner that makes it possible for you to understand it clearly, and got rid of those who didn't communicate with you in a timely fashion, it is time to get serious with those you have left. These are likely to be the best of the best from your list. They will all have a somewhat strong desire to win the job and will be interested in creating a relationship with you for the future. These are the contractors you would want to keep in touch with or enter into a business database if that is something that you do. Make sure you keep this in mind as you continue to interact with them, as they have already put significant time and effort into winning this job, and you will have to disappoint more than one of them by the time this is all said and done.

Compare the bids and see who is cheapest. My personal strategy is to look at any outliers who are grossly more expensive than the competition and throw them out right away. These are people who don't understand that investors work on strict budgets for a reason and that by the nature of the game, we cannot pay the same prices as regular homeowners would. Of those you have left, you likely have two or three bids left in contention.

My advice to you at this point would be to stop for a minute and consider that the price might not be the only factor worth considering here. If you have successfully whittled your list down to a modest number of names, it shouldn't be too much effort to do a little background work on the remaining names to find out who has the best reputation and whom you will be most likely to enjoy this experience with. I recommend waiting until this stage to start investigating your contractor's reputation a little more deeply because it's time intensive. But with a short list of two or three names, it's manageable. It would not be if you still had ten to fifteen to sort through. Even if you decided time was not an important consideration for you, don't forget that you may find a contractor with an excellent reputation whom everyone has loved—but if they won't draw the bid up for you in a way that works for you to easily compare it with others, they aren't going to be a good fit for you anyway.

When looking for people to give a review of your potential contractor, you can check the usual channels like Yelp or googling the contractor's name. In my experience, not many people leave reviews about their contractors online. If this is a contractor more likely to be working with investors, your odds of finding online reviews just dropped to almost nothing. No investors are going to be sharing information about their awesome contractors online. They are going to be much more likely to keep them a secret. This shouldn't come as a surprise.

Instead, a much better bet is asking contractors for phone numbers of former clients. If they are familiar with working with investors, there is a very good chance they will be giving you the number of former investor clients. This is good for you because these people will likely speak your language and will have a much clearer understanding of what you are looking to accomplish and what your needs and challenges will be. I've used this as a great way to work around the problem of investor-friendly contractors' having very few online reviews.

When you're speaking with the previous clients of the contractor, start with general questions about their experience. Ask them how they got along with the contractor, how the work turned out, how quickly it was done, and how experienced the contractor seemed to be. If you can get the people to open up, you should be able to tell a lot about their experience from their tone of voice. If you hear the cadence of their speech quicken and their voice get higher, that usually indicates excitement and is a good thing. If they give you a lot of positive information, this is usually something for you to consider a positive review and to worth noting.

If they didn't have a great experience, you are likely to get a much different conversation. Most people remember the bad things they have gone through much better than the good ones. They may forget to mention some of the things the contractor did well, but they will rarely forget to mention anything that caused them pain, stress, or disappointment.

That being said, if you get a bad review about a contractor, dig in a little deeper. Was this a first-time investor who didn't know what he or she was doing and may have been to blame for what went wrong? Did the person have unrealistic expectations about the contractor or the work that would be done? Often when something goes wrong, it is because of poor communication regarding the expectations of both sides. Don't automatically assume that because you are an investor that the other investor was in the right. Ask the referrals for as many specifics as they are willing to provide. Ask them how many times the contractors had to go back to fix mistakes they made, how proactive they were on solving problems, how well they stuck to the schedule, and how many good suggestions they provided. You want to get a really good idea of what kind of experience these people had because there is a very good chance you are going to have a similar one.

As you can see, these conversations may end up lengthy. This is why I recommend you wait until after you have your list narrowed down before you attempt to have them. Using this method to find a contractor, I ended up with a really good idea of whom I was going to be hiring and what kind of experience I could expect. The fact that most of the referrals will likely be other investors only makes the whole thing easier, since their goals were likely be very similar to yours.

NEGOTIATING YOUR BIDS

At this point, all you really need to do is choose the contractor you are most comfortable with and begin the process of renegotiating the bid you received. This should be easy for you because the work has been itemized and made very clear. You aren't negotiating the price of the entire job. Rather, you are looking at each individual item in the scope of the work and finding out how much cheaper the contractor can do it for. You want to know exactly where your money is going, when the job will be finished, and how you will hold the contractor accountable for the schedule of the work he or she gives you. The more specific you can make this whole process, the more control you can exercise over it, making sure things stay within budget and on time. You don't want to be doing the work of a contractor. That is what you pay the contractor for. But you do want to be doing the work of a project manager. That is why you need to oversee the schedule and budget. This will make it easier to do that.

Speak with all the contractors you are considering individually and ask where there is flexibility in their bids to reduce the price. Find out just what they will be doing, how many hours they anticipate it will take, and how they came up with the number they did. You will be surprised by how much you learn at this stage. When one contractor tells you it takes an hour to hang a door, and another tells you five hours, you'll get a pretty clear idea of who is shooting straight with you. You will learn a lot about the jobs the contractors will be doing, how long it takes them to do it, and what is involved in the process.

Once you find the contractor who seems to be the best overall fit, you simply need to hammer out the subject of how long he or she will take on the job. When I get to this step, I ask him or her to be very conservative and allow for plenty of setbacks. Once I get a number—say, eight weeks—I ask whether there is any reason the contractor shouldn't be able to finish this project within that time frame. Once he or she has said no, I include in the contract (which conveniently is now just your itemized list of the scope of work—score!) that if the work is done before eight weeks is up, I will include a small bonus to the contractor (typically 2–5 percent of the total job cost). Furthermore, I include that if the job goes over the allotted eight weeks, there will be a 5 percent reduction in the overall cost taken from the last draw. If the job goes over an additional week, another 5 percent will be withheld.

Many contractors don't like this, for obvious reasons. This is exactly why I ask them first how long they believe they will take and make sure they include a healthy cushion. It is important they understand they are entering into a contract with you (hence their name, *contractor*) and you expect them to uphold it—just as you will. I always make sure my contractors are paid what they are promised. I do my best to ensure they get the materials they need, and if I mess something up, I understand it is not their fault, and I pay the price, not them. I pay them on time and in full. Since I always hold up my end of the bargain, I expect them to do the same. If your contractor balks at the idea of being penalized for taking too long, *after* providing that time frame in the first place, it is very likely that contractor is not a person of his or her word and not someone who holds himself or herself to very strict standards. Set the tone right from the start that you are a professional and that this will be a professional relationship based on professional standards.

When it comes to picking out the materials, it's a very good idea to include your contractors in this process. Odds are they are doing this often and have their finger on the pulse of what is popular in home renovations. They also will have a good eye for how things will look when installed in the property. Any veteran will tell you that the products don't always look the same on the showroom floor as they do in the house. Experienced contractors can help save you money if you seek their professional opinion in matters such as these. They also are much more likely to know which stores have which products in stock and where to find the best prices and can even recommend good, cheap, popular renovation materials like laminate flooring and tile that works well in rentals. Leverage their experience and expertise to make things easier for yourself, even if you are the one paying for the materials.

In my own projects with a new contractor I've never worked with before, I pay for the materials myself and have them delivered to the property. I do this primarily to make sure I'm not overpaying for the materials. While this is a safer bet in the beginning of a new relationship, I still want the contractor's opinion when it comes to which materials I'll be using. A solid, typical process would involve my sending pictures to the contractor of how I want a particular phase of the rehab to look, then getting his or her input on which materials I should by. The following is an example of how this would look for a master bathroom remodel:

I go on Pinterest or Google or through pictures of my previous renovations and send to the contractor pictures of how I would like the bathroom to look. I include pictures of the shower tile, shower door, floor tile, and vanity. The contractor receives the pictures and compares them with what he or she has seen in different construction stores. Then the contractor tells me where my best bet is to find the tile or vanity and how much to expect to pay and also supplies me with the phone number and the name of a preferred associate for me to follow up with.

I call the store and get an e-mail for the associate. I send the pictures to the associate, explaining what I'm looking for. The store associate then compares this with what the store has in stock, and I compare it with what I've envisioned for the project. If I decide I like the material (say, shower tile), I get a price for it and see whether I can negotiate a discount. Once this is done, I work with the store associate to pick out the shower floor material, door, bathroom floor tile, and vanity. This helps ensure everything matches and allows me to pay for everything all at one time.

Once this is complete, I ask the associate to check on how soon the materials will be ready to be shipped. It's not common knowledge, but many stores don't keep everything in stock in their warehouse and have to put in orders to have it shipped in. You don't want to have half the materials show up at the house but the contractor unable to start until the other half arrives. Once I know what date everything will be available, I arrange to have the materials dropped off at the house on a date when the contractor knows they will be arriving. This means there is a much smaller chance that the materials will be stolen and a much greater chance that the contractor will be able to start as soon as the materials arrive. Pretty simple, right?

CHAPTER 6

UNDERSTANDING YOUR MARKET

Successful investing professionals are disciplined and consistent, and they think a great deal about what they do and how they do it.

—BENJAMIN GRAHAM

Now that you know how to find the team members necessary to run your business, it will only be a matter of time before you're buying investment property and on your way to building wealth. In a perfect world, you would just coast into the sunset or repeat the process to your heart's desire. As the passive income from your properties rolled in, the world of work, bosses, deadlines, commute traffic, and annoying coworkers would be a thing of the past.

But we don't live in a perfect world. Real estate investing requires oversight on your part. Some markets are very cyclical. They go up, down, and up again. Other markets are known more for their stability. No matter what market you're in, you'll want to keep an eye on things. Knowing whether you should ramp up your acquisitions, refinance, or exit your position is important as you manage your portfolio, the same way a careful farmer manages his crops. Your investments are your well-being, and you'd do well to treat them with the respect they deserve.

Every market, regardless of where it's located, is driven by some external factor that makes people want to live there. Job availability, wages, weather, local economies—they all have an impact on people's desire to live somewhere. As these factors shift, so will the demand for people who want to move there. As an investor, you want to make sure you own properties in areas that are experiencing a high demand for housing. This serves the dual purpose of driving up the value of your home as well as what you can charge for rent. It also decreases your vacancy and allows you to be pickier when choosing your tenants. Knowing the factors that affect demand in your market is vital to your success. Knowledge is power.

Some markets like Wyoming, North Dakota, and Texas are powered by the energy sector. When oil is up and jobs are plentiful, they see a rise in demand that usually corresponds with a rise in prices and rents. When the energy sector is weak, so are those markets. Blue-collar workers supporting families will move to these markets to take up jobs in the energy sector. The areas with the better schools, more space (likely suburbs), and low crime rates will flourish. Because energy tends to move quickly, it's not uncommon to see quick spikes in home prices as demand exceeds supply when the energy sector suddenly booms.

Other markets follow similar trends. Markets like San Francisco, Seattle, Denver, and Austin are powered by the tech sector. These cities are a hub for intelligent risk takers who are looking for a career in a field that is high risk, high reward. These markets are very desirable to millennials looking to have cutting-edge job experiences and employers willing to give them the freedom to do things their own way.

Understanding these factors puts you in a situation to proactively protect your investments and increase the odds of growing your wealth. Every market has a procuring cause for why people want to live there. Be it the weather, culture, type of jobs, city design, educational opportunities, or availability of affordable homes—it's your job to understand what that cause is and follow the trends that affect it. In this chapter, I will cover the metrics you need to know, how to track them, and how to store that information in a way that you can immediately notice whether it would be in your best interest to sell, hold, or buy more properties.

TRACKING PROPERTY VALUES

If you want to manage your portfolio well, you need to know what your property is worth. This should come as no surprise. If you want to know when or whether it's time to exit a market, you need to know how much equity you currently have in your investment as well as whether that equity would better serve you somewhere else. Tracking your home's value allows you to quickly determine metrics like return on equity (ROE) and gives you an idea of what options are available should you feel it's time to exit. You can do this by following the same steps you used in initially evaluating the property before you bought it. However, while looking up comparable homes on Zillow or using the Zestimate feature can get you a decent idea of what your house is worth, the most accurate value you can get is by having a comparative market analysis (CMA) run by an agent with access to the local MLS. If you have a good rapport with your agent, he or she won't mind doing this for you.

Agents use CMAs when trying to determine what to list a house for or what to offer on a home their buyer client is interested in. By using the search features of their MLS, they can input data like location, size, number of bedrooms, and other amenities and have the MLS search for homes meeting those criteria. Once these data are accumulated, the agents can look through the properties that show up and find ones that closely compare with the subject property (the one their client is interested in). By seeing what price the comparable properties sold for, agents can better determine what price the subject property is likely to appraise for. CMAs are commonly used by Realtors and are the most accurate way (outside an actual appraisal) to determine a property's value.

WHAT TO DO WHEN PRICES ARE RISING

Rising property values are a powerful wealth-building aspect of real estate. Historically, real estate has been a safe bet to benefit from appreciation over long periods of time. While real estate is cyclical and has its rises and dips just as other investment vehicles do, values of homes end up rising over time. A commonly repeated nugget of wisdom has been "Don't wait to buy real estate; buy real estate and wait." Real estate's appreciation potential is what makes it such a great "get rich slow" play. When your property eventually appreciates, it will give you more options to use this new wealth to grow your business. You'll want to have a good idea of what your options are so you're ready when this happens. You'll also want to know where you want to move your money, as well as how you're going to do it.

Successful displacement of capital is crucial to keeping your money earning its maximum potential. It's also important to consider that rising property values provide more opportunities than just selling your house and buying a different one somewhere else. Many doors open when your equity increases! When you find you have increased equity in your home, one of the first things you should consider is refinancing into a better loan. As your loan balance has dropped but your home's value has increased, you'll find yourself with a LTV ratio much more attractive to banks than it was before. If rates have dropped, or even if they haven't, you should consider a refinance into better terms. Times like this provide a great opportunity to get a fixed rate loan instead of an adjustable one and lock in better rates for the long term.

With this increased equity, you will also have the option to pull cash out of your property through the refinance to invest elsewhere. Owning a cash-flowing property where you've recaptured your initial investment is a great feeling and one heck of a sustainable model. Rising home prices make opportunities like this possible. Another great perk to increased equity in your property is the ability to access the equity through a home equity line of credit (HELOC). HELOCs are low-interest lines of credit secured by the equity in your property. Essentially a second mortgage on your property, a HELOC offers much more flexibility than a standard loan. Most allow you to make interest-only payments, and you choose how much of the line you want to take out. HELOCs provide a lot of flexibility when it comes to options of how you want to use your equity. You can draw the whole line and use it to finance a flip (then pay it back when you're done) or pull out smaller chunks as down payments for new rental properties. Rising values of your properties afford opportunities like these to gain access to your equity in creative ways.

There will come a time when you feel your property has risen in value so much, it doesn't make sense to keep it, as in 2005. For those who were homeowners during that time, I don't have to tell you how wealthy your house made you feel. Properties were increasing in value like crazy, and homes were being valued at prices that made no logical sense from any type of reasonable metric. If we were ever to see another market like that, it would make a lot of sense to sell while prices were high rather than refinance. What goes up must come down, and when a market goes up that much, you can bet there is going to be a correction at some point.

For most investors, it is unwise to speculate on rising home prices (buying a property that does not cash-flow positively on the hope or gamble that it will continue to appreciate so you can sell for more later). Don't make the mistake of assuming it's not important to try to buy in areas where appreciation is likely. As a matter of fact, getting out in front of where prices are going is one of the most effective things you can do to increase your wealth through real estate. If you aren't trying to understand what is happening in different markets that will lead to rising home values, you aren't trying to master real estate.

Converting the equity created through appreciation (forced appreciation or market appreciation) to cash flow is much easier and faster than converting excess cash flow saved up over time to new properties. The candid truth is that if you buy any cash-flowing property (assuming it is not in a war zone or will require ridiculous repairs), given enough time, it will more than likely make you money. The combination of inflation and loan pay-down alone is enough to make real estate investments look really appealing over a thirty-year time span.

While it is possible to just buy a random property and wait, it is much, much more effective to buy properties that stand a much better chance of appreciating more than others. Learning how to anticipate changing market trends is a crucial part of successful investing.

Don't make the mistake of assuming you have to either invest for cash flow or invest for appreciation. Do both! The best investments are those that cash-flow from day one and are also likely to increase in value more than your other options. When prices are rising, ask yourself where they are likely to rise faster and more consistently, and get into those areas first.

WHAT TO DO WHEN PRICES ARE DROPPING

Real estate is cyclical, and this means prices also sometimes drop. This can happen gradually or sometimes rapidly and violently. When prices are dropping, you want to be in a position to buy more property. Often this means liquidating what you have so you can be in a position to acquire more at lower prices.

When property values are falling, you'll be faced with a unique set of circumstances and challenges. It's not enough just to know *what* prices are doing; you also need to determine *why* they are behaving this way. Knowing the underlying forces behind why markets are adjusting allows you to capitalize on opportunities before others do and to recognize market shifts before they happen and exit expeditiously.

One of the great things about owning real estate is that even if prices drop, it doesn't hurt unless we sell. The fact that rental properties produce rental income gives us the unique opportunity to hold for very long periods of time compared with other investment vehicles. In general, a property's income-producing qualities are not very affected by its sale price. This is why a positive cash flow is so important. It is a hedge against unfavorable conditions and allows us to wait out the storm until it makes sense to sell.

Several factors cause home prices to drop, and the most common is a downturn in the economy. Other factors also play a role, like resetting loan terms or bad bank decisions that lead to more foreclosure activity—similar to what we saw from 2009 to 2012. When this happened, it became more difficult for most Americans to buy a home. This led to more people who were looking to rent and made it much easier for most landlords to keep their units filled. Even in a bad economy, real estate owners did well as long as their properties' expenses were covered by the properties' rents. While many property owners couldn't sell for a profit at that time, they *could* continue renting until market conditions changed.

Are you in an energy sector and oil prices have dropped? Were banks giving away loans people couldn't afford? Are the companies who provided the jobs leaving and never coming back? Knowing why prices are dropping helps you determine what to expect in the future. If there is reason to believe jobs are leaving and leaving for good, you may want to sell ASAP. If prices are dropping because of industry-specific reasons and you have cause to believe this is a normal part of your area's economic cycle, it makes more sense to wait it out.

So many people I know who bought around the market frenzy of 2005 gave up too early on their properties and came to regret it. In many areas, prices plummeted after 2005, and those who were not cash-flowing positively felt that the financial burden of a property that was sucking up cash every month was too strong to continue to bear. They sold for a loss or let the property go into foreclosure, assuming prices would never recoup. What's interesting is that by the year 2015, almost every one of those same properties was worth more than it was in 2005. If the homeowners who had let their properties go had held on, they wouldn't have lost a dime.

This is important to understand. It's the most influential fact that allows me to have confidence in investing anywhere I believe there are likely to be tenants who need a place to live. Prices can go up, or they can go down. I don't care as long as the rent covers my expenses. Decreasing home prices are not a problem if your property stays rented. You'll sleep very comfortably at night owning rental property that pays for itself compared with all the other homeowners who must continue making mortgage payments on homes they live in themselves. The wise investor never needs to fear a down market if it's managed correctly.

On the contrary, down markets should excite us! They are where the majority of investors build the majority of their wealth. If you understand the factors that affect market behaviors, and you understand your options regarding where you can invest, you won't need to fear shifting markets—you'll look forward to them.

INVESTING IN DOWN MARKETS, WHEREVER THEY MAY BE

When home prices are falling, opportunities to buy cash-flowing properties increase exponentially. To primary homeowners, they look forward to rising home values, as they can make them feel wealthier. Seeing a lot of equity in your home can feel pretty good, right? But as an investor, decreasing homes values is what should get you really excited.

The further a property's value drops, the less expensive it becomes to own. The less expensive a property is to own, the easier it is to find properties that will cash-flow positively. For areas where it was already easy to find cash-flowing properties, you'll see the opportunity to make even more money. Lower home prices mean smaller down payments, which means your money goes further. Lower home prices also mean lower mortgage payments, which means a higher return on your investment.

Real estate tends to behave in amplified cycles. When property values in one area rise, buyers become priced out of the area. This causes them to start looking in neighboring areas, which pushes prices up as well. As more and more markets see noticeable appreciation, this can create anxiety in buyers that leads them to pay more than they otherwise would have.

In this same pattern, falling prices can amplify things as well. As people see their homes lose value, they are much more likely to stop with upkeep, make fewer upgrades, and let them fall into foreclosure. This increases inventory and, by the law of supply and demand, decreasing prices. Buyers learn they can offer significantly below asking price, and the next thing you know, prices are being forced down from many different angles.

While this has traditionally been viewed as "bad" for the market, I say hogwash! I genuinely look forward to market downturns, as this is when investing becomes easiest. Most of an investor's time is spent looking for a "deal." Well, in market downturns, deals get easier to find. At times, everything can be a deal. This "fish in a barrel" effect makes investing much easier and much more fun.

When home prices are rising, you want to be looking for ways to increase your liquid capital. You can do this by selling homes and holding your profits in the bank. You can also do it by taking out HELOCs on your properties and holding the money while you can get it. I tend to flip properties more often in increasing markets. It doesn't matter so much how you do this, just that you do it.

When prices decrease, it's time to buy new properties. As many new properties as you can. Wouldn't you like to go back to 2010 and start over? You can bet that the next time a market crashes like that, I will be buying every solid, smart, cash-flowing property I can find. Decreasing markets should not be feared. They should be celebrated! Work hard to put yourself in a situation to capitalize on undervalued assets available for great prices because of market distress. If you're fearing decreasing prices, you're investing wrong.

One of the coolest things that happens when you invest out of state is you acquire the ability to take advantage of markets that are both rising and falling—in different areas. When you are invested in only one market, you are forced to play the hand you are dealt. Home prices are high, in which case you can flip, or they are low, in which case you can buy and hold. When you have systems set up in multiple markets as I do, a whole new list of options becomes available that really allows you to supercharge your wealth building. Moving capital from markets that have already risen to areas that will rise soon is a very simple way to grow your equity at a very high rate of speed while still taking advantage of the safety that income properties provide in protecting your wealth.

When prices are rising in an area you invest in, your equity increases but your buying opportunities decrease. This happened recently to many investors in Arizona, Nevada, Georgia, and Tennessee. Selling in a rising market will allow you to access your equity, but you'll lose it just as fast when you buy in that same rising market. "Sell high, buy high" is not a wise investment strategy and typically just results in higher property taxes and higher property insurance.

When prices are dropping in an area you invest in, your opportunities to purchase new properties are increasing, but the equity you have in your current properties is decreasing as well. Trying to sell your properties to get capital to buy more and take advantage of these new, lower prices isn't as enticing when you have to sell low. If prices have gone down far enough, all your excitement in looking at super-cheap houses is ruined by the fact that you don't have money to buy them. Selling low to buy low isn't a good investment strategy, either, and often isn't even feasible.

But what if prices were dropping in an area where you've been building a team so you could invest while prices were simultaneously rising in an area where you already own? What if you knew a Realtor in an area where prices had reached the bottom who could find you deals, but you also had one in the area where you currently owned who could help you sell? Wouldn't it be awesome to have the ability to move your equity from a stalled market to a more efficient market? This is basically having your cake and eating it too: Sell high, buy low. Or, more accurately, buy low, sell high, buy low somewhere else. I honestly do not know why more people are not talking about how powerful a wealth-building tool it can be when you can buy or sell in several different markets at a time, taking advantage of the strengths of each while avoiding the weaknesses. Having the option to do this is what allows you to supercharge your equity, rapidly increase your monthly cash flow, and protect yourself from losing wealth during market corrections. They are some of the big reasons I love being involved in several different markets and why I do not fear what any particular market is doing at one time. Protecting your wealth is just as important as growing it, and if you want to keep your money, you're much better off learning how to move it from areas where it can't do much for you to areas where it can.

RENTAL RATES

Previously we discussed how to find comparable rents in the market where you are investing. While the Internet is the most convenient and fastest way to check rents in an area, the most accurate method is to contact a property manager and obtain his or her professional opinion. Property managers hear firsthand the comments tenants make when they are looking for rental property. They know what amenities your competition is offering. They know how many other houses are available. They know the areas where everyone wants to live. They know what people can afford to pay. They know where the freeway ramps are, where the problem neighborhoods are, and what size houses are in demand. When it comes to knowing what you can charge for rent and which types of houses to buy, nothing beats the opinions of good property managers because they are the real estate agents of the rental world. Odds are property managers are going to give you information similar to what you found online. While this is usually the case, they can still provide more detail than you can get on a website. If they are experienced in the area you are buying, as you want them to be, follow their counsel closely and adjust your strategy based on their recommendations.

Once you know *what* rents to expect, the next step is to know *why* the rents are where they are. Property managers and, to a lesser extent, Realtors can be a big help with this too. Just like home prices, rent prices are a product of supply and demand. If demand is increasing in an area and supply is staying constant, you can expect rents to increase every year. Several things affect rental demand. Most are similar to what affects purchase prices for homes. When determining what current rental rates are, you also want to explore which direction rents are headed. I'll give you an example from my own experience.

Several years ago, I was buying in the Phoenix metro area. Competition had begun to grow as more investors realized demand was growing faster than prices were keeping up. As my competition became fiercer, I began seeing fewer opportunities to buy houses under market value.

A Realtor I was using found me a house in foreclosure about forty minutes from Phoenix. The house was almost 2,400 square feet, had five bedrooms and three bathrooms, and was a former model home. The Realtor estimated the home's value to be $125,000 and said we could buy it for $100,000 if we made an all-cash offer. The home required zero work to be rent ready and had sold for over $200,000 in 2005. Where I live in California, forty minutes is considered a short commute. In Arizona, where wages are lower, however, most people don't want to drive that far. I told my Realtor I believed the property was too far from Phoenix for me to feel comfortable with rental demand and that it would not work for me.

Before I gave up completely, I spoke with my property manager and asked what kind of rents I could expect. My property manager told me rents had been fairly low up to this point because of the sky-high gas prices. He then told me gas prices had recently dropped and he was seeing a ton of demand for the area. Tenants were sick of paying top dollar to live in Phoenix and realized they could save several hundred dollars a month and get a bigger house if they would commute. When gas prices dropped, my property manager saw a massive increase in demand for the area and could not find most of his tenants a place to live.

The rent demand had changed, and I almost missed it. Yes, it's true that if gas prices had shot back up, I might have faced the same problem. But by then, the tenants would already have been under a yearlong lease. Also, in the same way as I wanted to understand what drove rental demand, I also wanted to understand what drove oil prices. It didn't take long to realize America had begun drilling oil and was locked in a price war with OPEC. Both sides were trying to sell lower than the other in the hopes that the other side would run out of money first. It stood to reason gas prices were going to stay low long enough that I wouldn't need to worry about anything crazy happening. My thoughts were that if gas ever did get expensive again, rents would rise to a point where I was still making money either way, and I was right. To this day, gas prices haven't changed much at all, but rents have steadily increased.

I was able to present the seller (in this case the bank) with rent rates that averaged $750 to $850 a month. All the houses around this one had been leased when gas prices were higher. I wanted to show the bank that only investors would be making offers on these properties and the bank was asking for too much considering "market" rent. Using these numbers, I could negotiate a decrease in the asking price. When I closed on the property thirty days later, rents had risen substantially because of growing demand. More and more tenants and home buyers had been pushed away from the hot spots in Arizona in search of affordable housing. When all was said and done, I was able to rent the place for $1,100 a month. This increase in rent allowed me to later borrow 105 percent of the amount I bought the house for and still cash-flow positively. It's not too often I'm able to do this on a house that needs zero rehab and looks like a model home when I bought it.

This is an example of knowing the *why* of what a market is doing will benefit you. I was able to buy a model home only a few years old and get more than all my money back and still cash-flow well.

ANTICIPATING RENTAL RATE INCREASES

If you're a buy-and-hold investor, one of your goals is to locate the areas where you believe demand is going to increase. While it's rarely wise to plan on appreciation, it is still wise to make every effort you can to find areas where it can reasonably be expected to occur. While entire books have been written detailing how to do your own research to determine these areas, I've found much more success by simply developing relationships and collecting information from people who work in the areas where I want to buy.

As of 2017, many investors I know are buying in Indiana. Price-to-rent ratios are favorable, foreclosure inventory is relatively high, and many landlords who have owned large portfolios of homes have let their inventory deteriorate and now want to sell it. If I were to begin investing in a market like this, I would find the best property manager I could and begin asking as much as I could about the state of the local economies. Metrics like where are most of the jobs moving, where are the best schools, and where is the tenant demand greatest would all be incredibly useful for me to know. Understanding where the students in the local universities are living, and for how long they are living there, would be beneficial as well. Find out who needs to rent a property, and then find out what that person wants and whether that type of tenant is one you want to rent to.

Imagine if you could find the area where the jobs were expected to continue moving, narrow down where the best schools were, and cross-reference that with county tax information showing where the cheapest property taxes were. You'd be able to take that information right to your Realtor and ask him or her to search for deals in the MLS in that specific location. You'd be able to take that right to your whole-saler and ask him or her to start mailing more letters to that specific location. Heck, you could mail your own! Information like this is easy to find when you find the right people. Knowing it gives you an edge. What's even better is you can do all of this from the comfort of your own couch in your underwear with Cheetos-stained fingers.

I hear people every day make spontaneous statements like "What I really need to do is find out where the city is going to issue commercial zoning to next and go buy property nearby." Most of the time, this is spoken out loud and nothing is ever done. I wonder whether these people realize how easy this is to actually accomplish, how one well-placed phone call to the right Realtor can have him or her searching that information out *for* you so you don't even have to do it. When you have the right people on your team, acquiring information like this is easy, and acting on it isn't nearly as complicated as you may think.

The last advantage I'd like to present you with when it comes to following rental trends is increasing rental rates. By asking your property manager what upgrades tenants are paying more for, what level of materials are expected, and what your competition is offering, you can pass that information along to your contractor to make sure you get a finished product that tenants will want. If all the other homes for rent in your area have two bathrooms, you don't want to be the person with one. If your competition is offering refrigerators, you'll want to have one as well. The same goes for finishes like tile and linoleum, recessed lighting, and a landscaped yard. Find out what your competition is offering, and match or beat it. You'll be the one collecting a check every month, while others are lowering their rent and getting the leftover tenants.

Having your finger on the pulse of the rental community is important, but it's not hard! You don't have to do this research, put in the time, or gather the information yourself. You just need to know the people who do. It's not as if you have to seek out a private lawyer or researcher to get this information for you. Even more, these are people who *want* your business. They are excited for the chance to work for you to make money and show you what they can do. Too many people spend their time trying to acquire the information when what they need to be doing is trying to acquire the people who already have that information.

The best investors don't spend all their time looking for deals. They spend their time looking for people who have the deals. In the same way, you *don't* need to become the "market expert" in the area you are considering investing in. You need to know enough to be dangerous. You cannot be wholly ignorant. It's your job to pay experts for what they know. Stop trying to do everyone else's job, and start focusing on the stuff you enjoy doing. You'll be much better off for it in the end.

FOLLOWING EMPLOYMENT TRENDS

Another metric you'll want to follow closely as a real estate investor is employment trends. While rental rates let you know how much rent to expect in an area or on a property, employment trends let you know for how long you can expect to receive those rents and whether they are likely to increase or decrease in the future. Simply stated, jobs are the number one factor that affect housing demand. People move to where they can find work. People pay as much for a house they love as their job will allow them to pay. Hot markets follow jobs, not the other way around. If you want to be ahead of the crowd when it comes to buying in the next hot market, don't get caught up thinking you need to be in with the city planning department. Don't think you need to understand and memorize all the census data. The number one thing you need to know is whether the jobs are moving there and, if so, what kind they are.

The employment trends will affect the demographic of your tenant, the financial status of your tenant, and to a lesser extent the types of properties the local tenants are likely to want. You need to stay focused on these. Knowing the environment where your different properties exist is an important step in knowing how to get the most out of their potential. It's not enough to know what the employment situation was when you bought the property. This is something you'll want to con- tinuously monitor for the duration of time you own it. Luckily for you, the Internet has made it very, very easy to get a good grasp on what is going on in a particular market's economy. A simple Google search or browsing Yahoo's home page can tell you a lot about the state of the economy. Unemployment rates aren't hard to find; in fact, they are hard to avoid. Lots of information is available concerning where jobs are moving and what kinds of jobs are moving where.

For example, recently it was announced that Ford is canceling its plans to move a huge plant to Mexico. While to the novice investor this doesn't seem very pertinent to real estate, when you are monitoring the overall state of the economy and employment trends, this kind of information is really useful. If Ford ends up building a new plant in the United States, wouldn't you want to know where that is going to be? A new auto plant of that size would bring in a lot of jobs. Many of these workers would be family men and women. It would be reasonable to assume the need for housing would increase in areas near the plant. If you were considering investing in that area, news like this would be encouraging. Conversely, if you lived in Mexico and were considering buying land near the new incoming plant, you would definitely want to know whether plans for the plant were canceled before you completed the purchase. This is a small example, but it reflects the importance of keeping an eye on employment trends.

That is just one illustration of the importance of understanding employment trends in areas you are both considering investing in and already investing in. If I had already bought the land, intending to build homes to sell, it would be wise of me to adjust my strategy to build rental units once I realized what kind of jobs would be moving into the area (and the accompanying wages). It doesn't take a hedge fund manager, Harvard business school graduate, or genius-level IQ to be able to follow the employment trends of a particular area and see the writing on the wall regarding how it will relate to changing demand. Anyone can do it now that we have the Internet and Wi-Fi at every coffee shop.

UNDERSTANDING YOUR TENANT POOL

It's important to know where jobs are moving. It's also important to know what types of jobs are moving where. This is an area where specificity matters. If you're looking at buying in an area where tech-happy hipsters are flocking, you'd be wise to invest in areas close to downtown near lots of public transit. You want to give the people what they want. Those who move to be closer to tech jobs tend to favor great restaurants, trendy clubs, fashionable bars, and lots of Wi-Fi. They don't mind living with several others in close proximity, since they often have just left college and are used to the dorm lifestyle. Some will be happy to just have their own shower!

These tenants tend to care much less about a car, a large yard, space from their neighbors, and the quality of the school districts. If you're considering investing in an area where tech jobs are moving, it would be foolish to buy the house in the suburbs with a three-car garage and a large backyard for playing catch. This crowd may not own a car at all and will rely on the subway and bus system to get around. They aren't thinking about playing soccer with their kid in the park across the street or being able to watch the children from the kitchen while they cook. They surely won't be paying extra for an amenity like that. While you may get by on renting out run-down properties to these twenty-somethings who are happy to finally have their own place, you'll also have to consider that their employment is anything but reliable. The tech industry giveth, and the tech industry taketh away.

Conversely, if you're considering an area and you're seeing a lot of big corporate jobs moving in, you will likely be catering to an entirely different crowd. If Wells Fargo, Berkshire Hathaway, or PG&E is moving its headquarters to an area you're looking to invest in, you're going to be seeing an influx of middle-aged, white-collar, family men and women looking for places to buy or rent. If you go big and buy a twenty-story condo complex in the heart of downtown (near public transit, loud bars, and yoga studios), you might be disappointed when you can't find anybody who wants to rent the units. Where are they going to park their Mercedes? How are they going to sleep at night with all the noise outside?

They will be better impressed with features like large backyards, pools, multiple covered parking spaces, four-to-five-bedroom houses, and proximity to parks. The quality of the school district will matter much more to them. Upgraded features like granite countertops, stainless steel appliances, and custom-built showers will provide a wow factor that will impress their friends when they entertain. Having several bedrooms for all the children will be important. A downstairs mother-in-law unit might get you an additional 15 percent in rent. Having an open floor plan will be huge for them.

These are tenants you can comfortably assume will be OK with rents being raised every year. As they move up the corporate ladder or get their yearly raises, they'll be able to afford the rising rents and will appreciate the feeling of living large that you have provided. Most of these tenants will have a pride of ownership and take better care of the property. Their kids will sink roots into their local schools, they will get involved in Little League and PTA programs, and they will make friends with the neighbors. These tenants will be less likely to leave your property to move in with their buddy a few blocks away. They will be more likely to value their credit and want to avoid an eviction.

I realize I just presented two polar opposites, but can you see the pattern I'm getting at here? Knowing what kinds of jobs are moving into your area helps you determine what types of tenants are too. Being aware of information like this allows you to construct an investment strategy that will maximize results. Doing a great job on a property that no one wants yields the same exact result as doing a terrible job on one: vacancy. It's not enough to be good at what you do; you also need to make sure that what you're doing is something people want.

Just as with other areas of investing, don't get sucked into thinking you need to do all this work and research yourself. You have assets on your team you've constructed. *Use them.* Your property manager is a great way to accomplish this. He or she is more likely than you to know which employers are moving into an area because your manager will be the one fielding the phone calls from the prospective tenants. If tenants whom he or she manages stop paying rent and say it's because they lost their job, the property manager knows what kind of jobs they are losing and why. Your property manager oversees your units, but it's not just *your* units. He or she is managing everyone else's too! Leverage this kind of information. Communicate with your property manager often and listen to what he or she is saying. You are already paying him or her to manage your property—why not leverage your manager for market info as well?

Ask your property manager and real estate agent what types of occupations they are seeing from their client pool. After all, if you know what kinds of tenants are moving to a specific area where you're buying and you're keeping an eye on the employment industry, it reasonably stands to assume you may catch wind if things start to shift. An easy way to do this is by checking with your property manager every quarter and asking whether he or she is seeing more people falling behind on their rent, more people unable to handle rent increases, or a decrease in tenant demand. If my property manager tells me that one area of town is becoming less desirable, you can bet I'm paying attention and trying to figure out why.

A personal example involves the only rental I've ever sold. I noticed on this one Arizona property that rents were just not keeping pace with inflation. While prices had risen immediately after I'd bought the property, they had leveled off and stayed pretty much constant, while all the rest of my properties were appreciating healthily.

When I began prodding my property manager and Realtor for more information, I found out the city had issued new building permits after rezoning the area, and new homes were being built in a brand-new development about fifteen minutes closer to the area where my tenants were commuting to work. This new development was much more desirable compared with mine, as tenants did not need to commute as far. Tenants and home buyers were all going to that area first, and it was causing demand in the area where my home was to drop. Nobody was looking to move where I owned, since there were plenty of properties closer to the jobs that were comparable with mine. Once I realized this, I asked how many more homes were going to be built. The answer was ... a lot.

Seeing that the winds had shifted against me, I quickly put my house up for sale, collected my equity, and moved it to a growing market with a much healthier rental demand. I was able to get out of a bad situation and into a good one because I asked questions every so often about the condition of the overall market, not just about the condition of my property. Since I sold the house, its value has not risen at all. I was able to turn the equity from that one house into three different homes, each of which cash-flowed about the same as the original. This led to my tripling my monthly cash flow and borrowing more money to have my tenants eventually pay down, and the homes I bought have all increased in value (and had built-in equity when I bought them). This one move was very good for my overall net worth as well as for my passive income—imagine if you could replicate this several times over.

Simply put, the job market is the number one factor that will influence both the rate you can charge for rent and the value of the house. Home demand, including prices and rent values, is a product of the job market and accompanying wages. Learn to understand it and follow it closely.

CHAPTER 7

WORKING WITH THE MARKET

Look at market fluctuations as your friend rather than your enemy; profit from folly rather than participate in it.

—WARREN BUFFETT

One of the very best feelings in real estate investment is when you see your carefully selected, diligently rehabbed, and closely managed properties appreciate in value. Very few things can grow your wealth as quickly or as easily as seeing your equity grow by significant amounts as you ride a wave of rising home prices.

As investors, we can't make the market do anything. The market is going to do what it's going to do. We can work as hard as we want and spend as much effort as we want. The only way our efforts really help us are in putting us in a position to score from that great wave. Think of things like working hard to save a down payment, researching the area in which you want to invest, and putting the time into building your team. Once you're there, you're looking to catch that big win. That win can make or break your whole day. All the hard work you've done has been to put you in a position to see your new worth rapidly rise while you just enjoy the ride.

If things have gone well and your properties have increased in value, you're left with more options than you had when you started. When investing, options mean opportunities. The option to sell your properties in one market and move to another is present when it wasn't before. The option to sell and sit on your money is a possibility as well. You also have several refinancing options or equity lines of credit you could consider.

So what do you do? How do you know whether it's time to sell and reinvest or whether you should sit tight with what you have and not get greedy? After all, you make your money when you buy. If you can find more good deals, it would stand to reason that it would be wise to sell something that's already increased in value and move it somewhere else. This becomes an even easier decision if building your cash flow is your number one goal. While real estate investing provides many different ways to build wealth, this can become confusing when you're trying to compare one advantage with another. If all you're considering is which area is likely to appreciate the most in value, the decision is usually very simple. If you throw into the mix that one area may not appreciate as much but has a much stronger and more stable rental market (leading to more cash flow), the decision can get a little trickier. If you want to know how to move your wealth around, it's very important to establish a common denominator. If you don't do this, you can't really make a sound, logical decision.

CREATING AN APPLES-TO-APPLES COMPARISON

Before you can know whether you should move your equity to a new market, you first need to establish an apples-to-apples comparison. It doesn't matter which metric you use, as long as you're using the same metric for both possibilities. Different investors have different goals and therefore will have different criteria with which to evaluate their options. You need to decide what is most important to you and make that the standard you use for comparison's sake.

To illustrate this point, I'm going to start with comparing the cash flow in your current property to the cash flow you could expect if you bought a different property somewhere else. Since many of this book's readers are buy-and-hold investors, and most buy-and-hold investors do so for cash flow, it makes the most sense to start there.

When it comes to the purposes of determining and measuring cash flow, the most commonly used metric is return on investment. ROI is a bread-and-butter term thrown around in all kinds of investing, not just real estate investing. It is the functional equivalent to the return you would expect on your money if you put it in the bank at a predetermined interest rate. Its most simple definition would be "the percentage of your initial investment you get back in a year." ROI is determined by taking the amount of money your property makes you in a year and dividing it by how much money you invested (typically your down payment). The higher the ROI, the better return you're receiving.

For example, if your ROI is 10 percent, you could expect to get 10 percent of your initial investment back per year. After ten years, you would have recouped all your investment and paid yourself back. To calculate ROI related to real estate investments, it's a very simple formula.

(Monthly cash flow x 12) divided by initial investment

So with a house that generates $500 a month in rental income profit where we put $50,000 down, it would look like this:

$500 x 12 = $6,000 divided by $50,000 = 0.12 (12 percent)

This investment's ROI would be 12 percent.

ROI is valuable because we can use it to very easily compare one investment with another. Thinking about investing in the stock market where you can expect to earn an 8 percent return or buying a rental property instead? Find the ROI of the rental property you want to buy, and if it's more than 8 percent, it's going to make you more money. Voilà.

Now, real estate is of course a little more complicated than that. There are more benefits to rental property than just the cash flow (ROI). There is the loan pay-down, potential appreciation, tax benefits, and more.

The real value in calculating ROI comes when you are comparing one investment with another specifically to determine which will cash-flow more.

I've said earlier how cash flow shouldn't be the only reason you invest. It's one of the reasons but not the only one. For the purposes of this portion, we are going to ignore every other benefit to investing for the purposes of focusing on cash flow to simplify the process of determining whether you should sell in one market and buy in another. While in the real world you should compare all aspects of an investment (potential for appreciation, tenant desirability, "headache factor," strength of financing, and so on), you should still learn how to run an apples-to-apples comparison of properties. This is how we do that with cash flow.

ROI is the easiest way you will determine the return you are making on your money. The thing with ROI is, it can be misleading, especially in situations where properties have appreciated a significant amount after you bought them. Real estate follows patterns, but they aren't the same across the board. Prices tend to increase much faster than rents in appreciating markets. They also tend to fall much faster than rents in depreciating markets. Sometimes rents increase when prices stay the same. This discrepancy in behaviors causes the performance of your investments to change over time.

While this is clearly true, many investors will never realize it. The reason? They are evaluating the performance of their property using only ROI, and ROI is not a great metric for evaluating the performance of a property over a significant period of time.

As the initial down payment on an investment stays the same, only the income accumulated by the property changes in the ROI equation. Simply put, this means if your rents go up, your ROI will go up. If your rents go down, your ROI will go down. Because rents rarely ever drop, at first glance it appears a property performs better every year than it did the year before. The investor is pleased, and not much more thought goes into it.

This is where people are making big mistakes. ROI is useful, but it's *most* useful when determining the expected performance of a property upon initial purchase. It's even better for comparing performance between properties. It's *not* great for determining the performance of a property after you've owned it for a period of time. Here's why:

In most cases, you should be evaluating the performance of your property based on its current equity, not the initial down payment you invested. Now, at first, your down payment is the exact same thing as your current equity. Unless you got an awesome deal with built-in equity, of course. For the majority of purchases, your down payment pretty much becomes your property's equity. Because of this, calculating your initial ROI is an accurate indication of your property's potential.

After you've owned the property for a while, things may change. Your loan is slowly being paid off, increasing your equity. When your property appreciates significantly in value, your equity will be increasing significantly as well. In this chapter, we are also determining what to do when your properties' values have appreciated. When this is the case, ROI just won't cut it anymore.

If you put $30,000 into a property and it's bringing you back an ROI of 15 percent, you may be very pleased. But what if the property has appreciated $100,000 since you bought it? That's a lot of equity sitting there that is doing nothing for you. If all you did was calculate ROI, you would have no idea how vastly your property was really underperforming. You also likely wouldn't realize the amazing opportunity you had to move that equity into a different market when you could convert the return on equity (ROE) in your property to a much higher ROI than it is currently producing.

Boom.

The magic of ROE.

UNDERSTANDING RETURN ON EQUITY

Return on equity isn't talked about much. I don't want to see any of you make that same mistake.

Your ROE is determined by taking the amount of money your property makes you a year and dividing it by the amount of equity you have, not the amount of money you originally invested. It is a much more accurate way of determining how your property is performing than simple ROI. Let me explain.

I bought a property in 2009 for $195,000. I put $48,750 down. As of today, this property cash-flows $685 a month after all expenses and the mortgage are paid. This is effectively an ROI of 16.86 percent ($8,220 a year divided by $48,750). Now, at first glance, this looks like a very good return that most investors would be happy with. If this were all I considered when determining whether to sell a property, I would have to find an opportunity to make better than a 17 percent return before it would be logical to do so.

However, this property has appreciated to a value of approximately $380,000. My current loan balance is about $130,000. This gives me approximately $250,000. Assuming I would have to pay a Realtor's commission to sell the house and some closing costs as well, if I were to sell it, I would likely walk away with about $225,000 left over. If I use this number as my equity, I can calculate the ROE of this investment.

My ROE would be:

Yearly income ($685 cash flow x 12 = $8,220) divided by equity ($225,000) = 0.036.

The return on my equity is 3.6 percent. Not quite as impressive as the nearly 17 percent I was making on my ROI that had me feeling pretty smart.

If I were to sell this house and buy somewhere where I could achieve a much more modest 12 percent ROI, my cash flow would jump up to $2,250 a month. Compare that with the $685 a month the property is making me now. Seems like a no-brainer that it would be better to sell, right? At least if my primary concern were cash flow, that is. The big difference in the amounts of cash flow is the difference between my current ROI and my potential ROE.

This is why understanding that in the long-term buy-and-hold investment game, understanding your ROE is absolutely crucial to the speed at which you grow your portfolio. I'm leaving nearly $1,565 on the table every single month between what I could be making and what I am now. ROE matters, and it becomes an even more important metric when you begin opening yourself up to the amount of options available to you when you can invest anywhere.

One of the reasons investors don't talk about ROE much is because for a long time, if you sold in one market, you had to invest in the same market. It was very difficult to sell a house where you had a lot of equity and invest it in the same market but hope for a better ROI. If you invest only locally, your options to sell a property and move the equity to somewhere better become limited. As real estate is local, if you're selling high, you're also likely to have to buy high. This makes it much harder to put that equity into play.

When you invest in different markets, you can take the properties that have appreciated a good amount, sell them, and move the money into a market that is primed for a good run. This can be a great way to grow your equity at an accelerated rate. If I were to sell my property with approximately $225,000, I could buy five new properties where I put $45,000 down on each. If each of these new properties eventually increased by $50,000 (or I forced that equity with solid buy prices and skillful rehab work), I would have grown my initial equity from $225,000 to $475,000. This is even more impressive considering it all started from an initial down payment of $48,750.

This same concept works for cash flow. If I were to take my initial cash flow of $685 and move the $225,000 in equity into five different properties that each cash-flowed at 12 percent ($45,000 down on each), I would end up with the $2,250 a month I mentioned earlier. This is more than a 325 percent increase in my monthly cash flow. If you are investing in different markets, this suddenly becomes a very real possibility for you. This is one of the huge advantages out-of-state investors have over those who invest only locally.

TIMING THE MARKET

While we will never do everything perfect when it comes to real estate investing, we can still try to. In the San Francisco Bay Area, where I live, many homes have already reached their 2005 highs. This means that houses here are selling for as much as, or sometimes more than, what they reached in the highest real estate peak we've ever seen. This is a time when I would consider selling to maximize my ROE. However, in this case, I want to keep holding. Why? Because the market shows that prices may still continue to rise because of the market and employment trends in the area.

Understanding what drives a market is paramount when making decisions on where to move your equity. I follow my own advice on knowing market trends, and I study local employment trends. I know tech jobs are flooding to the Bay Area—and they are high paying. I know that the Bay Area culture is very desirable right now, and tech companies (and the millennial IT workers who accompany them) are all moving here. I also know that new homes haven't been built much at all since the crash. There is a severe lack of inventory with a simultaneous rise in both housing demand and job wages.

What does this mean for real estate prices? It means demand has begun to skyrocket and supply has remained constant. There is good reason to think that prices will keep rising. In fact, with wages rising fast, it's hard to see what could stop them from continuing to do so. Now, this is admittedly a gamble. I have no idea what prices are going to do. Neither do you. All I can do is make the best decision I can with the information available.

I've chosen to wait and see how much higher the market will go. I believe the facts, market trends, and laws of economics support my decision. In these situations, you should weigh the risk against the reward. If I see prices start to drop, I'll have the option to put it on the market fast and try to sell before they go down anymore. If I see lenders making risky loans, I'll have a good idea another crash is imminent. When you buy a property correctly, you don't need to fear what the market does. You just need to know what your options are for when it shifts.

That being said, there are usually signs an economy shows before it collapses. Just as a good wave can be seen making its way toward you if you know what to look for, market corrections give clues just the same. A few of the easiest to recognize are:

- A significant increase in the average number of days that available homes are sitting before going into escrow
- Abnormal lending practices such as more adjustable rate mortgages, 80/10/10 loans, negative amortization loans, and interest-only payment periods

- A noticeable pattern of companies leaving the area
- Sellers' having to offer significant concessions to buyers

If you're starting to see effects like these in an area where you've invested, it would be a good idea to calculate the ROE on properties you own and compare it with the ROI you can receive in other areas of the country where you're investing. Neglecting to do so limits your options and at the same time limits your ability and opportunities to grow your wealth.

THE "HEADACHE FACTOR" AND OPPORTUNITY COST

It's important to consider potential positive outcomes when moving your money between markets. Cash flow and appreciation are both great wealth-building tools. As important as these factors are to real estate investors, there is another one to consider—the headache factor.

Money is good. It's the reason we do this. It's not all there is, though. You also need to consider how much time you will be putting into managing the property, how likely the tenant base is to cause you problems, and how much sleep you'll be losing over things going wrong. As investors, we all love money, but not all money is good money. Ask anyone who has chased the spreadsheet magic of a 2 percent property in a war zone whether they disagree. Simply put, some properties are going to cause you much more grief, stress, lack of sleep, and headaches than others. For most of my investing career, my philosophy has been to settle for a modest ROI in exchange for highly desirable properties that would serve me well long term. I get very busy, and I know that a property that demands a lot of my time, attention, and creativity to keep profitable is going to *take* money from my pocket as it pulls me away from other endeavors in which I could have been making more.

Problem properties take up so much of your time and resources that they ultimately can end up costing you money in the end that you could have made elsewhere. If I focus on this, I cannot focus on that. If I buy this property, I cannot buy that property. In economics, we refer to this concept as opportunity cost.

Opportunity cost refers to the money, opportunity, or other thing of value you lost when you turned your resources to another. If you skipped work to go shopping, we all tend to think of the money you spent shopping as what the trip cost you. Opportunity cost points out you also lost the money you had the opportunity to make by going to work that day. Yuck.

If you're a house flipper and your project runs two months over schedule to complete, you may lose out on another deal in which you could have made more money by reinvesting your profits. That extra money you lost out on would be the opportunity cost for your project going over the deadline. Successfully limiting the money, time, and opportunities you lose out on is an important strategy for real estate investing. It's not just what you pay that matters; it's also what you miss out on. This concept isn't unique to money. It also applies to time, effort, and energy.

With buy-and-hold real estate investing, you want your properties to be as passive as possible. Meaning, you want them to take up as little of your time as possible. Selling a home in a great area to improve your cash flow might sound great on paper, but in practice it's not always that simple. There is more to think about than just cash flow. Quality of life matters too.

When considering moving your money from one area to another, don't forget to ask yourself how much time and energy this will take. Selling investment property isn't always simple. Often it involves getting a tenant out of the house, making repairs and upgrades to prepare the home for the market, and then meeting with real estate agents to choose the one you want. Once the house is listed for sale, you will be conversing back and forth with your agent, going over offers, and obtaining information necessary to complete the sale. Selling a house takes some work.

Once the house is sold, there is also obviously work involved in finding a new one. Finding the right agent, searching for homes, making offers, signing forms, evaluating numbers, doing research—this all takes time. Once you find a home and your offer is accepted, you'll be reviewing inspection reports, natural hazard reports, and title reports and meeting with property managers and contractors. And this is all before you even get started with paying them to do their work!

All this time will take you away from other possible money-making opportunities. If you're in school, it will pull you away from your studies. If you're in sales, it will pull you away from your clients. If you value your family time, you'll be losing some of that too. Don't neglect to consider the price you will pay to get all your ducks in a row to sell one property to buy another.

This is a great way to build equity rapidly and then transfer it to cash flow, rather than try to save cash flow for a long time to build wealth. Too many investors get caught up in the idea that saving cash flow is the way to build wealth—it's not. Wealth is created most quickly by buying below market value and creating equity through wise decision making and management. Concentrate on building equity first, then turn that equity into cash flow later in your career when you need to live off it.

With this strategy in mind, you need to be very careful that you're not moving money into areas that look good on paper but cause major headaches. It can be really tempting to consider moving some of that big equity into markets with big rental yields. It's not until after you own and are trying to manage the properties that you realize how much work goes into them and how much of your anticipated profit gets soaked up in repairs, vacancy, damage by tenants, and capital expenditures. You don't want to buy a job. You want to own an investment. Knowing what you're buying is really, really important.

Understanding the headache factor of an area is crucial. Learning how to sniff these areas out and avoid them at all costs is crucial to your success. The strength of real estate as an investment is in large part because of its passive nature. When done right, managing a rental portfolio shouldn't take much of your time or attention, especially once it's been stabilized. One of the biggest contributors to a negative experience in real estate investing is buying in one of these high-problem areas and ending up wanting to pull out your hair rather than focus on better things in life.

HOW TO DETERMINE THE HEADACHE FACTOR OF AN AREA

First off, you need to understand that investors *not* knowing the types of areas they were investing in caused a lot of people to lose a lot of money for a long time. Situations like these gave out-of-state investing a bad name. An ol' California boy like me sees a big, gorgeous home for only $125,000 that would cost over $500,000 here. Thinking he's got a steal, he ties it up, brags to his friends, and puts it on the market to rent out. To his dismay, the only tenants he can find want it only as a grow house for their hydroponic marijuana operation. One police raid, three broken doors, nine HOA violations, and $10,000 worth of damage later, and that ol' California boy realizes why nobody else was buying that home.

This doesn't need to be you! In today's environment, there is absolutely no excuse for something like this happening. If you've followed the steps outlined thus far for putting an out-of-state team together, you have everything you need to prevent a disaster like this from happening. Horror stories are the price of admission for the uneducated, and that's no longer you.

I know we are all eager to know what the house will rent for so we can plug it into our spreadsheet or calculator. Analyzing a property is a straightforward, clean process. I'm here to tell you that's not even one of the first three questions I ask. Before I ask what a property will rent for, I want to know what kind of neighborhood it's in. Don't chase rents; chase information, chase desirability, chase equity.

This is why communication is so important. My property manager needs to know she's still getting my business even if she tells me to stay away from a property. My Realtor needs to know she'll make a commission on the next one. My contractor needs to know if I don't buy the house, I'll still offer to pay him for his time. He also needs to know that if I end up buying a house in a nicer area, he'll make more money because I'll do more upgrades.

To sum this up, the trick to avoiding bad areas is to get good, honest information about the area the house is in. If you want accurate information, you need to have the right people. If you want to have the right people, you need to have the right ecosystem where you have aligned their interests with yours.

IMPROVING YOUR PORTFOLIO'S PERFORMANCE

Another factor to consider when looking for ways to decrease your headache factor is to consider reducing your ROI. The difference in

ROI between a 2 percent property and a 1 percent property is huge. The difference in the headache factor between the two is often just as huge!

Remember, money on a spreadsheet is not the same as money in your hand. One eviction can eat up six to nine months of cash flow. One bad tenant who causes several thousands of dollars of damage can eat up over a year's worth of cash flow. It was the tortoise who won the race, slow and steady. Not the hare who tried to speed out ahead and got lost.

Sometimes (and by sometimes, I mean usually) it's better to take a modest return on your money over the sexy return that never works out. If you have a good tenant, you may not want to raise the rent if it means losing him or her. If you're in a good market that has room to rise, steady employment, increasing demand, and a good tenant pool, it may be wise to just stay put. Make sure you're looking at the big picture and weighing all your options. It's not all about pure cash flow on paper.

Let me give you an example of how this would look.

You have several California properties that have increased in value and now have $500,000 in equity after sales commissions and taxes. You are considering moving this money into duplexes in North Texas because you love the future upside of North Texas, the demographics, the job opportunities, and the state's friendliness toward landlords. You are considering brand-new duplexes from a builder with a great reputation in an area you would encourage your mother to live in. You also feel very confident that the tenants will take good care of the homes, that the homes will hold up well, and that the experience will be easy to manage for the property manager. The only negative you can think of is that you can't buy them for very far below market value because this is new-home construction.

Your plan is to put $50,000 down on each and buy ten of them. This should net you a 10 percent return, or $4,166 a month. Appreciation is likely, since the area is growing, jobs are flooding in, and the city is limiting the amount of new building permits it issues each year. Before you pull the trigger on buying them, you see a post about another investor who is buying in South Bend, Indiana. This investor is talking about how many doors he can acquire, how amazing the cash flow is, and how unbelievable the ROI will be. You start to doubt.

If you move your money to South Bend instead, you can buy houses for $50,000 each! Rather than finance ten duplexes with $50,000 down, you are considering buying ten houses for $50,000 each—all cash. Each of these houses will rent for about $800 a month, and you anticipate a return of 20 percent. This comes out to $8,332 a month. Double the estimated Texas returns! The South Bend properties are all about thirty to forty years old and are so cheap because they need significant capital improvements.

This South Bend opportunity has got you second-guessing yourself. It's hard to say no to 20 percent returns, and that spreadsheet magic is really weighing heavily on your mind. Before you take the plunge, here are some points you should consider.

1. Most lenders have a minimum loan value of $50,000. That means that at an LTV of 80 percent, your cheapest-priced property that you could finance would have to be $62,500. The properties you are looking at are all around $50,000. This means they would not qualify for conventional residential underwriting, and you would have to either find commercial lending or not finance the properties at all.

2. Your anticipated capital expenditures on the Texas side will be minimal, since these are brand-new construction properties built by a great builder. Your anticipated capital expenditures in South Bend will be 15 percent of gross rents because the properties are older, in an area with weather that beats up on homes more, and lived in by tenants much less likely to appreciate and take care of appliances, plumbing, and other features of the home.

3. The pride of ownership you will get from your tenants in North Texas is expected to be much greater than from those in South Bend. This means fewer repairs, fewer maintenance requests, and less damage when the tenant moves out.

4. The rental demand in North Texas is high, and everyone knows it. Tenants will be much less likely to object to rising rents or become a headache, since they don't want to be asked to leave because rental inventory is hard to come by. In South Bend, you are likely to have the opposite problem. Your research has shown there are a lot of rentals available and not a lot of tenants. You are much more likely to have tenants balk at rising rents, especially

if they don't have steady employment or built-in raises.

5. You've determined the average tenant in North Texas has been renting for three to four years at a time. Conversely, the average tenant in South Bend rents for nine months. This means your vacancy rates are anticipated to be three to four times higher in South Bend.

6. In addition to the vacancy rate, you can expect to "turn" the property (make it ready for new tenants) three to four times as often in South Bend. This means repainting, re-carpeting, and so on, that much more often.

7. South Bend weather beats up on roofing and pipes and causes dry rot on the properties. Texas weather is much gentler on your properties, and repairs will likely be much less.

8. Over the following one to five years, North Texas is expected to see home price appreciation of approximately 5 percent. South Bend is expected to see maybe 1 percent.

When all you are looking at is a spreadsheet that shows South Bend returns' being double those of North Texas, it's easier to assume South Bend is the better market. When you step back and look at the big picture, it becomes apparent this isn't necessarily the case. There are several factors at play you need to take into consideration when deciding on where to invest. If you fail to account for the things mentioned above, there is a very good chance you will end up seeing your productivity suffer as your time is sucked into these projects, your wealth decrease as your properties suck up all the income, and your desire wane as this becomes less fun and more of a headache.

In this example, North Texas may very well end up being the better option even though it's much less impressive on a spreadsheet. Make sure you consider accepting a lower ROI and less headache over maximizing your potential cash flow but handicapping your ability to enjoy life.

TIMING YOUR LEASE RENEWALS CORRECTLY

If you're investing out of state in buy-and-hold properties, the scenario will inevitably come up when you want to sell a property that is currently occupied by tenants. This can happen for a variety of reasons. Sometimes someone approaches you with an opportunity that is too good to pass up. Maybe you need to make the balloon payment on an overdue mortgage. Maybe some partners of yours find an apartment complex they want to do a joint venture on, and you want in. Maybe your research has shown a market correction is imminent, and you want out. Regardless of what opportunities you may find yourself with, there *will* come a point when you want to sell a property that still has a tenant. Allow me to present you with some options for how to avoid this if possible and how to manage it smoothly when not possible.

One strategy I use is to have all my leases expire in the middle or beginning of summer. It's no secret that the real estate market is hottest in the beginning and middle of summer. It's also no big secret that tenants don't want to move in during the middle of summer because they won't have much time to find a new place in a school district they want. For families, most moving decisions are centered on the school year. They want to be moved into their new home and settled in with time to register their children for the new school year. This creates a crunch around later summer to find a new place to buy or rent. Trying to find a new house to rent in the middle of summer, when everyone else is also looking to rent, is not fun.

I set things up this way for three reasons.

1. The first reason has to do with raising the rent. If I raise the rent, the tenant will be more apt to pay the higher rent than try to frantically find a new place to live within a short amount of time. This puts me in a stronger position to ensure I'm always on the front end of rising rents and my vacancy period is less.

2. The second reason has to do with a tenant's deciding not to renew his or her yearly lease. Should this occur, I have the option of selling the property at the peak of the home-selling season. If I've already decided to sell, I don't need to come up with creative ways to get my tenant out of the house before I can put it on the market. Simply not renewing the lease and having the tenant vacate makes for a quick and seamless transition should I determine selling is in my best interest.

3. The third reason is I find that often (but not always), rents tend to track in a direct relationship with home prices. This means

that as home prices rise, rents do too. If I want to find the best time to sign a yearlong lease, I want to do it when home prices have just begun to rise and rents likely will have also. There is also a psychological advantage in tenants' seeing homes becoming less affordable in the middle of summer and not wanting to leave my property to buy one during a seller's market. If I can take advantage of home buyers' fears that homes are becoming too expensive, I am more likely to get them to re-sign their lease with me.

If you're a buy-and-hold investor, the last thing you want is a property to become vacant in December or January, during the holidays. Nobody is looking to move or buy at a time like that. Your house is almost guaranteed to sit vacant for much longer. In renting terms, this is a "buyer's market." Fewer tenants looking for somewhere to rent means the tenants have more negotiating power when it comes to demanding a lower rent amount. By arranging for my leases to expire in the peak of the real estate market, I put myself in a better situation that costs me nothing but makes a huge difference in the number of applications I get and the quality of tenants to choose from.

CASH FOR KEYS

While setting your leases up like this decreases your chances of needing to have a tenant break a lease before it's up, it's still not a guarantee. Should you find yourself in a situation in which you need to sell but the tenant doesn't want to just leave, you're going to need to take some steps to make it worth his or her while to do so. This can be a big headache as a landlord, and we want to mitigate that.

As an investor, this solution may pain you. We are trained to pinch pennies, balance budgets, and count costs. Having to pay your tenant money to break the lease may hurt, but it's often your best option from a financial standpoint. A powerful lesson to learn is you simply cannot make people do something they don't believe is in their best interest. Even if they are morally in the wrong. This is why so many good, experienced investors embrace concepts like cash for keys and note holders embrace deed-in-lieu. They know it's better to lose the moral battle to win the business one.

Should you find a tenant who doesn't want to move, your best bet is to offer him or her money to break the lease. You should also make an effort to help the tenant find a new place. If you're using a good property manager, this step could be very easy because sometimes there is a similar property the person can move into—and you can even offer to pay a small percentage of the new rent for the first year. If you want people to do something that is difficult, make it easier for them. By taking the initiative and showing you have found the tenant a better property than the current one, he or she will feel you care. By paying for moving costs, offering cash, or even paying for part of the new rent, you are making it easier for the tenant to subconsciously cooperate with you. People are much more likely to cooperate with someone when they believe that person cares.

In addition to the stress you avoid by operating this way, take a minute to think about the benefit you bring to your property manager. This is much better than having to manage angry people. Taking steps like this will help solidify your relationship with your property manager in a way that will earn his or her respect and help your manager to see you as an ally as well.

ACCEPT SOME HEADACHES

> *You don't have to see the top of the staircase to take the first step.*
>
> —MARTIN LUTHER KING JR.

Thus far, I've been discussing how to avoid headaches in your portfolio once you've already achieved a certain level of success. When trading in equity that came via previous good decisions, you want to make your life better, not worse. However, there are times when you may be willing to accept properties that come with more of a headache factor than would be ideal because it's still in your best interest to do so. Many times, this is based on your level of investing success.

That phrase "beggars can't be choosers" can apply here too. Sometimes we have to start investing in areas that are more problematic and prone to bigger headaches because it's all we can afford. Sometimes they're the only places where we can get financing, or the person backing your deals refuses to invest anywhere else. For whatever reason, you may find yourself trying to pick up steam in areas that are higher on the headache factor spectrum, and this doesn't mean you're doing anything wrong. Sometimes you have to just play the cards you're dealt.

If you do find yourself in a market notorious for its challenges when it comes to being a landlord or dealing with bad weather or the unavailability of deals, try to look for ways to minimize the problems. One great strategy is to spend more time looking for a rock-star property manager who handles the tenant base skillfully instead of just hunting for deals all day. If you put the cart before the horse and don't get a strong system in place before you start bringing in properties to manage, you may find the experience much, much more frustrating. If you can successfully make the experience easier on yourself, you'll find yourself much more likely to throw more effort into your business, and better results will follow.

Another important factor to take into consideration is that if you can learn how to manage rentals (and people) in these very worst of situations, you can probably learn to manage properties in *any* situation. When I first became a deputy sheriff, I started off working in a maximum-security prison. When I left and became a police officer working on patrol, I was often told by my training officers that I did a really good job of handling the most dangerous suspects. Working in a custodial setting, I had become used to communicating with and understanding the most dangerous people. When I left that setting, I had confidence that I could police in any neighborhood, no matter how bad, because I had already been surrounded by the worst. This can be your same experience when it comes to investing. If you can learn how to write up an airtight lease for the toughest tenant to follow, you should have no problem at all with managing a portfolio in more desirable areas.

If you do find yourself as one of these people who are forced to start in a rough market, your goal should be to build up enough equity to get yourself out of there as soon as is reasonably possible.

This is a tough goal but a worthy one. Should you get to a position where you are able to start looking in a better market, the question you will be faced with is: Does moving my equity somewhere else make sense for me?

While this is obviously a complicated question, generally speaking, there is a very good chance the dilemma you will be faced with is trading in a strong, cash-flowing portfolio of stabilized properties for the opportunity to start from scratch and try to replicate this process in a new market. It very well may feel like taking a step backward. If you find yourself in this dilemma, ask yourself what your end goal is.

If you are close to retirement and feel you just want to coast at this point in your career, it may be best to hold what you have and manage it as well as possible. If you're still looking to expand, however, I would encourage you to consider trading in some of that ROI for properties that will be much easier to manage and have a greater likelihood of appreciating over time.

When looking for these new markets, try to remember that you've done well so far and you deserve to find a market where you don't have to deal with such headaches. If you've put together a successful portfolio of properties at this point (in a tough area to boot), you have likely acquired a knowledge base and skill set that should allow you to make money in markets that aren't as difficult or as frustrating to manage. You have, in effect, earned the right to start investing in better markets. I highly encourage you to take advantage of that. Most people become accustomed to their present environment and don't ever realize how things could be better somewhere else. Real estate markets can be like that too! Here are some examples of things I've found that people who are operating in difficult markets fail to consider while continuing to invest in their present market:

1. Some states have much, much friendlier landlord laws than others do. Tenants know this and won't cause you trouble because they already know they will lose in court.

2. In some areas, there is a much higher "pride of ownership" when it comes to the tenant base. While the tenant may not own the home, there are certain cultural environments where it's socially unacceptable to let your house get trashed, and tenants face

positive societal pressure to keep your property looking clean and well kept.

3. Some areas are better known for having businesses that want to retain their employees. These good jobs keep their employees and want them to be promoted and stay with the company. This means consistent raises and tenants who are less likely to run into financial trouble.

4. Many cities limit the number of new homes that can be built per year. These areas tend to see greater home price appreciation, since supply is limited by governmental quotas. This creates higher demand for rental property as well.

5. When you're buying in rough markets, housing inventory tends to be older. This leads to higher repair costs. Newer properties break less and need less maintenance.

6. Newer homes tend to have better technology. Better insulation, better foundations, better roofs, newer appliances, upgraded electrical systems, and so on, are all likely present in newer homes. Old houses come with bigger code problems. This is unavoidable in older markets, where you tend to find bigger headaches.

7. In markets with more expensive homes, you find that capital expenditure becomes a smaller portion of your rental income. A roof costs roughly the same for a $30,000 house as it does for a $200,000 house—but the percentage of the gross income is much different. Appliances, plumbing systems, paint, flooring—they all tend to cost the same regardless of the price of the house.

8. When you invest in better markets, you tend to find better support staff. The very best contractors, property managers, lenders, and agents don't want to spend their time in low-profit, high-headache areas. You'll spend much more of your own time trying to find quality team members in areas that score high on the headache scale.

As you can see, there are a lot of reasons why it's advantageous to move your system to an area better suited for long-term real estate investing. Less headache often means more enjoyment. It's almost always better for long-term success. Real estate isn't like picking stocks. We aren't trying to choose a winner and then cash out as soon as we can. No, it's more like planting seeds or trees. We make wise decisions when we plant, and then protect and nurture these decisions as they grow. When the investment or seed becomes mature, we make the decision to harvest the tree or collect the fruit. Because the whole process takes place over several years, the most important decision you can make is where you plant your seeds. It's the one thing you can't change about your investment. Houses tend to be heavy and difficult to move.

BUSINESS BENEFITS OF DECREASING YOUR HEADACHE FACTOR

So far, I have mentioned practical benefits of decreasing the number of headaches your property will provide, things that make sense from an analytical standpoint regarding the individual properties themselves or the individual people managing them. Now I'd like to mention some of the indirect benefits to making the job easier on yourself by decreasing your headache factor. When it comes to real estate investing, we want to make sure we are focusing on the whole picture.

The most important benefit of decreasing your headache factor is the reduction in time it takes for you to manage your business. As you already know, time is money. High-maintenance portfolios are not fun, not productive, and not good for business because they hinder our performance and slow our growth.

You may be thinking you can avoid this by having a property manager take care of your portfolio. That's a nice thought. Unfortunately, it's a bit naive. Properties that require a lot of your manager's attention will inevitably require a lot of yours as well. When it comes to how a property manager tends to your properties, you typically have two options:

1. The property manager approves expenses below a certain dollar amount determined by you. This will almost always lead to his or her approving everything that comes through to keep the tenant happy and paying and your becoming very upset when you see all your "cash flow" disappearing on its way to the pockets of the maintenance man.

2. You make the property manager run everything by you first, which will inevitably result in your feeling like the manager yourself.

As you can see, it doesn't take much before the property manager's problems are your problems. Frankly, this is OK. It's your business, and no one is ever going to care about it as much as you do. Property managers aren't magicians. They can work with only what they are given, and if you're giving them a crummy product, they are likely going to have a crummy experience. This means before long, you will too. If you want to be a productive business owner, you need to be looking for new ways to expand your business.

Do you think Elon Musk is in the factory running a machine? No. Elon is in his genius laboratory coming up with great ideas—he passes the task of assembling the products on to employees who handle the details of running the company so he can focus on the big picture stuff.

If you want to make your portfolio grow, you need to be focused on finding and acquiring properties, not working out a payment plan with a struggling tenant. You are better off developing new relationships with great deal finders than fixing broken roof tiles. There is no way you can do that if you're constantly being contacted by the property manager about a new late payment, a new eviction, or a new vendor that needs to be sent out to repaint your newly vacant property.

You get the point here. Free up your mind for its highest and best use, and watch better results follow. I've had this experience in my own career, and I've found it's worth sharing with others.

When I first began investing, I was investing only in B+ properties. I knew this was a good long-term strategy, and it ended up being true. My problem was I didn't get to reap the benefits of investing in B+ properties because I was too busy trying to micromanage them. While the issues that came to my attention were very easy to solve and should have been left to my property manager, I felt I needed to be involved in the entire process.

My property managers must have hated me. I wanted to know every single detail that was going on in the homes. How the grass looked every month, what the outside deck looked like, how many times tenants had guests over, how many cars were parked in front of the house, all of it. I thought managing a property meant micromanaging it, and I was the worst. I quickly found that owning rental property was no fun. Every bit of bad news had the power to ruin my entire day. This all led to my eventually hating real estate and wanting to get out but feeling trapped and as though I couldn't.

It wasn't until I let go of my self-imposed expectations of perfection that I finally started to enjoy this whole business. It came to a boiling point one day when a drunk driver crashed into the fence of one of my properties. My insurance company originally told me that it would be paying, then that the driver's insurance would be paying, and then that nobody would be paying. This got me pretty upset. I caught myself thinking about how I should have prevented this, and I was a fool for buying a house on a corner lot. Of course this happened—look how easy a house on a corner lot can have a car run into it.

As soon as I heard myself think this, I realized the absurdity of my thoughts on this topic. I quickly realized I had been doing this the entire time, and it had been creating a horrible experience for myself. I had been holding myself accountable for things I had no control over and ruining the entire experience for myself. Every time a water heater needed a pilot light relit or a spray for pests was needed, I was blaming myself for buying the wrong property.

Once I realized no human being could reasonably be expected to anticipate the problems I was having, I quickly adjusted my expectations. At that point, I just started to budget for unforeseen problems and accepted that things could be expected to be found broken or to need repairs after I closed on a property—especially during the first year. It was time for me to adjust my expectations to account for that.

Once this happened, it changed my whole experience. Rather than feeling like a failure when my property manager called, I just shrugged it off and let him work it out. As real estate investing became more enjoyable, I started to get more and more excited about searching, analyzing, and offering to buy more houses. These were the beginning steps of when I fell in love with the whole idea of being a real estate investor.

THE 1031 LIKE-KIND EXCHANGE

The final tool you should have a basic understanding of when it comes to moving from one market to another is found in the Internal Revenue Code Section 1031. This section of the tax code has to do with provisions to avoid paying capital gains taxes on profits made for certain, specific investments when handled a certain way.

Now, I'm not a CPA, and when it comes to this stuff, I definitely talk to my own accountant and recommend you do the same. With that in mind, I'd like to give you the general gist of how this whole process works because it plays a pretty big role when it comes to out-of-state investing and moving your equity from one area to another.

In general, a 1031 like-kind exchange is a way to sell an asset and move the gains into a new asset without paying taxes on them. In essence, you're just deferring paying these capital gains taxes so you can reinvest the proceeds rather than pay them to the IRS. Cool deal, right? For real estate, this means, in practical terms, selling a property and moving the profits into a new property without realizing any of them. According to IRS.gov, a like-kind exchange is:

> Properties are of like-kind if they are of the same nature or character, even if they differ in grade or quality. Personal properties of a like class are like-kind properties. However, livestock of different sexes are not like-kind properties ... Real properties generally are of like-kind, regardless of whether the properties are improved or unimproved. However, real property in the United States and real property outside the United States are not like-kind properties.

In a nutshell, this means you can exchange one type of rental property for another without paying taxes on it, if done correctly. Now, please keep in mind, you want to talk to your CPA before you do this, since there are several rules to keep in mind and it's easy to mess this thing up. I've heard several people know just enough about this process to be dangerous but not enough about it to keep themselves safe. A few of the rules that can hurt you if you don't understand them correctly:

1. Upon selling your property, you have forty-five days to identify new properties with which to close on. You can't buy just anything.
2. You then have 180 days to close on one or more of the identified properties. There is no allowance made for weekends or holidays.

3. There can be no "constructive receipt" by you of the funds. Meaning, a third party needs to maintain control of them after your property closes. The funds are then put into the escrow of your like-kind or a replacement property later. If you take possession of the money, my understanding is you just messed the whole thing up.

4. And lots more!

While accountants should be familiar with this process, it doesn't mean everyone else is. The important thing to remember is, it's a powerful tool to help you move assets from one market to another. One of the biggest arguments about ever selling a property is the fact that you must pay taxes if you make money on it. We have the awesome ability to delay paying those taxes until later in life, when our capital has had a chance to grow and significantly increase.

If you're curious to learn more about how to effectively pull off a successful 1031 like-kind exchange, speak to your title company about whom it can recommend to advise you, and speak to your accountant or your real estate attorney. You want to make sure you do this first, before getting yourself involved in selling the house, because there are several hoops that need to be jumped through and restrictions that need to be met. As a California Realtor, I must have my clients sign a form that indicates whether the property is going to have funds held by another party as part of a 1031 exchange. If you miss checking this box, the IRS could receive information from the title company about capital gains taxes being due that will complicate or ruin your plans.

Don't be that guy! Measure twice and cut once. Prepare for your exit, plan for your acquisition, and be guided by the experts when it comes time to execute. This is an awesome tool to be kept in the arsenal of the real estate investor, and it becomes even more powerful when it's wielded by the out-of-state investor. When done right, this can really supercharge your equity buildup and help decrease your headache factor at the same time.

CHAPTER 8

MANAGING OUT-OF-STATE PROPERTIES

Teamwork is the ability to work together toward a common vision. The ability to direct individual accomplishments toward organizational objectives. It is the fuel that allows common people to attain uncommon results.

—ANDREW CARNEGIE

Ah yes, here we are: the chapter where I get to address the question of how any of this is even possible. Without question, the issue I have found more people have with out-of-state investing is how they find and rehab a property thousands of miles away when they can't be there to see it. The thought of managing an out-of-state rehab project can be daunting, but the thought of missing out on potential millions in equity is even worse.

A lot of work goes into real estate investing, no matter where you live or buy. Searching out a new market, finding the place you want to build your team, acquiring all the right players, and then scooping up properties is all for nothing if you can't find a way to get them ready to rent out or sell. Rehabbing is a crucial part to real estate investing, and the process looks very similar to how we do it in our own back-yards, with a few variations or extra steps involved. The familiarity in understanding the fundamentals of a rehab project gives us the confidence to take this show on the road.

For most people, the overwhelming urge to "be there to see it for myself" is enough to convince them that managing a rehab proj-ect from thousands of miles away is too much to take on. For those who don't understand how simple the process can be, it looks like a gut-wrenching proposal. Letting someone mow the lawn or do some landscaping may seem plausible, but when it comes to sending tens of thousands of dollars across state lines, it can begin to feel too risky to be prudent.

There are just so many things that can go wrong! How do you trust your contractor? How do you know the work is being done? How do you know your contractor won't take your money and run to the Bahamas, never to be seen again? I get it. I went through all these emotions once too. It's scary! What I'd like to propose to you is that the fear you're feeling is really just an emotional response to not feeling in control.

Buying a turnkey product that is already rehabbed is something people can more easily stomach. This seems to be why most out-of-state investors are just turnkey buyers who fancy themselves inves-tors. Truth is, it doesn't take much skill to buy something where the work has already been done and completed by someone else. The emo-tional control required to buy a turnkey home is so much smaller, it's no wonder most people take this route. It's sold as "safer," and it can certainly feel that way when someone else has already completed the project. But is turnkey really safer? Is it the best way to invest your capital? Let me ask you a few questions that may reveal that turnkeys aren't as safe as you think. Then I'll explain how you can do it yourself and save a lot of equity.

When you buy turnkey, you are relying almost exclusively on the word of the turnkey provider that the investment is sound. This can be troublesome considering the person selling you the property is the same one providing you with the deal. What the seller of the property considers a "good" neighborhood may not be the same as what the objective advice of your property manager ends up being. Furthermore, the work has already been done, and therefore you cannot verify it was done right. You cannot choose your own contractor or research that the materials used were the best for rental or resale demand. All the heavy lifting is already done, but you don't know whether it was done correctly. It's a crapshoot, and this doesn't even consider the numbers of the whole thing.

Turnkey products, even when done amazingly well, are still best suited for the very wealthy who just need an easy place to drop their cash. When you buy a turnkey product, you are paying top dollar for the convenience of a job that is already done. Many of these are sold over fair market value and advertised because of their strong ROI or cap rate. This means that uninformed investors who just get starstruck at the idea of an "easy" double-digit return never realize they are paying so much more for a product than they would have if they had bought it and assembled it themselves.

You aren't going to get wealthy or increase your net worth very fast by putting money in someone else's pockets through buying turnkey homes. The idea is to do the work and keep the money for yourself. That's why you're reading this book! Learning how to manage rehabs, even out-of-state ones, is not a complicated process, and you don't need to be a genius to figure it out. Turnkey providers have learned this process themselves and now replicate it on the homes they sell to their buyers. If they can do it, and I can do it, there's every reason you can too.

I routinely get told that what I do isn't possible. Even when I tell people I do it, they still tell me it can't be done. Speaking from experience, I'm telling you that not only is it possible to rehab out-of-state investment property, but you can also flip houses to sell as well. These are houses I've never seen, that I have no reason to go see. Houses in neighborhoods I myself have never visited or driven through. Projects I manage remotely with such specificity that I choose the style of the tile, color of the cabinets, type of backsplash, brand of appliances, and type of bathroom fixtures. What I've found is that the process for flipping a house out of state really isn't any different from the one for flipping a house a few blocks away (I just did that, too, and it became clearer than ever how the system is the same regardless of where the property is located.)

If you want to add built-in equity to your properties (which you should), you are going to have to learn how to rehab a property well. The best deals can often be found on the worst homes. It's possible to buy and own real estate without ever having to learn how to manage it. It's also possible to ride a bike without ever taking off the training wheels. While it's possible, it's still a lot slower, and you're a lot more restricted on where you can go and what you can do.

I'm going to give you all the tricks, techniques, and tips I've learned along the way from doing this over and over. I'm going to share what worked, what didn't work, and how to make the whole thing as painless as possible. By the time we're done, you're going to see it's not much different from everything else we've been talking about, and this is *totally* doable if you do it right.

Many investors avoid houses that need a lot of work because they are afraid to deal with contractors. This is OK! It's a whole new world that requires a whole new skill set and knowledge base. Contractors need to be communicated with directly. If you are more of a passive personality, this can feel intimidating. You need to learn their lingo. If you don't understand construction, it can feel like being the only skinny guy in a gym full of monsters and not knowing how to use the machines. Nobody likes to be that person, and it's understandable to want to avoid this.

What I'd like to propose is while anything and everything can seem intimidating at first, most things in life are not nearly as hard or as intimidating to learn as we originally think. Managing rehabs is no exception. Once you learn the basics, the fundamentals of what stuff goes into a home rehab, you'll find that most of the work is the same in each project and that managing a rehab can be familiar and even monotonous with time.

It's an amazing concept that you can take a run-down dump, fix it up nice and shiny, and then sell it for a healthy profit, all from miles away—never having seen it once. It's an amazing feeling when you successfully buy a slumlord's rental needing major work, shine it up like a polished gem, and rent it out. This feeling gets only better when you know it will be in your personal portfolio and making you money and being enjoyed by your tenants for as long as you'd like.

I'm excited to be able to show you just how possible this is. Through a lot of trial and error, I've been able to put together a system that makes rehabbing a rental or a flip as easy out of state as it is down the street. Like that farmer who has mastered the art of planting, protecting, and then harvesting his crops, you, too, can learn how to grow crops anywhere you want, with total confidence and full control. It's time for you to learn how you can start taking advantage of opportunities to build wealth wherever they may be.

GIVE YOUR CONTRACTOR INCENTIVE AND MAXIMIZE YOUR RESULTS

Management is nothing more than motivating other people.

—LEE IACOCCA

As discussed earlier, the process of finding a good contractor is done primarily through the process of getting great referrals from great contacts. Rock stars know rock stars, and you want to be in touch with as many as possible. Once you've found the contractor you're ready to start with, it's time to get the ball rolling.

THE CONTRACT
If you've followed the instructions so far, you will still have that itemized bid you agreed on with the contractor when you were choosing which contractor to work with. The itemized bid should include the full scope of work, the price for each line item, and the agreed-on time frame for the project. It's a good thing you kept it because this is

going to be a very easy way to form a contract with him or her (I am not an attorney and do not give legal advice, so please consult your attorney for questions about contract law). Since you already have an itemized scope of work in place (with built-in prices ready to go), you won't need to waste any time haggling over the cost. All you'll need to determine is how long it will take for the work to be completed, how you will handle unforeseen problems, and how the contractor will be paid along the way.

I love using this method. I already have the itemized bid saved in my e-mail folder, and it doesn't take long for me to open the bid, add some quick verbiage about deadlines, bonuses, and penalties to it, and forward it to the contractor for his or her signature. This saves me time, but more than that, it saves me brainpower! By keeping everything simple, I can keep several balls in the air at one time, removing the fear of missing out on a good deal.

ENSURING YOUR PROJECTS FINISH ON TIME

When it comes to a rehab, there are two things that tend to go wrong: (1) The cost of the rehab goes up, and (2) the time of the rehab runs too long. Projects going over the projected timeline cost you money indirectly in several ways:

1. Any hard-money costs associated with the project are extended.
2. Your vacancy periods are extended for a rental.
3. Your holding costs are extended for a flip.
4. Your "velocity of money" is slowed.
5. Your opportunity cost increases as you miss out on other deals before you can reinvest the money.
6. The people managing your projects get worn down the longer the project lasts.

In this section, we are going to talk about a few ways we can prevent these from happening. While no project is perfect, it is definitely better to get the place rehabbed and ready to rent or sell as soon as possible.

Psychologists have found that negative reinforcement (think of being allowed to step onto the grass from the burning hot sidewalk after completing a task) is much more powerful than positive reinforcement (think of being given an ice cream cone for completing a task). People respond more strongly to the removal of adverse stimuli than they do to the addition of pleasant stimuli. Understanding this can give you an advantage with people to help your business. In my business, I make it very clear in the beginning what my expectations are and why it's in the contractor's best interest to meet them. When it comes to motivating people, there are two basic schools of thought. They center on the positive and negative reinforcement styles I mentioned earlier.

So which of these methods works best for managing and motivating contractors? What about real estate investing as a whole? Is there a simple way to know whether positive reinforcement or negative reinforcement works better overall? What it really boils down to is finding a reasonable compromise between the two methods. Through trial and error, much thought, and many long conversations with contractors I use often, I've come up with a great system for doing just that.

The process is simple. If you want to motivate someone the right way, include elements of both. I offer contractors a bonus if they finish on time and impose a penalty if they finish late. Once they've told me how long they will need, I usually add a week to this number to be extra careful and then write this time frame down on the itemized bid. I type in a clause that says something along the lines of: "Full scope of work to be finished and approved by owner in [*however many*] weeks. If the project is finished ahead of this deadline by a certain number of days, contractor will be paid a 5 percent bonus based on the total job. If the work runs past this deadline, contractor will be assessed a 5 percent penalty for the first week. If the job runs longer than a week over schedule, contractor will be assessed an additional 5 percent penalty. Owner to retain final rights of approval for quality of work completed."

CREATE ACCOUNTABILITY THROUGH PAYING A BONUS

I include this clause for several reasons. First, I want the contractor to be very sure that when he or she tells me eight weeks, I expect eight weeks. Contractors are often used to working according to their own time frame and don't manage time well. Secondly, this gives the contractor one last chance to give me a more realistic finish date before signing the contract. I don't want pipe dreams. I want reliable time frames. Thirdly, I want to give the contractor incentive to finish the job on time. By having him or her agree to a penalty for being late, I'm introducing negative reinforcement into the contractor's psyche (rewarding my contractor by helping him or her avoid an undesirable consequence—late fees). By offering a bonus should the job finish early, I'm also providing a form of positive reinforcement into his or her psyche (fostering a desirable outcome—the bonus).

This may sound simple, but this one easy step can help avoid so much conflict during the process. By giving my contractor extra reason to stay on track, I help avoid arguments, anger, and miscommunication throughout the process. By giving my contractor a healthy desire not to lose money by falling behind, I give him or her extra incentive to stay on track. By allowing my contractor to provide the time frame to finish the job, I remove any argument he or she could make regarding my unrealistic expectations because I do not "know the industry." By giving an extra week on top of the number my contractor gave me, I crush any argument that exigent circumstances occurred. By spelling out exactly what the bonus and penalties will be in the beginning, I guarantee my contractor won't be caught off guard when I'm upset and say I'm not paying.

Sometimes simple is best. While this may seem like a concept too simple to be effective, I've found that not only does it help me weed out bad contractors in the beginning, but it also helps to ensure a healthier and positive experience with the contractors I choose.

CREATE ACCOUNTABILITY THROUGH ADVERTISING

Once we have an agreed on a contract, my next step is to share with the contractor that I am a real estate investor and there will be professional pictures taken of the project once completed. The pictures will be top quality and highly detailed. They will be heavily advertised through multiple media. I make sure the contractor knows that the property will be listed for sale and his or her name will be given should anyone ask who did the work.

Furthermore, I explain I'll also be sharing the pictures all over social media and on my own website. My intent is not to scare, intimidate, or bully the contractor. I say all of this with a very pleasant demeanor and continually reinforce that I chose him or her for a reason and that I love the work he or she has done. My real intent of these conversations is to build up my contractor subconsciously so he or she really wants to wow me. I want my contractor to feel that if he or she hits a home run here, his or her business can really take off and go to a whole new level. This is an important concept that all the people you work with should feel.

I don't want to intimidate my contractor, but I do want my contractor to know I'm an influential investor and will have a large impact on his or her business, good or bad. If my contractor does bad work, many people will see it, and his or her reputation will suffer. If my contractor does good work, he or she can expect a ton of referrals as more and more investors see the quality of the work. If you've chosen the right contractor, the reputation of that person's business will mean everything to him or her. Making it clear up front that the work is not being done in a vacuum will provide even more incentive to make sure the contractor is managing his or her workers and subcontractors that much better.

By the end of our phone calls, my contractor should know that he or she is going to get free advertising one way or another. May as well make sure it's positive.

PAYING FOR MATERIALS YOURSELF

When you're first getting started with your contractor, you may want to exercise a little caution and make sure you're not being taken advantage of. One of the easiest ways to handle this is by choosing and paying for your own materials outside the contract. While this may take some more time and effort on your part, there are several advantages to doing so. I recommend that if you're just getting started with buying out of state, or just getting started with an individual contractor, you order and pay for the materials yourself.

The first and most obvious benefit is that your contractor cannot overcharge you for the materials if you are paying for them yourself. While I don't want to scare you from ever forging new relationships with different vendors, the fact remains that you can get taken advantage of in this business, and you should be taking steps to make sure it is less likely to happen. One way unscrupulous contractors earn more money on the job is to charge you more for the materials than they actually cost. When a contractor gives you a bid for a specific, itemized task, he or she will typically charge you a rounded-up number because the contractor does not know exactly how much materials will be needed, what they will cost, or other pertinent information. This isn't inherently dishonest (contractors may justify this price to pay for their time in choosing the materials, paying for them out of pocket, picking them up to bring to the project site, and so on), but it is vague at best, and that's not good for you as the investor.

Some people try to avoid this problem by asking for receipts from the store. While this is a good idea and can help with tax write-offs, it's still not foolproof. If you are using common materials (which you likely are if it's a business rehab), your contractors can easily buy more than they will need for your project and save the materials for the next one. They can also return the extra materials at the end and get money back that isn't likely to be returned to you. By paying for materials yourself, you make it much more difficult for this to happen.

Another benefit is in the fact that you will learn a *lot* more about construction, materials, and design when you take the burden on yourself to pick the materials. When paying for something like floor tile, there is more than just the tile that needs to be paid for. The backer, grout, and adhesive are all extra costs you may not have taken into consideration. There are also transition pieces that need to be paid for and stains for certain kinds of tiles to make their natural features more pronounced. If I hadn't bought the materials for my own projects, I would never have learned about all the extras that go into rehabbing a house.

Buying materials yourself also offers you the added benefit of being able to search for the best prices. While most contractors will make some form of effort to pay less for materials, it really doesn't benefit them much to spend a lot of time trying to do so. If you are doing the research and making the calls yourself, you can ask store representatives to show you what they have on sale or ask them which materials they would like to sell most and see whether they are willing to help you out on the price. Overall, it is a tremendous learning experience to do this a few times and really see just what goes into rehabbing a property. I recommend that you do this at least once.

One final benefit of paying for the materials yourself is that you earn the credit card points and other discounts. You're already paying for the materials. You may as well get the perks, right? Some credit cards offer substantial cash back. This starts to add up when doing $10,000 to $13,000 renovation projects. If you earn even 1 percent cash back on your card, this starts to add up to substantial savings when repeated several times over. Other than the cash back on your credit cards, some stores offer discounts when using their in-store credit. Perks such as zero percent interest rates on balances and 1–5 percent discounts aren't uncommon from DIY stores looking to earn your business on large orders.

This is an underrated way to become a better investor. We want to understand the business really well while eventually distancing ourselves from it. If you can successfully learn more about what goes into a contractor's work, you can avoid wasting time and money. While this is likely to strengthen your relationship with your contractor, it is also likely to help you find ways to run your own rehabs much more efficiently.

ADDING VALUE BY ADDING YOUR OWN TIME

When you pay for materials yourself, you know exactly what you're paying. There is no discrepancy between you and the contractor, no opportunity for miscommunication, and no reason for you to feel you're being cheated. By ordering materials and having them dropped off or picked up by the contractor, you also remove any argument he or she might make to buy the materials and then squeeze some more money out of you.

By picking out and paying for the materials myself, I maintain a degree of control over the project and its cost. In addition to avoiding the contractor's charging me more than what the materials cost, I can also make sure I'm not overpaying for materials that could be found cheaper elsewhere. Most contractors work with homeowners who are basing the scope of their work on a fixed budget. These people are used to watching HGTV shows in which the clients say, "I have $15,000 to spend on the kitchen." While it's important not to go over budget, it's foolish to think that all money spent in the kitchen will bring the same amount of value. As an investor, I don't think solely in terms of a numerical budget. My goal is to come in under budget, but that is not my only concern. It's not even my primary concern. My primary concern is to add as much value as possible to the property I've bought while keeping costs within reason of what is typical for the area the property is located in.

That being the case, I'm not going to approach my material selections the same way as a homeowner who just doesn't want to spend more than the allotted amount. I'm looking for the best materials I can get for the money—I don't necessarily want to go find some tile that is under $3 a square foot just to stay within budget. I want to find the *best* tile that is as close to $3 a square foot. Again, my goal is to add as much value to the property as possible. This includes upgrading to certain features like tile floors and granite countertops at times to cut down on future repairs likely to be needed if I use inferior products. It also includes making the property as aesthetically pleasing as possible to attract better tenants and obtain a higher appraisal price once the rehab is completed. As a rule, you always want to be looking to add as much value, for as low a price, as possible.

Which brings me to my next point about how to manage contractors (and it applies to more than just contractors). They will never care as much about the quality of the project as you do. Before you start complaining about how unfair this is, I'm just going to go ahead and make an assertion based on general human nature. While there are some people out there who genuinely want to see you succeed as much as they want to themselves, most of us can agree that this is the exception, not the rule. Most people will always do what is in their own best interest. I expect this of people. This doesn't mean your contractors are going to walk into Home Depot and buy the first stove or tiles they see. The majority of them will make efforts to find something that matches, looks nice, and is still within your budget. However, they probably aren't going to put as much effort into finding a really great product, and you shouldn't expect that of them.

In the above example, I mentioned how I want to find the best tile I can for $3 a square foot. Generally, with rehabs, you want to make every effort to stay on budget. However, there are times when this isn't always in your best interest. As you are making phone calls to various tile supply stores to find something that will work in your kitchen, you should always be asking what they have on sale. Should you come across a store that has a gorgeous travertine on clearance for $3.25 a square foot, when it is normally $7 a square foot, do you think it would be wise to turn it down because it's "over budget"?

If you're leaving this task up to your contractor, he may call you to ask if you're OK with going over budget. But he may not. You don't want to risk not getting that call because he's on the phone with someone else, thinking about where he wants to have lunch, or in the middle of an argument with his wife via text. Many times, your contractor will just be thinking, "Find something under $3 a square foot to make my client happy." He could easily walk right by this perfect travertine and not even notice it. If you want to add the most value as possible to your project, it behooves you to maintain as much control as possible. You are much, much more likely to find better prices, better materials, and a better overall deal when you are doing the work yourself than when you have someone else do it, even a licensed contractor.

Now, keep in mind, this will take more of your time. If you're operating at an extremely high level, it may not be worth it for you to choose all your own materials. Some people are better off putting their time into finding more deals or putting more effort into their job to increase their income. No static formula exists for the best approach. As you are determining what is best for you, keep in mind that everything starts off slow and gets more efficient in time. In the beginning, you will spend hours and hours as you call different stores and ask about prices on different items. After having done this successfully, you'll find you have saved contact info for the various personnel at the stores you call and are beginning to establish relationships with these people. With persistence and time, you will eventually get to a point where some of these employees will be calling *you* with good deals. It's not uncommon for DIY stores to call preferred clients when vanities, appliances, flooring, and other popular items are on clearance. As you develop these relationships and repeat these transactions, it gets easier, smoother, and quicker each time. Once again, we find ourselves becoming more efficient as we become more proficient. As systems begin to take form, you'll find it takes much less of your time to perform each task than it did when you first started.

In addition to receiving notification when certain products are available at good prices, you'll also find that you'll use a product you like and tend to stick with it. For a specific type of home I buy in Jacksonville, I use the same shower tile, same bathroom tile, and same vanities. I have used them enough times that all I need to do is have the contractor let me know how many square feet I'll need, and I can send an e-mail with my order directly to the head of the department of the store I buy these materials from. What once took several hours on the phone now takes all of 20 seconds via e-mail. A quick confirmation with my contractor to determine when he or she wants the product delivered, and I can have the entire order set and ready to go. This efficiency is what allows me to manage several projects at a time, from wherever I am in the world, without feeling overwhelmed or stressed.

The same rule applies when negotiating prices for the rehab work that needs to be done. In the beginning, you're dealing with many different contractors, many different bid formats, and widely varying bid amounts. As you work more and more with the same contractors you'll begin to become familiar with the way they write their bids, the prices they bid for certain jobs, and the speed at which you can expect a response. The hardest time is the first time—each step gets easier after that. If you quit before you've established a system, you will have done all that hard work for nothing. Don't let that be the case! Remind yourself daily that the hardest day was yesterday, and you'll find the encouragement to keep going. Building a system takes time and hard work. Maintaining a system is much, much easier.

USING YOUR CONTRACTORS' HOUSE ACCOUNTS TO SAVE YOU MONEY

If you want to save even more money, ask your contractors whether they have an account at the store you're buying your materials from. Many contractors often have accounts where they are registered, like Lowe's and Home Depot. These accounts offer them a discount as high as 10 percent sometimes. When buying materials in California, I'm able to call and order them under my contractor's name. This gets me 10 percent off regular items, plus an additional percentage on clearance items.

Whenever I'm using a new contractor, I always ask right away whether he or she gets a discount at any DIY stores that might be useful. If the contractor does, you can bet that store is one I'll call to get prices on necessary items like flooring, shower tiles, paint, vanities, appliances, baseboards, lumber, and more. Controlling the cost of your rehab is very, very important. Coming in under budget can have a big impact on your bottom line, especially when multiplied over the course of several projects. Take a minute to think about how a little effort on your part can create such a compounded effect on your savings over time. What if you could combine all the methods I've shown you in the same project? Let's take a minute to envision what that would look like. You come up with a contract between you and the contractor that you feel is a great value to you and the job. Your contractor allows you to purchase the materials under his or her name. This gives you a 10 percent discount right off the bat.

In addition to that discount, you contact the Pro Desk at Home Depot or some other specialist at the store of your choosing. This rep can help you find items in great condition that are on clearance. You're able to purchase items that would typically be much more expensive than what you're able to buy them for. Maybe you find last year's model of appliances or a type of tile the store ordered too much of. Maybe the store has leftover granite someone ordered and never picked up. It could be any number of things, but you are able to find them. You decide on buying the materials the store has on discount and arranging the style of your project around them. You've now earned yourself a great discount on materials that typically would have been too expensive for your project and another 10 percent discount on top of that. Once you have your order complete, you ask for free delivery to the job site because you're taking these clearance items off the store's hands. These types of requests are often granted because customer service reps are often given permission to include perks like this to help clear up warehouse space.

Now, of course this won't always work out so cleanly. Sometimes you can't get free delivery, or nothing that interests you is on clearance. While there are often things like this that you cannot control, what you *can* control is the amount of effort you put into looking to save money in these ways. Did you find a tile you love, but it's not on sale? Ask for a picture of it and start e-mailing it to all the other tile providers you can find on Google. Ask whether they have anything that matches and give them the price you're willing to pay. All too often, we make one effort, are unsuccessful, and assume it can't be done. This is why most people don't have long-term real estate investing success. Heck, this is why most people don't have *any* long-term success.

The main reason that this whole process deters people is they walk into it expecting it to happen for them. The reality is, you have to make it happen. You do that by putting your own time into finding these materials at a great value. You do this by persistently exploring every avenue available to you before settling. You look to find the most valuable materials, at the cheapest price, and once you find them, you remember how you did it. It gets easier and easier each time.

Take the time to develop the persistence it takes to find good deals on materials and seek new opportunities. It helps your subconscious form an idea of what to expect when looking for properties. You'll save money on those items and learn techniques that will help you in every other aspect of the investment cycle. Take the time in the beginning to learn these techniques. Find what works for your personality. Make the effort to sharpen your investing sword. You'll find the financial benefits will serve you for much longer than the initial money you save on the rehab.

HOW TO MANAGE PAYING YOUR CONTRACTOR

Believe it or not, the way you pay your contractor matters. Contractors are people, too, and as people, they need to be both motivated and held accountable. Human beings are fallible. We operate best when we are in an optimal state of mind. Many self-help and motivational speakers like Tony Robbins and Hal Elrod spend a great majority of their energy helping their listeners achieve an optimal state of mind. When you are in what Tony Robbins calls a "beautiful state," you will find that solutions to complex problems come to you more quickly. A positive attitude is much easier to maintain. Your motivation to complete tasks on time is higher. The quality of your work, no matter what is it, will naturally be closer to your potential than to "just good enough." Living in a beautiful state helps you to live and work out of your optimal self.

Think of a time when you've been in the zone. A time when it seemed that as soon as problems popped up, you were knocking them out right away. Solutions came to mind effortlessly and quickly. Your attention to detail was flawless, your desire to please was at its peak, and creativity flowed from your pores. For athletes, they talk about time slowing down: Hand-eye coordination improves, and their brains think faster. For businesspeople, it feels as if they can see right through the negotiators on the other end of the table and know how to handle them.

Knowing this, I want to create an atmosphere for people working on my projects that takes advantage of these factors as much as possible. I want my contractors to be both motivated to do their best job ever as well as concerned that if they don't finish on time or with good work, it will hurt their business. I *don't* want to resort to intimidation, threats, harassment, micromanaging, or other negative efforts of control. I *do* want to appeal to my contractors' own internal, natural, and organic desires to do what is in their own best interest and the best interest of their business. Part of how I do this is in my personal interaction with the contractors before, during, and after the project. While your interactions with those you partner with are important, they're not the only things that are important. You also want to create a *system* in which your contractors have incentive to do their best work, keep you happy and coming back for more.

HOW TO PAY YOUR CONTRACTOR

While your contractors will be motivated by several things including the promise of more work, the referrals you will bring them, and the natural reward of a job well done, there is nothing more important to them than the money you're paying. The wages they earn will be the number one thing that motivates them to get the job completed. Your contractors know that if there is a dispute regarding the quality of the work, it could disrupt their getting paid. If you included a penalty for the project taking too long, they know they won't be getting paid as much. It is the desire to make money that motivates them to make progress every day toward completing your project.

Most contractors want to make sure they get paid. If you leave it up to them, they will most likely ask for payment up front for the entire job. This is not a good plan for you. While in a worst-case scenario, your contractors could take the money and run (trust me, there are all too many stories out there of people who were ripped off this way), even if they don't do that, you've just removed the biggest incentive they have to perform a job well done. If you want to keep your contractor honest and motivated, you don't want to give them everything up front.

My favorite way to approach this with a new contractor I've never worked with is to ask which of the jobs in our contract he or she will be performing in the first two weeks. This is usually work like the demo, installation of cabinets or countertops, exterior paint, or plumbing or electrical. By looking at our contract, I can quickly determine exactly how much money the contractor will need to complete the work (comes in handy, right?). If I'm wiring the money directly to the contractor, this is how much I will wire. If I'm using a third party such as a property manager, this is how much I'll tell that person to release in the first draw to the contractor. The contractor should be able to use this money to buy any needed materials and to pay his or her people for the work to be completed. When you include only enough money to pay for the first phase, the contractor knows you're going to be checking his or her work and will be performing it under the mind-set that someone is going to be checking it. We all tend to perform better when we know someone is going to be evaluating what we do, so it's important to create this atmosphere right from the start.

VERIFYING YOUR CONTRACTOR'S WORK

After the allotted period of time, the contractor should notify you that the initial work has been completed and that he or she will need more money for the next phase. If you're not notified, it's best to take the initiative and find out when your contractor will be finished. The goal behind checking in isn't to micromanage your contractor. You're trying to make sure dead time doesn't occur while he or she is waiting for the next draw before continuing to work. Once the first phase has been completed, you'll want to find out what projects will be tackled in the next phase. The process for the second phase will be like the first. You will want to determine how much money your contractor will require for the next phase and wire that to him or her. It's important to time this right so your contractor has the money in time for the next phase.

Plus, electronic payments make this simple: If you want to set up a business checking account for your own business, all you need is your contractor's checking account number and the bank's routing number. By creating an "account" in your online banking system with your contractor's info, you can easily wire your contractor money without the hassle of trying to use a credit card. This will often create an easy-to-track way of knowing exactly how much you've paid to each contractor when it comes time to prove to your lender how much you spent on improvements (many lenders will let you borrow only against the price you paid for the home plus the cost of improvements). If you save your contract, you'll have the grand total easily available, but in the case of an audit, it's always nice to have as much info as possible.

To verify the work was completed, you'll need some way to know. The easiest method is to ask for photos and video. While video can give you more of a bird's-eye view, pictures allow you to really get an up-close and intimate view of the work itself. Smartphones now have cameras powerful enough to show you everything you need to see. The grout on the tile, the way the granite was cut on the counters, the paint streaks on the cabinets, or how straight the tiles were aligned in the shower. By asking the contractor to send you pictures and videos of completed projects, you can see for yourself that the work was done and that he or she is ready for the next draw. As a reminder, be sure to store all the pictures and videos you receive from your contractor in the appropriate folder in your e-mail.

SAFELY PAYING YOUR CONTRACTOR

Following this process, you will continue to send draws of money until the project is complete. I've found that most jobs can typically be done in about three to four draws. As you become more and more familiar with your contractor, you can eventually remove this four-step-draw process altogether. With some of the contractors I work with, I'm able to send the full amount right away and know the work will still be done on time. With others, I send an initial draw and send the rest when the work is complete. If I'm not using a third-party buffer system (I'll explain how that works in a bit), this is the best way for me to make sure the contractor gets paid, my work gets done on time, and the work gets done well. I can also make sure my money doesn't end up in a numbered account in the Cayman Islands. While this is the safest method, it's clearly not the most efficient. Being extra cautious with a new contractor requires extra steps to ensure your investment is safe. Anytime you have extra steps, you lose efficiency.

As you build trust with your contractor, you'll slowly start to feel more comfortable paying him or her in larger lump sums that are more convenient for both of you. The important thing to remember is you are cautious for two reasons.

1. You want to make sure your money is safe with someone you don't know well yet.
2. You want to make sure your contractor is motivated to do great work as fast as possible.

As the two of you become more familiar with each other, the issue of your contractor's running off with your money will quickly become irrelevant. Real construction businesses that are run successfully make more money with repeat business than by ripping people off and skipping town. If you're worried that someone will take off with your money, focus your efforts on finding a contractor with a good reputation, plenty of positive reviews on Yelp, and a long history of staying in business. The shady people in any industry may find themselves lucky enough for a quick score, but they rarely if ever find any long-term staying power. Finding a company that has been in business for a significant period of time is one of the most solid ways you can prevent any unscrupulous behavior. If the company was engaged in the type of behavior we all worry about, odds are it would have been outed as a fraud a long time ago. Before the final draw is made, you're going to want to make sure they have finished the entire job. Remember, if you included a clause that penalizes the contractor for finishing late, it will be hard to get that money back once you've already paid him or her. You'll likely need to take the contractor to court in a civil case and hope the judge rules in your favor. Even if you win, there is a good chance your court fees will take a huge bite out of the money you get back—and this doesn't even count the time spent locating documents, preparing your case, and actually showing up in court. In situations like these, it is always better to avoid paying the final draw until you've been able to confirm the work was done and done in a way that satisfies you. If you pay the final draw before you've confirmed everything is to your satisfaction, you've put yourself in a situation where the contractor is not motivated to finish the job. You've also lost your leverage in persuading them to redo things that need to be repaired in a timely fashion.

In any negotiation, project, or task, you want to maintain leverage whenever possible to protect your interests and keep your profit margins as high as possible. A motivated contractor is a good contractor. By sticking to a system that pays for the work after it's been completed, you ensure that your contractor stays in the right frame of mind—from beginning to end.

THE PARTNERSHIP MENTALITY

I've mentioned a few times that I believe it's important that your team members are viewed as partners, not employees. I've found this to be important in just about every aspect of investing, and it's twice as important when investing out of state. What makes out-of-state investing possible is the fact that you have others working as your agents—ensuring the job is done the way you want and handling the things you cannot do yourself. If you want to make this as easy on yourself as possible, you'll want as many people as possible looking out for your interests as if they were their own. Enter partners.

Having partners when investing out of state is vital. You can't do it without them. This shouldn't surprise you. So many pieces are needed to complete a project, and all those pieces need to work together. Think about the rehab alone. Your contractor is trying to juggle the painter with the carpet guy and the sheetrock guy. Each of them needs to do a part of the job before the others can do theirs. This system works the same way. Your real estate agent knows what styles buyers in the area want. Your contractor knows how to put them together. Wouldn't you want input from your agent on the design for the house he or she is going to need to sell?

Your property manager knows what tenants in the area expect and what your competition looks like. Your manager knows which houses have plain-Jane tile countertops, which have landscaped backyards, which have upgraded appliances, and which need at least three bedrooms. If your property manager is going to be the one renting the place out for you, wouldn't you want his or her opinion involved in the rehab?

Since it often behooves us to gain input from certain team members like agents and managers, it only makes sense to take that one step further and ask them to verify that the work was done according to plan. So when I'm working with a contractor for the first time and want to make sure the work was done correctly, I'll send my agent by the house if it's a flip and send my property manager if it's a rental. Most people love being asked for their opinion. It makes us feel valued and important. When we are asked for an opinion on something we are specifically an expert in, it feels even better.

If you can make your team members feel as if they are a part of this project, it will be much easier for them to willingly help you in monitoring it. I always refer to it as "our rehab," "our design," "our property." I want my property manager to feel that he or she has been there every step of the way, from inception of the idea to delivery of the finished project. If you ask for input in the design, you further build that bond between your property manager and the property as he or she becomes more emotionally invested after having picked out some of the materials. You are helping to remind your project manager that it's in his or her best interest, as well, for this project to work out.

When investing in an area you can't physically go to, you are extra vulnerable. You need a lot more advice, assistance, guidance, and help than when the property is located somewhere you can manage it yourself. The best investors don't burden themselves with tasks that don't cater to their skill set. Investing out of state forces you to take advantage of the abilities of others. If you're going to do that, you really need them to *want* to help you. You need them to feel connected to you, your property, and your business. Having others feel connected to your success is crucial.

Since I know someone will be stopping by the house to check on things, I want to take proactive measures to ensure this will be easy for that person to do. The simplest method I've found is to have either the agent or the property manager leave a combination lockbox on the front door of the house and to text me the combo to get into the house without a hitch.

This comes in handy because vacant houses can attract a lot of unwanted attention—especially if they are in rent-friendly areas where many of the other homes are not owner occupied. When someone is stopping by to look at the progress of the work, it's one more car in that driveway and one more person going into the house. The neighbors or any troublemakers won't know it's a real estate agent or a property manager. They'll just know people are stopping by the house and it's being watched.

Ask your property manager what you can do to help his or her business. Property managers love referrals as well. Post something on social media about how amazing your manager is and leave contact information or add him or her as a friend. Ask what resources your property manager could use. He or she may need a great handyman who can show up and fix things without much notice. Do you think there's a good chance your brand-new all-star contractor you've spent so much time finding might be useful to your property manager? Do you think you could ask your contractor to recommend a handyman your property manager could hire? What about a great roofer, plumber, electrician, or landscaper? If you can find your property manager good, capable blue-collar workers to perform specific tasks better and cheaper than whom he or she is currently using, you'll prove your value to your manager and win him or her over to your side.

MAKE IT EASY TO WANT TO HELP YOU
While your agent and manager are going to be helping you out quite a bit, it's important to remember not to treat them like a packhorse. If they feel as though they are being sent to the property to just make a video and leave, they are much more likely to lose interest. You want

more than that. You want them to be giving you their *opinion* of what they think of the work. Ask them whether the flooring matches the walls and whether the rainfall showerhead works. Ask them anything and everything you can think of. If I know asking someone for their opinion is going to make them feel special, I'll ask it every time—even if I know it's not likely that I'll use it on a project.

Maybe I'll use it next time. Maybe they saw something I didn't see. Regardless of where they are coming from, it's important to know that nothing they say can hurt your project. Worst-case scenario is it will be neutral. Even if you don't benefit directly from their opinions on your design, you can definitely benefit directly from their noticing that things were not constructed correctly. I've had third-party agents point out that tiles were cracked, that the baseboard was missing, and that water was leaking and would have ruined the floor.

Property managers are used to putting out fires. They know what phone calls they are likely to get from tenants about broken issues in the house. Experienced contractors will know very well how garbage disposals can be an area of weakness. They will know that HVAC units frequently go out. They will know that dishwashers often leak, seals wear out, bathroom showers leak and lead to dry rot, and roof tiles eventually cause a leak as well. Property managers know where the weak points are in a home. Leveraging their experience by having them look things over can save you potential problems later.

More important, when I take their advice and change something, these people feel they are a valuable part of the process. And they are. I rely on so many other people for so much advice sometimes, I feel as if the only person in the whole project who is not needed is me! I've learned to love that feeling. If I can find someone else to help me with things they understand better than I do, it will always be better for my business in the end.

CHAPTER 9

FINDING MATERIALS

*If you think good design is expensive, you
should look at the cost of bad design.*

—RALF SPETH

After several back-and-forth e-mails, phone calls, and negotiating,
you and your contractor have finally agreed on a budget that works
for each of you. You have a good idea of what you'll be paying and feel
much better now that your numbers are worked out. It's always a feeling of relief once your rehab budget is squared away, and it's always
tempting to start looking for the next deal while you're waiting for the
contractor to do his or her thing.

But wait! Your job is likely not done. Materials need to be chosen
and an overall design needs to be collaborated on between you and the
contractor. If you're me, you aren't feeling too great about this part.

If you got your start watching HGTV flip shows, this will probably be your favorite part of the book. While it may be intimidating at
first, once you learn how to do this, it really does become one of the
most enjoyable parts of the process. Having the ability to take an ugly

property that most likely nobody else really wants and turn it into a beautiful, clean, sparkling gem is one of the most rewarding parts of real estate. The feeling of accomplishment is incredible! I know several house flippers who like the money but are absolutely addicted to the restoration process. They love solving the puzzle of a distressed property and putting the pieces together to make it something others are fighting to own or rent. With practice, this can be you.

The ability to design a rehab is one of the most confidence-inspiring aspects of the entire process. While I could write another entire book about home design, people have already done that. I'm going to concentrate on the basics you'll need to get through this, then give you some techniques for how to put these basics into play when investing out of state. The most important thing to remember is it doesn't matter where the house is when you're designing the rehab. The only factor that distance plays in this process is the fact that different areas can have different design preferences.

Knowing this, we will want to spend some time running our ideas by other experienced people who are used to the area where we own the property and know the tastes of the locals. Common sense dictates this is a good idea. Log cabin, rustic, and weathered type materials may go over swimmingly in Montana or Wyoming. But if that's your taste, you wouldn't want to use that same design style in Oakland or San Francisco, California. Some areas love big, grandiose elements, while others prefer subtle and elegant finishes. Learning the preference of the people you're marketing to—whether it's to sell or rent—is of the utmost importance.

If you prefer to dig in and do the research yourself, the good news is it's never been easier with the Internet. Even the most artistically irrelevant, design-flawed, and creatively helpless person can find whatever they need on the net with inspiration from Pinterest, Houzz, and Tumblr. These three sites are created to inspire design ideas and help people search for products that will assist them in renovating homes. While most of these users are homeowners doing their own house, nothing stops us from taking advantage of these same resources for our own purposes.

R&D (RIP OFF AND DUPLICATE)

The benefit of websites like Pinterest, Houzz, and Tumblr is that others have already done the work of designing a beautiful project and you get to take advantage of their success. Who doesn't love that? When it comes to a task in which you are unfamiliar, unskilled, or inexperienced, it can feel like a long climb to get from the bottom, where you're starting, to the top, where you want to be. Whenever possible, don't reinvent the wheel. It takes effort to blaze a trail, but it is much easier to follow a beaten path. Following the success of others can reduce stress, minimize mistakes, and save us a lot of time and money in the end.

If learning the process of rehab is like climbing a steep mountain, it makes sense to follow the path of those who have gone before you. Hence the process of R&D. While most people understand the popular acronym to stand for "research and development," I have to give credit to my good friend Andrew for sharing his version with me—rip off and duplicate.

Andrew was a chemical engineer before he was a real estate investor. While he's an incredibly intelligent person, chemical engineers aren't exactly known for their creativity or keen eye for interior design. The problem is, Andrew wanted to be a full-time house flipper. A big part of flipping houses is redesigning them so they are appealing to the broadest number of buyers possible. Designing a house rehab in a way that turns off potential buyers can cost a lot of money in the end. The house sits and sits waiting for someone to like it, adding to your cost. The ability to get your money back to reinvest in the next project is slowed. Opportunity cost builds, and your bottom line feels the pain. Surely you can see how this could be a problem.

Andrew taught me that he learned to copy the systems of people who were good at things he wasn't. By watching how successful people ran aspects of their businesses that he didn't understand, Andrew was able to model their systems and make good money in the house-flip niche. Andrew eventually called this process R&D because he was "ripping off" someone else's great idea and "duplicating" it for himself. Several years later, Andrew is running a successful flipping business while also syndicating large multiunit apartment complexes across the country. Andrew had learned how to copy other people's systems and turned his weaknesses into strengths. This empowered him to take advantage of his own strengths like crunching numbers and marketing for deals without having to worry that his weaknesses like interior design would prevent him from succeeding. This is exactly why I learned to use other people's design ideas to motivate, inspire, and provide direction for my own remodels. R&D is where it's at!

The concept of R&D is what makes websites like Pinterest, Houzz, and Tumblr such effective tools for your business. The users of these sites end up putting together some of the very best and most popular design ideas and then leave it right there for people like us to duplicate. It is the availability of resources like these that opens doors and makes it possible for me to have confidence that I can flip or rehab rental property anywhere, anytime, any style. If some of your own limitations are holding you back, you should really feel better knowing just how much is out there to fill in the gaps that your lack of experience leaves. Not having done something before is only a problem if you believe there is no way to find the answers you need. When you stand on the shoulders of people who have come before you, you'll find you can see much further than you ever thought.

FINDING DESIGN INSPIRATION

I've already mentioned websites that will inspire creativity for design. If you're not quite feeling it, or if doing it yourself and spending an hour or so online looking at pictures feels too burdensome, there are plenty of other ways to find design ideas to help you with your project.

One of my favorite methods is to reach out to other people and ask for their opinion. Now, in this case, I'm not referring just to the members of your team. I'm actually talking about just anybody. There is a world of people out there who are interested in doing exactly what you are doing but aren't doing it themselves. So many of these people are willing to give free advice, and even put their own time into helping you, if only they knew you wanted or needed it. Let me give you a few examples of easy ways you can get design ideas from others.

SOCIAL MEDIA
The number one, hands-down, most effective way to reach large

groups of people and make it easy for them to engage on this topic is through social media. By saving a couple of pictures of design ideas you're considering and asking people to vote on their favorite one, you can have an abundance of feedback in very little time. Let's take Facebook for example.

The first and easiest way you can use a site like Facebook is to put out a post that says something like this: "Hey! I'm redesigning a house in [insert city/neighborhood] to serve as a great rental property for some lucky tenant. I'm looking for design ideas for the kitchen and bathroom that can stay within [insert budget]. Here are a couple of pictures of how the kitchen and bathrooms look now. Any suggestions are appreciated. Dinner on me if you provide the best feedback!"

Something like this is inviting and fun and helps make people feel as if they are involved in your project even though they have no monetary gains to be made. While they aren't being paid monetarily, they *are* being compensated emotionally. This is such a powerful incentive for people. By allowing them to share their design ideas, you are allowing them to essentially sharpen their own ax and feel as though they are helping you out in the process. This becomes a win-win for many people who are interested in real estate investing but not able to do it themselves. They win because they get to experience the fun in the challenge of designing something under budget. You win because you get free advice.

You can ask people to reply directly to your thread or to e-mail you instead. Obviously, the more people who follow you, the larger number of a replies you're going to get. This is a great time to point out that if you want to be a good real estate investor, it's important that people know that. You should be seeking out others who are interested in real estate investing and friending or following them. You should be looking for mentors and people who have had success that you enjoy learning from and following. You should be searching out trending real estate topics and following those who gave opinions you felt were insightful or helpful. The point is, you want to be part of a bigger community exactly for reasons like these. We refer to "networking" so much, it ends up getting a bad name. People often imagine networking as forcing your business card onto people who probably don't want it and telling them you're looking for deals.

In reality, networking is much more than this. It is developing contacts, resources, and encouragement from others who will assist you in your business. When you come across situations like this, the importance of networking really gets highlighted. Imagine if you had a strong network of experienced home flippers, aspiring real estate investors, and construction workers who could all give you great feedback on how to design your own remodel. With no exaggeration, it is conceivable that you could literally get all the feedback you need from one post on social media to complete this portion of your project. If people sent you pictures form their own remodels, then told you where they got them and what they paid, you could choose to rip off their own design and duplicate it as your own. While this may sound too easy to be true, stuff like this happens all the time. Don't ever take for granted the power of others who are interested in and excited about real estate.

For some of you, this response isn't as likely to work. You may not have enough of a network built up to make this feasible, or you may not know people who feel comfortable dishing out their opinion that easily. That's OK. There is another way to use Facebook for this purpose that works just as well.

Start off by taking some time on home design websites to find pictures you think might work well for your remodel. Send ten to twenty of these pictures for the kitchen, and another ten to twenty for the bathroom, to family members or friends in the industry you believe would provide you with a good opinion. Ask these people to choose the four pictures they like best for the kitchen and the four they like best for the bathroom. Make sure they understand they are choosing based on the colors and styles, not the elements of the pictures you won't be using (the size of the bathroom itself, the layout of it, and so on).

Once you get your top four that everyone seems to like most, you're ready to present them to the public. Post a question asking which of the four pictures everyone likes most for the project you're working on. The post would read something like this:

"Hey, everyone! I'm working on a home remodel and need your help! I can't decide which of these four styles would look best on my latest project. It is a townhouse in [insert city] built in the 1950s and could use some love. If you would please check out these four pictures that are labeled 1–4 and let me know in the comment section which number you think would be best, I'd be super appreciative. I'll be sure to post a video of the finished project for everyone to see, so give me your feedback and stay tuned to see how things turn out."

Once you post the question with the four pictures, watch how quickly the feedback starts rolling in. What's awesome about this survey is how easily viewers can look and vote on their favorite style. It is literally one click to comment, one keystroke to vote, and one more click to post. It doesn't cost your viewers much time at all to participate, and it doesn't cost you anything at all to get free opinions on design styles when you don't have much confidence in your own taste.

These kinds of posts are very popular and usually get lots of feedback. Your viewers get to see what you're up to, give their input without much effort at all, and participate in your design. I find that posts like these often arouse a lot of curiosity in the viewers and get them thinking about their own remodels. If you end up choosing a style they didn't vote for, they'll be left thinking they could have done this job better than you. This fills people with confidence and often lights a fire to start getting more serious about their own investing. If you choose the same style they voted for, it can leave them feeling like a home design master and do a lot to increase their own confidence in real estate investing. Why does this matter to you? Because the more involvement you get from others, the better. No matter how they vote, the result is likely to be more interest from them in your project. They are going to want to ask you more questions, follow and like your future posts, and start to wonder how you can help them to do what you're doing. The more interest in your business, the more likelihood you'll find people able to bring useful resources your way. Many joint ventures, partnerships, and private money lenders have been found in similar ways. You never know just how much influence you can have on others until you start sharing what you're doing yourself.

If you want to really ramp up your social media involvement, consider posting a video online that your contractor, agent, or property manager took when walking the house initially. You know, that same video I told you to have someone take when going over to check things out and send to you so you would feel better knowing the house had a roof and a toilet? That one!

By posting the video for others to see, they can get an even better idea of what the flow of the house will be and what would work best in certain areas. If you want to use this style, post something like this:

"Hey there, guys, wanted to post a quick video of my latest flip project in [insert city]. As you can see, it's still in the "before" phase. I like to think of it as a blank canvas! I have about [insert budget] to spend on the remodel. I'd love it if you'd take a minute to watch the video and let me know what recommendations you have on the remodel. Any and all advice is appreciated. Excited to see what I can do with this baby!"

A post like this gets people thinking creatively. While I like the idea of posting the pictures because it's less effort to get people to vote for what they like best, it also limits the amount of feedback you can receive. If you have some passionate followers, you may get a lot of feedback with a lot more detail than the picture method might provide. With the video, you're looking to have people tell you what kind of countertops, cabinets, flooring, appliances, paint, and so on, they think would look best in the house. If you keep the conversation stimulating by commenting on their posts, you may get even more people building on the recommendations of others. If one person is inspired by the idea of a countertop-cabinet mix, that person may recommend an awesome backsplash he or she found and send a picture of it to illustrate the idea. If this ends up being something you like, a quick copy and paste of this picture sent in a text to your contractor might be all it takes to get the ball rolling on your brand-new kitchen. Facebook is great because it's easy to communicate, keep up-to-date, and share ideas. Start harnessing those same powers in your own business to make up for the areas where you feel you're lacking!

E-MAIL

While using Facebook might sound good to some of you, others may prefer a more private approach. Some people don't feel comfortable putting their information out to the public. Others don't like the idea of so much advice coming from so many people they don't feel comfortable with or already have a strong relationship with. Still others don't even use social media (I didn't have anything until I became a licensed Realtor a year or so ago myself), so this wouldn't be a viable option. Whatever the case may be, if social media isn't for you, that's not a problem. There are other ways to use technology to receive feedback without putting your business out there for the whole world to see.

One of the easiest methods is e-mail. Personal, private, fast, and flexible, e-mail provides ways to communicate that can provide the same result with less exposure. If you want to get feedback from a list of people regarding which design ideas they like best, simply attach the pictures or video to the e-mail and write a message something like this:

> "Hey there, wanted to reach out really quick and see whether I could get your feedback on some design ideas I'm looking at for a kitchen on a house in Kansas City I'm rehabbing. I've included four pictures of four different styles, and I would really like to know which one is your favorite. As you know, I value your opinion and would really love it if you could reply with which of them you think is best. I've labeled them 1–4. It shouldn't take too long, and I'd love to see what you think. Thanks!"

You should have a high response rate with this because it doesn't take much time for the people to check out your pictures (curiosity alone will ensure a lot of them take a look) and even less time to type a number and hit Send. While the message is always going to be pretty much the same, there are several ways you can deliver the e-mail.

1. Write a mass e-mail and send it to everyone whose opinion you'd like to receive. Be sure to email everyone in the blind carbon copy line (bcc) so it is more private.
2. Write a personal e-mail to everyone you want to question, and copy and paste the text into each e-mail.
3. Use a provider like MailChimp to do this job for you.

Writing a mass e-mail and sending it to everyone is the fastest and most efficient way of the three to gather this info. All you have to do is attach the pictures or video one time to the e-mail, choose everyone in your address book you like, write the message one time, and click Send. While you can get a lot of exposure this way and save yourself a lot of time, you also are likely to suffer a lower response rate. Part of what makes people want to reply to you when they receive your e-mail is the pride and privilege they feel in being asked for their opinion specifically.

It feels good to be sought out individually. It feels even better when the e-mail states someone is being sought out specifically. You lose a lot of the impact this can have when you send the same e-mail to so many different people. Additionally, it's getting tougher and tougher to defeat e-mail providers' spam filters for this kind of thing. Even when you're sending a personal message to your own friends and associates, some e-mail providers won't let you send to more than five people at a time. This can make the whole thing pretty labor intensive, when the original goal was to save you time.

Remember, while it's not a lot more work to use e-mail than social media to send your surveys out, it's *much* more work to tally up the responses. There isn't a very quick way to determine how people answered you when you have to go through and open each e-mail to see what the recipient said. This can end up costing you a lot of time. It's tough to beat Facebook when it comes to ease of use and efficiency for these kinds of things.

If you use this method, you may want to add each person's name to the top of the e-mail for a personal touch (start it off with "Hey Brenda, Hey Bobby ...," and so on). This method can work because copying and pasting can save you so much time. By adding the recipient's name to the beginning of the e-mail, you may be including just enough of a personal touch that you won't offend that person and still get a response.

If you're looking for a higher response rate, or you don't have a large group of people to question, it's better to write each person an individual e-mail. This method is the least offensive and will therefore lead to the recipient's feeling much more inclined to respond to you. Simply use the same message provided in the earlier method but enter only one recipient in the "To" field.

Make sure to remember to include your attachments in the e-mail. When you are sending out several e-mails to different people and trying to do it as fast as possible, it's easy to neglect this step. Make sure you let them know you will keep them in touch with the project and updated on how it's turning out. Again, the more interest in your project you can create, the higher likelihood that others will take interest in you and remember what you do.

USING MAILCHIMP

In my opinion, using a service like MailChimp to communicate with your audience is the perfect hybrid of the first two methods. MailChimp allows you to collect e-mails through people signing up on your website. If you don't have a website or don't have an interest in collecting e-mails, you can still use it to send e-mails to large groups. What's more, most of the features you'll need from MailChimp to perform this task are free.

The Forever Free plan offered by MailChimp is an awesome asset for investors, small business owners, and other marketers looking to use a service like this on a small (that is, no) budget. Under this plan, you're able to send 12,000 e-mails per month as long as you have fewer than 2,000 subscribers. Since none of us using this program for this purpose are likely to have numbers anywhere close to that, you should be able to avoid all the fees associated with it while still enjoying tons of its perks.

The beauty of MailChimp is you can send the same message to large numbers of recipients without anyone knowing someone else received the same e-mail. Cool, right? Not only can you send an e-mail to large numbers of people, but you can also even track who opened it and looked at it. While this isn't as important of a feature for sending out surveys like this, it does come in handy when you're marketing to different people. If you want to use MailChimp this way, all you need to do is manually enter the names of the people you want to send the e-mail to. Once you've built up your list, simply paste the message you want to send, attach the images, and watch this awesome program do all the work for you. You can even tell MailChimp what time of day you want the e-mail to go out. Cool, right?

I love this feature because it liberates me from having to match the time I'm available to work with the time I want others to receive my e-mail. It's no secret there are times of day when you're more likely to get someone to check an e-mail than others. Sending a message like this in the middle of someone's work morning wouldn't be a great way to encourage that person to open it. Sending it when people are winding down for bed, watching TV after dinner, or sitting on a train or bus while commuting to work would make much more sense. While some business coaches have this process down to a science, all it takes is a little common sense to improve your chances of getting the response you want.

PERSONAL BLOG

If you run a personal blog or website, this process can be made even easier and probably a lot more fun. When posting on social media, you are likely looking for the opinion of anybody interested enough to reply. Some of these people will be following you because they are interested in real estate, but many of them will just be people connected to you through everyday life. While hopefully you get some good feedback, the odds of it being from someone with a lot of knowledge aren't as great unless you've done some killer marketing.

A blog, however, is a bit different.

If you run a real estate blog, most people who follow you will be interested in real estate. My website, www.GreeneIncome.com, is a real estate blog where I share articles, podcast appearances, media appearances, tools for investing, and more. One of the most popular aspects of the site is the portion where I share the deals I'm working on. People can see what income properties I bought, how much I paid, how I found the deal, what my numbers are, and all the other information I choose to share. I pull back the curtain and show people exactly how I do what I do. The same goes for my rehab projects. I share pictures, videos, numbers, prices, and all kinds of other aspects that go into home flipping and rehab projects. People follow me because they are interested in learning more about investing and want to see what I'm up to.

If I were looking to get opinions on what type of materials I wanted to use, what are the odds people on my site would be interested in sharing theirs? Pretty good, I imagine. I mean, have you *seen* the BiggerPockets forums? They are *chock-full* of people bending over backward to share their opinion on real estate—much of it unsolicited. People love to talk real estate. Finding the places where these people are is a great way to get free advice—and build up your network as well.

A post with pictures and a way for people to vote on the site is an awesome way to show your followers what you're up to and get free advice in the meantime. If you don't have your own blog, odds are you do follow someone else's (or maybe several someone else's). Why not send them an e-mail and ask whether you can post a survey on the site for their viewers and followers to vote on? You would get exposure to an audience you don't have, and they would get a cool promo to advertise and drive more traffic. If you have a substantial social media following, you could post about the survey on this website and introduce a whole new audience to this blog who wouldn't have seen it before. These win-win scenarios are always great practice for investors to start getting used to. You may not have the blog, but you do have *something* of value to offer people who do. Once you find that, you can take advantage of their resource to accomplish your mission.

BIGGERPOCKETS

Hands down, if it weren't for BiggerPockets, I wouldn't have had the confidence to stick with investing when it felt as if no one else was doing it. I wouldn't have become a millionaire by the age of thirty, I wouldn't have the opportunity to help others achieve financial freedom, and I wouldn't be writing this book. BiggerPockets has taken many of the principles I'm talking about right now and amplified them to reach a level of success seldom seen in anything else.

I know of no better place than the BiggerPockets forums for posting questions and getting immediate, qualified, intelligent feedback. This is the equivalent of posting a question about how to shoot a free throw and having NBA players responding to you. If you want to know how to budget for your rehab, which materials to use, or anything else real estate related, BiggerPockets is where you want to be. If you want to get the most bang for your buck, you need to be posting your question in the forums.

The process is about as simple as it gets. Simply hover your mouse cursor over "Community" on the top of the page, then choose the bright blue button at the bottom of the drop-down that reads "Start a Discussion." This will take you to a page where you can enter the category in the forums where you would like your question answered. Some of the applicable categories would be:

- Real Estate Investor Marketing Help and Advice
- Do It Yourself
- Deal Diaries
- Rehabbing and House Flipping
- Contractors

Next, you'll enter the title of your post. A few good ideas would be something like:

- Help! Need advice choosing materials for my flip.
- Attention: Please vote on the best choice of material for my bathroom remodel.
- Survey—Vote on the style for my new kitchen rehab. Opinions needed!
- Can't decide between tile and laminate flooring on a duplex rental. Need your help!
- Choose the best color for my new flip's interior paint. Pics included.

Once this is done, all you need is a brief entry in the text box explaining what your problem is and how you would like others to help you solve it. It doesn't need to be much, just enough for the other members to understand how they can assist you. BiggerPockets is full of people who love to help!

Once you've got your narrative spelled out, you're almost done. Just take a quick minute to attach your pictures or video or your links to them, and you're set. You'll find the area to attach them at the very bottom of the text box. Look for the words *Picture, Video,* and *Link.* That's about as easy as it gets to receive free, insightful, and diverse advice from other investors all over the world.

If you were lacking confidence in your ability to choose rehab materials or create a design concept, there's really no good reason to let that hold you back. With so many investors ready, willing, and able to help, your odds of coming up with a great design are looking fantastic. Don't think you need to know it all to do it all. Sometimes the view is just better sitting on the shoulders of giants.

GETTING SAMPLES FROM YOUR CONTRACTOR

Never hire someone who knows less than you do about what he's hired to do.

—MALCOLM FORBES

While getting samples from others can be a quick and powerful way to come up with design ideas, there may be some of you who don't have enough contacts with much to offer in this area. Whether you're the only one interested in real estate in your circle, or you don't necessarily want others knowing what you're doing, the social media or e-mail survey may not be the most efficient or desirable option. Don't worry. I've still got an ace in the hole I haven't shared yet!

Opinions from who do this for a living are the best. While it's great to get ideas from everywhere you can, you're likely to get the best ideas from the person who does this for a living—the contractor himself or herself.

There are so many reasons your contractor will be very likely to provide you with design ideas. A few would be:

1. Your contractor likely takes pictures of all projects (or at least the ones he or she gets enough creative control over) for business marketing.
2. Your contractor is a person and, just like other people, knows what he or she likes, what comes out looking cool, and what he or

she would do in his or her own home. If you ask for an opinion, your contractor will most likely share it. People like doing that, and your contractor is a person.

3. Your contractor likely secretly fantasizes about doing what you're doing. Who wouldn't? These people bust their butts daily to make a beautiful project out of a dump and fight hard to save you money (if yours is good). You really think your contractor wouldn't want to be on the other end of this equation? I guarantee you most contractors wish they could be working on their own projects and making $50,000 on a flip instead of $10,000 on the manual labor. If you want the opinion of someone who has been mentally putting together the perfect design for years, ask your contractor what he or she thinks.

When you think about it, there are very few people who are more qualified to give you a great design idea than a good contractor. These people see this stuff every day for a living. They know what turns out looking good in real life and what looks good only on the showroom shelf. They know what colors are in because they see what others are buying. They know what styles are in because they know what's sold-out in the stores. If your contractor is working with you as an investor, you're probably not the first one the contractor has worked with. He or she is likely used to others looking to do exactly what you're doing who are not exactly sure how they want to do it.

Additionally, your contractor likely doesn't work only with investors. There is a very good chance he or she also works with homeowners remodeling their own homes. Generally speaking, homeowners spend more money on their projects than investors do. They choose nicer, pricier materials. A homeowner isn't looking to use their home as an income stream. They just want to live in it. They are looking to create a design that makes them feel good to be a part of and leaves them feeling comfortable. Because of this, contractors who work on homeowners' projects see a wider variety of styles, designs, and materials. They are more likely to have been exposed to beautiful concepts and creative designs than someone who looks only at the bottom line (like you, the investor). The amount of different designs their memory has to pull from is likely much more diverse than yours.

Why does this matter? Because your contractors likely have exposure to more concepts than you do. They've seen the beauty that a little extra money can provide as well as the penny-pinching methods that an investor needs. They can likely help you find the best of both worlds. They may remember that project they did with the beautiful marble flooring complementing the glass backsplash and how it really made the kitchen pop. They may also remember that they saw a tile very similar to that marble flooring for a quarter of the price and a backsplash that looked very similar but was on sale. By combining the cheaper materials with the killer design concept, they can help bring a flair to your flip that will really help it sell while still keeping your project under budget. And many of them are hoping you'll let them do it!

WHEN THE DESIGN IDEA IS FORMED

With all these methods available to you, you should now have been able to come up with a design concept you feel comfortable with, even if you're no Martha Stewart. Once you've got the colors, style, and an idea for what kind of materials you're going to use, all you've got to do is start looking for the best prices. While your contractor may have a good idea of where to buy, you may feel more comfortable doing some of this legwork yourself. Once you've got the pictures for what you'd like, the heavy lifting is already done. Calling different home improvement stores and asking to speak to the design specialist can be a quick and simple way to get in contact with the people to help you find the materials.

My favorite method is to call the store, ask for the kitchen specialist, and e-mail or text him or her the pictures. Once the specialist knows what I'm looking to do, that person can go take pictures of the product on the floor and send them back to me. Many of these stores also have pictures on their websites that the specialist can direct you to so you can find something close to what you're looking for. If that store doesn't have what I need, I simply ask whether the specialist knows who does. It usually doesn't take too much time before I get directed to the store that does have what I'm looking for and the associate who can help me find the materials I want.

When dealing with stores like Home Depot, Lowe's, various tile or cabinet stores, and so on, you'll find that most of them use model numbers. A great tip is to write down and save these model numbers because you may want to use the same materials again in a future project. Another great reason to note the model number is you may want to send it to their competition, show them the original price you received, and see whether the competition can beat it. By sending the model number to another store, the representative can quickly look at the store's own inventory and see whether it has anything that matches.

If you find a different store with a better price, you have two options.
1. You can buy the materials from the store with the cheaper price.
2. You can go back to the original store and ask the rep to beat the price of the competitor.

The option you choose will depend on the totality of your circumstances. If you are looking to buy all your materials from one place to make it more convenient to pay and pick up the materials, you may want to ask that one store you have in mind to drop the price. If you're planning to buy more than one kind of material from the same store (for instance, appliances as well as tile or countertops), you may want to ask for a discount on the overall order. Many stores will give you this discount when making one large order, so sometimes it's in your best interest to ask. If you're unable to procure a discount for buying all your materials in one place, your next bet is to shop around and find which stores offer you the best price on each individual material.

One thing to remember is it never hurts to ask for a reduction in price. The worst someone can say is no, and if you ask respectfully, the associate likely won't even be bothered you did. If you want to save your contractor some time, gas, and headache, at the very minimum ask for a free delivery of materials. By coordinating with your contractor what day and time he or she would like the materials delivered, you can score major points. Your contractor may be willing to go pick up a truckload of laminate flooring, appliances, paint, and tile, and take it to the house site, but I can pretty much guarantee you he or she doesn't want to. Asking to have the materials delivered for free on a large order is likely to be accepted by the place you're buying from and is a nice gesture to show your contractor you are looking out for him or her as well.

DETERMINING THE VALUE OF UPGRADES

Ah, the age-old question of how much is too much when it comes to upgrading. This is an often-debated topic with two schools of thought. Each side tends to be dug in deeply on its opinion. While it's hard to ever win someone from one side of the argument to the other, I do believe there is merit in hearing out both sides and trying to glean whatever wisdom we can from each. While they typically represent polar opposites on a spectrum of value, I find that the battle lines are more often drawn based on the investor's opinion of tenants.

If you're like me, you have had mostly good interactions and experiences with the tenants in your properties. I typically buy in B+ to C+ areas, and I have never had a unit trashed or destroyed. While I have had to deal with a handful of evictions, nearly every single one of them came from a property I bought with a tenant already inside. As soon as they learned rents were going to be raised, they stopped paying and forced me to start the eviction process. If you've had an experience like mine, odds are you don't worry too much about having a tenant trash a property. Most properties I buy are occupied by tenants who want their security deposit back. They also want to make sure their rental record stays clean and they get good recommendations from previous landlords. These tenants are motivated to take care of my property because they understand it's in their own best interest to do so and are mature enough to carry that out. When dealing with experiences like these, it's not hard to want to provide the best property possible to get the best tenant and the highest rent possible.

Not everyone is so lucky. Many landlords have gone through nightmares as tenants lied, refused to pay, refused to move out, and then trashed the property in protest. Just one tenant like this can have a serious effect on an investor's psyche. Knowing how hard you've worked to create a clean, safe, and desirable property creates a bit of an emotional bond with the project. Seeing it destroyed by an uncaring stranger can be really discouraging and leave a taste in someone's mouth so bad, he or she will never want to invest again. It's not hard to see how someone who's had an experience similar to this will not want to take the risk of being burned again. Seeing the beautiful cabinets you elected to put in your unit ripped to pieces and scratched to death is enough to make your blood boil. Seeing the beautiful laminate flooring ruined by the claws of a dog that wasn't allowed per the lease in the first place can be a gut-wrenching blow. For someone who has experienced this, it's easy to see why he or she would be as cautious and mistrusting as possible.

This is why I believe we get such opposing and polarizing views when it comes to upgrades. The emotional experience we go through as a landlord can really cement our position. I say all of this because if you're reading this and trying to decide which upgrades you'd like to make on your next project, it's important to understand your own preconceived feelings on the matter and why you may have come to feel this way. The best opinion is an objective opinion, and the mind that is free of emotional burdens will usually make the best decision. If you understand the way you subconsciously tend to lean on this topic, you'll have a better opportunity to control yourself in this aspect of real estate that often gets people in trouble.

IT'S NOT ABOUT THE JUST LOOK—IT'S ABOUT THE VALUE

Simply put, your goal is to spend the least amount of money you can to add the most value as possible to your project. This is not an easy task. In the beginning of my investing career, I was a self-admitted cheapskate. I added or repaired only what was absolutely necessary, and I believed if people were renting a property, all they needed was a roof over their head and running water. I got away with this for a while because everything I was buying was move-in ready and already in great condition.

When the economy started to get better, real estate prices started to rise. To buy properties at prices that still made sense as rentals, I, like most people, was forced to buy properties that needed more work, were more distressed, and would require more time, effort, and attention to make rent ready. The training wheels had come off. Now in addition to finding, analyzing, and closing on a property, I had to learn how to rehab it as well. This took some time, and mistakes were made as I got better at learning how to estimate repairs and choose upgrades wisely. Mistakes were made that affected my success. After some significant trial and error, I started to gain confidence in my ability to get the most bang for my buck when it came to rehabs. This skill became one of the most important I've ever developed as an investor. When I learned I could do rehabs better and cheaper than other investors, I was able to buy properties that didn't make financial sense for them to buy. In essence, I kept building, while others fell into a holding pattern. Several years later, I'm sitting pretty, while they are still sitting on the sidelines waiting for prices to drop.

This is what separates real investors from those who just bought well during a recession—namely, the ability to buy an underperforming asset (the property) and make it a performing asset while simultaneously adding value through increased equity. This is how the wealthy grow their wealth and the wise see opportunity where the timid or inexperienced see only obstacles. This is what you want to learn to do if you want to be able to buy in any market.

Spending less but getting more is really the same principle we are working under when looking for a great deal, right? Rehabs work the same way. If we spend too little and don't make the property at least equal to that of our competition, we'll suffer. If we're renting it out, we'll have problems with high vacancy and low rents. If we're trying to sell it, we'll have problems with time sitting on the market before selling and with purchase price.

Conversely, if you overdo your rehab, you'll find you reach a point of diminishing returns that really eats into your bottom line. You will hurt your ROI and risk having tenants damage your expensive upgrades. If you spend too much on your flip, you'll find you've out priced yourself in your market, and nobody wants to pay too much to own the champagne house surrounded by beer-bottle neighbors.

So how do you know how much is too much or whether you're skimping?

When we tell ourselves we have a $15,000 rehab budget, how did we choose the $15,000? Often, it's because we were trying to come in at a certain percentage of ARV (after repair value) because we believed this will make for a "successful" investment. The answer I learned is that it's not about hitting a magic rehab number. True value comes from getting great deals that add value to your property, regardless of what they cost.

Let's say for a moment you decided you wanted to buy an investment property in the $100,000 to $110,000 range. You search and search and find a few possible deals where you might be able to buy something in which you can add $15,000 in equity while getting a 15 percent return on your money. Not bad by most standards. Now let's say that while searching, you happen to find a property for $130,000 that will have $35,000 in equity and return you 17 percent on your money. If you can afford it, would it be wise to pass up this deal because it's "over budget"? Your "budget" is a number you came up with based on who-knows-what criteria. If we are being honest, many people choose a budget just because it's a nice round number and sounds reasonable. In this case, you would be passing up the better investment to buy a lesser-performing investment simply because the price point of the $100,000 to $110,000 homes was "under budget."

Rehabs work the same way. If you need to replace the countertops, conventional wisdom may say to go with tile countertops because they are the cheapest option. Your odds of coming in "under budget" are much better if you spend as little as possible on the countertops. If that's all you're thinking about, tile is the way to go. But what if your contractor knows a great granite installation guy and also happens to know that granite is on sale for $250 a slab at a granite expo? A quick crunching of the numbers might reveal that going with this handsome granite over plain tile will cost only 12 percent more but would have a significant positive impact on the overall value of the house. You may get it rented more quickly and for more money because the granite shows great in the pictures. Your granite countertops might be what drives the buyers to your flip over the competition's if buyers aren't used to seeing it. While it would be foolish to spend top dollar on this granite upgrade, what if the 12 percent increase were more than made up for by getting multiple offers on your home and being able to entice buyers to offer their highest and best? What if the house sat on the market for three weeks less and the reduced holding costs were more than the 12 percent you spent on the upgrade?

The same can be true for cabinets, stainless steel appliances, tile flooring, new vanities, and other upgrades. Always ask, "What is my *best* option?" By best, we mean what will add the most value for the least amount of money. I'll give you some specific examples, as well as some general overall philosophies that will help you get the most bang for your buck and set you apart from your competition.

WHERE IS YOUR MONEY GOING?

First off, when asking myself which items will get me the most value for my dollar, I've learned to differentiate upgrades into two categories.

1. What are the aspects of this rehab that I *need* to do for the house to be livable and in line with my competition?
2. What are the aspects of this rehab that would be nothing but additional perks? Nice but not necessary.

The items that fall into group one would be the cake. The items in group two would be the icing. Depending on where your property is located, you may not be able to justify anything that is icing. Your odds of being able to add some icing will be significantly better when flipping a house than when buying a rental property.

Items in category one would typically be as follows:

- Roof
- Cabinets
- Appliances
- Flooring
- Paint
- Countertops
- Windows
- Showers
- Vanities/bathroom cabinets
- Lighting
- Fences
- Screens on windows
- Blinds
- Sinks
- Toilets
- Doors

These are items that just about every property is going to need to be considered livable. While the list is far from exhaustive, the point is these are all items that a home would need for a buyer to be able to use financing to buy it or a renter would need for the home to be legally eligible to be rented out. These are your "cake" items. You are going to need them in some form or fashion for your investment to be worthwhile.

Items in category two would be more like the following:
- Outside fixtures such as birdbaths or other water features
- Built-in bookshelves
- Rock, stone, or brick decorations on accent walls
- Rainfall showerheads
- Upgraded mirrors
- Kitchen backsplash
- Upgraded baseboards
- Crown molding
- Surround sound speakers in house
- Alarm system
- Exterior landscaping
- Heated floors
- Security cameras
- Skylights

The category-two items are not necessary for a property to be livable but may be just what you need to impress buyers, or, in rare cases, renters (I've yet to see a tenant who demands crown molding in the house, but I'm sure in some high-end rentals or vacation rentals, this is standard). These items are the "icing on the cake." In most situations where you, as an investor, are rehabbing a property, these items will be overkill, and you should stop dead in your tracks if you find yourself wanting to include them, and seek outside counsel to ensure this is wise.

The reason we focus primarily on the category-one items is that we are much more likely to get a good return on our money for these. Odds are you are going to need to replace these items at some point (possibly right away, when you buy the property). It makes much more sense to upgrade something if you need to replace the entire item than it does to replace an item that's working fine with another that is nicer. When I mention upgrades, many people assume I'm talking about ripping out a perfectly fine tile floor to replace it with nicer tile or taking out a gas stove that still works to replace it with a shiny new model. Don't make this mistake. It rarely makes sense to upgrade an item that is still working and has life left in it.

Our primary goal during a rehab is to make sure our money is going toward projects that add value to the property. If I haven't said this enough, please hear me now: value, value, value. I've split the different kinds of upgrades into two categories primarily because it's important to note that certain kinds of upgrades are more likely to provide value in investment property than others are. When you're investing out of state, it's really that much more important to know that the upgrades you're doing are worth the cost it takes to do them for the people in the area where you're buying. As we move forward, I'll be discussing some of the best ways I've found to add massive value to a project for the minimal amount of money you can. These are time-proven tricks to make sure I get the absolute most for the money I spend. It's not enough for me to come in under budget; I want to come in over value.

IS THE JUICE WORTH THE SQUEEZE?

When it comes to investment property, this is a question we are constantly asking ourselves (sometimes late at night when we are supposed to be sleeping). Any fool can choose supplies or negotiate with a contractor to make sure his property is under budget. But if the project looks boring or isn't quite up to snuff compared with that of the competition, the joy of an under-budget project will quickly turn into the stress of a home sitting on the market waiting for a seller or tenant to want it.

We want to avoid that. I'm calling on you to step outside a boxed-in way of thinking. Conventional wisdom suggests a budget is a number you come up with that serves as a target you must strike. Budgets are necessary to keep you on target and are used as a sort of measuring stick to ensure you don't wander too far from your intended goal. Instead I want you to start thinking about rehabs the same way you look at buying investment properties. When we are looking for deals, we have certain criteria.

This same concept exists in your rehab just as it does in your acquisition. This same hunter mentality, careful eye for a bargain, and creative vision can serve you throughout the entire process—not just in the beginning, when you're trying to buy. If this is a skill you've been developing, it's high time you started to put it to use in more aspects of your business than just finding the deal. Start using it to make the deal come alive. Start using it to increase your profits. Start using it to reduce your headaches. Start using it in the rehab process.

HOW TO "HACK" YOUR CONTRACTOR

The term *hack* is being used more and more in real estate investing to refer to "house hacking" (a term coined by Brandon Turner at BiggerPockets). House hacking is any process where you buy a house and, through the process of renting portions of it out, can own the property without paying for it. Useful for those who want to save money and popular among those first starting out in real estate, house hacking is a pretty powerful concept.

A cool method I've learned has to do with "hacking" your contractor. All people have strengths and weaknesses, and I've learned that it's best to capitalize on these strengths. In some cases, contractors hire others to do the actual work and just oversee the project. In others, they do the work themselves. But in most cases, you'll find it is some hybrid or combination of the two. Once you understand this is how contractors work, you can start to look for ways to play to their strengths while avoiding their weaknesses.

If you want to get the most use out of your contractors, start by asking them what work they can do themselves and what work they have subcontractors for. Ask them what type of work they are finding they get the best prices from their subcontractors for. If your contractor tells you he or she has a killer tile guy, you might want to ask how cheaply he can do the kitchen or bathroom floors. If your contractor tells you he or she has a landscaping crew that works cheap and fast, you may want to consider asking how cheap that crew can landscape your backyard and what design options they have.

We all have our areas of expertise. Some contractors got their start framing houses and will be very familiar with and skilled in hanging drywall or adding additional square footage to a house. Others were roofers and can repair a roof where others would just add a whole new one. Ask your contractors how they got started and which aspects of the job they enjoy most or feel most comfortable doing.

Do ask how they got started and what they like doing most in a project.

Don't ask this during the initial interview phase or with a judgmental or investigatory tone.

You don't want your contractors to feel pressured to tell you what you want to hear. You do want them to feel free to be honest and maybe brag a little about the areas they're most comfortable with. Getting sellers to open up helps you find out more about their situation, motivation, and bottom line. This can help you make better offers. Getting contractors to open up helps you learn more about their foundation, background, and bottom line.

Once you find out a little more about them, start asking how much they'll need to add certain jobs onto a project. I recently found out my contractor had run across a subcontractor who could build beautiful projects with stone. This particular subcontractor was looking for work. Guess who was able to get an amazing stone wall built around his entire fireplace instead of just the mantel for $600 instead of $1,000. This guy! That stone wall became a huge focal point of the flip and was well worth the money (prices included materials too). If I hadn't been asking my contractor more about where he feels he can bring the best value, I never would have been able to get such an awesome feature for such a cheap price. Contractors can be hacked just like everything else; it's time you started hacking.

THE UPGRADE HACK

Since we've already broached the topic of hacking a house, hacking a contractor, and hacking anything else you can get your hands on, I'd like to take a minute to point out a unique way to hack your rehabs that no one else (as far as I know) has come up with: the Upgrade Hack.

Upgrade Hacking occurs when you already have to replace an entire item (countertop, floor, shower, and so on) or make some form of change on your property that is going to cost you money. The concept is based on the premise that since you're already going to be spending something, sometimes spending a little more can get you a big difference in quality. Now, certain choices that wouldn't make sense if you weren't already going to replace something start to make sense. When considering how to Upgrade Hack, we are going to weigh the cost of the cheaper version against that of the upgraded version to help determine how much more you'll have to pay for the better quality. You'll often find the upgraded version isn't much more than the cheap version but that the value it brings can be significantly more.

The trick is that you are *already* going to be doing some work that will cost you money. You aren't going to be paying full price for an item to replace something that already works just fine. On the contrary, you will typically benefit from this technique only if you have a certain amount of money budgeted for an item to be replaced and you had intended to replace it with the cheapest material possible.

For instance, I recently purchased a property in North Florida with an ARV of approximately $110,000. This isn't the Taj Mahal. It's in a blue-collar neighborhood with great schools, and it will rent for around $1,100 a month. Once my contractor got inside, he informed me the appliances were crap and needed to be replaced. Before delivering the news, he took the liberty of getting me a price for a new stove, range hood, microwave, and refrigerator (I've got him trained well, right?). The total cost for all four items was about $1,500 if I went with the standard white color and base models. While this was the most economical, I still took a minute to look up how much stainless steel appliances would go for at a Home Depot in the area. Turns out Home Depot had them on sale, and I could get the same four appliances in stainless steel and slightly nicer than base models for $1,800.

For $300 more, I was able to get appliances that were significantly nicer and made a huge difference in the presentation of the property. If I rent the place out, tenants will be pleasantly surprised to see stainless steel appliances in place of standard, old, white appliances. If I sell the place as a flip, buyers will be drawn to my property when the pictures on Zillow look nicer than that of my competition (more buyers mean more leverage, and leverage is everything in negotiating the sale of your property). This is a mixed neighborhood, where some of the properties are worth over $200,000 and others are worth

$50,000. Putting in stainless steel upgrades will push me closer to that upper echelon of houses I want to be compared with when the rehab is completed and it's time for the appraiser to come.

While it's tough to know how much value an appraiser is going to give a property with upgraded appliances, it certainly can't hurt! Conventional wisdom would say don't put anything in a rental that is nicer than you need. I say if I'm able to find stainless steel appliances that are $500 off because they are last year's model and I'm buying a package deal, it would be foolish to pass that up because of "conventional wisdom."

Many people fail to see the value in this because they look at the stainless steel appliances as an $1,800 upgrade. It would be foolish to spend $1,800 just to upgrade the appliances on a property likely worth $110,000. Normally, this would be true. However, if you take into account that I already needed to replace the appliances and my base rate was going to be $1,500, buying $1,800 worth of appliances suddenly becomes possible for only $300 more.

While appliances are somewhat of an easy Upgrade Hack because they can often be bought in bulk for discounted prices, this same principle applies to more than just stainless steel appliances. If you are looking to upgrade items to nicer models than you originally anticipated and combine this with looking for sale prices, you'll often find you can do the upgrades for significantly less than you would have thought. If I'm being brutally honest, I've had so much success with this method that now I almost *expect* to be able to use it to get nice upgrades on just about every project. When it doesn't work out, sometimes I feel cheated!

If you're able to combine several different methods of Upgrade Hacking on one project, you can expect to see significantly more value in your project than you may have anticipated for not much more work or money on your part. I've compiled a list of some of the very best ways to add massive value for minimal money. I recommend as you walk your investing journey, you always keep an eye out for the following ways to make your projects look far better.

PAINT

Paint can cover a multitude of sins! If you can change only one thing on a house, it should usually be the paint. Paint is almost always the most bang you'll get for your buck. It hides bad smells, creates modern style, and makes an old home look new again. When it comes to choosing how to paint a house, obviously you want to choose neutral colors that are popular with the most amount of people. In addition to that, consider going two-tone.

Two-tone paint schemes look more professional and noticeable. One of the strongest elements in a good design element is contrast. A bright, creamy white on your accents, baseboards, and trim really pops when set against a darker color on the walls, creating a wow factor for very little money.

In addition to contrast, an important element in a great design scheme is the way different aspects complement each other. Certain colors mesh well and bring the best out of other parts of the home. If you negotiate a two-tone paint scheme when dealing with your contractor over the price of the paint, you're even more likely to get a great price.

FLOORING

If you want to Upgrade Hack your flooring, there are several ways to do it. One of the very easiest is to use beautiful, amazing, high-quality products whenever you have a small portion of space. This creates the appearance of massively high value but doesn't cost you much money. The trick is that flooring is purchased at a price per foot. If you can buy expensive materials but need them only in small quantities, you can make an incredible impression at an affordable price.

I use this technique most often in bathrooms. Because most homes don't have large square footage in guest bathrooms (or master bathrooms in older homes), it doesn't take much tile to cover the floor. If it would cost $100 to buy the cheap tile to cover the floor but you elect to buy the expensive, imported stuff for three times as much, you're still paying only $300. The difference of $200 to create a huge impression is often well worth it.

SHOWERS

In my experience, most investors don't fully understand the impact a beautiful shower can have on a home buyer or a tenant. Some buyers make up their minds to buy the home as soon as they see the master bathroom. While showers can have a huge impact on a buyer's or tenant's emotions, they don't always have a huge impact on your budget! The secret is that most showers aren't very big.

If you are buying a rental and have a fully functioning shower that is clean and serviceable, you most likely shouldn't change it out. However, if you're like me and most of the houses you buy look like a cesspool of neglect, you will find yourself often having to replace shower stalls. It's in situations like this that you can successfully Upgrade Hack a shower.

When you're buying severely distressed property, it's not uncommon to find the showers have not been maintained and need to be replaced because of common issues like mold, mildew, faulty seals, busted and worn pipes, and worn-out grout.

A tile shower is the nicest option you'll have in a rental. Because the area that needs tile itself isn't large, going for nice, expensive tiles won't cost you a ton. A nicely tiled shower will really make a difference to your buyer or tenant, and if you already had to rip out the shower, it won't cost you much more to use the upgraded materials.

Another great idea that is surprisingly cheap when you Upgrade Hack is to add a rainfall showerhead. On my last project, the plumber charged me $60 to run the pipes over the shower because we had already ripped it out. The rainfall showerhead and diverter pipe were $200. For $260, I was able to add a luxury item like a rainfall showerhead to my master bathroom shower. Can you imagine having that in your advertising photos? Much of the cost in items like this is in the installation. When you already have a demoed project, you'd be surprised at how little it can cost to upgrade.

CABINETS

Kitchens make houses. They are the most crucial part of any rehab. If you want to create a great kitchen, you need to have a strong design, starting with the cabinets. Unfortunately, cabinets aren't cheap, and they have limited options.

You can either replace the cabinets or reface the cabinets. As a buy-and-hold investor, you will almost always find that if the cabinets are still in serviceable condition, it is better to reface them. Want to Upgrade Hack your cabinets to make them look brand-new without paying much for it? I've got a few ideas for you.

The first is that cabinets can be repainted. While this is a labor-intensive job, it isn't impossible to find someone to do this for $500 to $900 depending on where you live and the size of the project. Freshly painted cabinets (dark paint works best for this) can make a kitchen look a thousand times better.

After painting them, buy new fixtures for the doors. Matching them to your appliance color is easy and really makes the cabinets look great for very little extra money. When done well, your kitchen can look brand-new for a fraction of the cost of new cabinets.

If the cabinet doors are too worn, consider buying only new doors and painting the existing frames. Since the doors are what most people see when looking at a cabinet, they are the most important and will give you the most return on your dollar. Upgrade Hacking cabinets is easy if you have the right strategy and find the right person for the job.

COUNTERTOPS

Since we are talking about kitchens, let's move on to countertops. They are a huge part of the kitchen and usually the first thing people notice. Beautiful counters can sway a buyer to want the house on sight. While everyone loves them, they aren't exactly cheap. The good news is, upgraded countertop materials like granite and quartz have become much cheaper over the years and in many areas are now downright affordable.

If you already have to remove old, molded, or out-of-style countertops (such as Formica or laminate), you may be surprised at how cheaply you can purchase granite countertops. A simple and easy Upgrade Hack is to find granite on sale at the store for your rentals or purchase nicer granite for your flips. In many areas, I'm able to buy the granite for an entire kitchen for $1,200 to $2,500. Not that bad! With granite this cheap (and always durable), it makes sense to install it in your projects whenever you can.

The trick to making this Upgrade Hack happen is finding someone who can install it skillfully and cheaply. If you can find a good granite person, you've struck gold. I typically pay $700 to $1,500 for installation depending on the size of the kitchen and the number of cuts needed. This means that for $1,900 to $4,000, I'm able to put granite countertops into a project instead of cheaper, uglier materials. This boosts my ARV for both appraisals and flips.

ADDING EXTRA BEDROOMS

The other Upgrade Hacks we've been referring to have been ways to add a few bucks to the deal, but adding bedrooms in the right situation can turn a good deal into a home run, and experienced investors know this.

While there are myriad ways that adding another bedroom can be useful to the buyer or renter, the main reason this can add so much value is in the way single-family real estate is valued in America. When dealing with commercial real estate, the value of the property is determined by the income it brings in. While you may be buying residential real estate to generate income, the banks and the buyers don't care. Residential real estate, regardless of the purpose for which it's being used, is valued by comparing it with other residential real estate in the same area. More specifically, it is valued by comparing properties similar in size, floor plan, and amenities.

FOUR SIMPLE FACTORS TO DETERMINE VALUE

1. What is the location?
2. How many square feet?
3. How many bedrooms?
4. Is it upgraded?

While this may sound oversimplified, I believe if you start paying attention to how people talk about housing, you'll see it's true. We can't change the location of a property we have bought, but we can change the next three factors. I'll discuss adding more square feet (number two) next, and we have already discussed ways to get more value out of upgrades (number four). So right now, I'm going to take a minute to explain how you can Upgrade Hack *your entire property* by adding bedrooms.

As I've explained, residential real estate is valued by comparing it with other properties using the four main factors of value I listed. Agents determine listing prices for their houses using these four factors, appraisers determine appraised values based on these factors, and buyers determine what they will pay for properties based on these factors. This makes these four factors pretty important. If you think about it, this book is primarily about how to improve each of these four factors to make your property worth as much as possible for as little money as possible.

If you think about it, the whole reason we are looking to invest out of state is because of the number one rule! We are looking for properties in a location that is more advantageous to our investing goals. Once we find those properties, we look for ways to improve the other three factors of value to get the very most out of our investment!

When your house is compared with other houses, a big factor in that comparison will be the number of bedrooms. The number of bedrooms has become so important because it's one of the most commonly asked questions by home buyers and tenants. Residential families buy residential homes. In general, the more bedrooms (that are usable) your property has, the more money it will be worth.

When your property is valued by others, they will be comparing it with other properties with the same number of bedrooms whenever possible. Since properties with more bedrooms are typically placed in more expensive "tiers" than those with fewer bedrooms, you can add significant value to your property by increasing the number of bedrooms. Up to this point, the upgrades we've been discussing have been for the purpose of increasing your home's value *within its specific bedroom tier.* What we are talking about now is making changes to move your property's value *into the next tier*! That's why I've said this is where you should start paying attention!

The simplest way to determine whether adding a bedroom is a good idea is to ask your agent or a reliable team member whether four-bedroom houses are worth much more than three-bedroom ones, or whether three-bedroom houses are worth more than two-, and so on. This is the very first step. If the answer you get back is "not really" or "not much," there is no need to keep asking. This Upgrade Hack applies only if you can add *significant* value by adding bedrooms.

In my experience, however, I've often found it *does* add significant value. In all but the cheapest markets, you're likely to see a healthy amount of appreciation by adding a bedroom or two. Something to keep in mind is that the law of diminishing returns applies in this hack. Namely, turning a one-bedroom into a two- will usually be huge. Turning a two-bedroom into a three- will also be huge. Turning a three-bedroom into a four- will still be pretty good. Turning a four-bedroom into a five- may not add as much value as you expected, and so on. There comes a point when adding bedrooms doesn't do much for you.

There is also the fact that you aren't likely to find many one-bedroom homes, and if you do, they probably won't have enough space to add a second bedroom. So in all practicality, you usually find there is massive value in turning a two-bedroom property into a three-bedroom property and very good value in adding a fourth bedroom, and then it can be hit or miss with adding a fifth. With this understanding, I concentrate primarily on looking for two- or three-bedroom properties with more square footage than the surrounding models. This gives me a higher chance to successfully Upgrade Hack a bedroom.

For example, in Florida where I've recently been buying, there are several well-established and popular neighbors near commuting centers and great schools where houses rent out immediately. Problem is, many of these houses were built with two bedrooms and one or two bathrooms. While the area is great, the houses are slowly becoming functionally out-of-date as it gets harder and harder for today's families to work with a two-bedroom house. This means there is a large demand for three-bedroom houses but not much for the two-bedroom ones. In the same neighborhood, two houses next to each other can have values that differ 30–40 percent. This is crazy!

If redoing your kitchen can make sense to add 5 percent to the value of your home, can you imagine what adding a bedroom to add 40 percent can do? There are few things, if any, that can have this much impact on increasing the value of a property. So knowing this, you want to know the area you're buying in and what the difference is in price between two homes with similar square footage, similar location, similar upgrades, but different bedrooms.

Once you've found an area where adding a bedroom makes sense, your next question is to your contractor. You want to ask, "How much would it be to add a bedroom?" Your contractor is going to ask you what area you want to use to convert it, and we will discuss that next. But for now, give him or her a generic example just to see whether the price is less than the value you can expect to add. Remember to remind your contractor that you'll need a closet made and a window possibly added, as well as wall, and a door frame and a door installed. With this info, your contractor should be able to give you a decent rough estimate on how much it will cost.

If the rough cost isn't worth the value you could expect to see in return, go ahead and stop right here. You tried, and it wasn't worth it. But if it still sounds reasonable, you should proceed to the last step.

The last thing you'll need to decide is also the step that more often than not becomes the primary reason you can't use this Upgrade Hack. To add a bedroom or two to a home, you need a place to do it! Not just anywhere will work to place a bedroom. You don't want to put one jutting off the kitchen for example.

Ideally, you are looking for a space that's not being used correctly. The space will preferably have a window and room for a closet and be located in a portion of the home that is far enough away from the main living area that it won't be too noisy for people trying to sleep or too awkward for them to walk outside their bedroom door and find themselves staring at the front door or the kitchen refrigerator. You also want the space to already be part of the existing square footage of the house if possible and to be within insulated walls. Remember, in most areas, a bedroom is expected to have a closet, a window, a doorway that can be closed, a ceiling height of at least seven feet, and at least seventy square feet of space.

I've picked up a few common tricks over the years from the success I've had in adding bedrooms. I've also included some good ideas for areas where I'm actively looking now to add bedrooms and therefore add value to real estate. Some of the best are:

- A large storage area added onto the square footage of the house attached to the laundry room
- A den in a home with sufficient space to put a computer or work desk elsewhere
- A bonus room with no door
- A playroom that is large enough to split in half to create a bed-

room and still have half the playroom

- A family room/living room/great room combination with multilevel flooring
- An unfinished attic
- An unfinished basement
- A large mudroom
- An unused California room (an indoor-outdoor living space)
- Any Florida room (or sunroom)
- The third-car space in a three-car tandem garage
- A large sitting room near an older home's front entrance

The point of this Upgrade Hack is you are taking an area without much inherent value (many of the spaces listed above are nice additions but not crucial) and replacing it with an area with *massive* value—an additional bedroom. The big trade-off is what makes this so powerful. In addition to creating more value, you are also hopefully lifting your property from one tier of comparables to a completely new tier of comparables—with much higher values.

Simply put, adding bedrooms in the right situations is a very powerful value-add move that can supercharge your returns. In fact, it is so powerful, even if you don't have existing space to add a bedroom in the house, you might consider adding space to accomplish just that.

EXTERIOR ROOM ADDITIONS

While many people don't consider spending the money to add on to a house, I've found that there are many situations in which it's in my best interest to do so. The value of an addition to a home is in the fact that:

1. You can increase the square footage.
2. You can cure whatever problem is preventing the property from reaching its full potential.

If you are looking to add square footage, keep in mind that you'll have to go through the inspection process in the city or county where the property is located if you want this to be recorded. While I always recommend you complete this process when adding on to a house, it's especially important if you want the tax assessor's office to record the additional square footage in public info—a major selling point if you're flipping the house. If you're looking to cure a problem that's preventing the property from reaching its full potential, this can be a great way to do it. I'll share an example from my own portfolio as an example.

A year ago, I purchased a two-bedroom, one-bathroom home from another investor. The property was appealing to me because it was turnkey ready and in a part of Arizona where those looking for affordable housing were being pushed. Because I made an all-cash offer, I was able to buy it for 20 percent below market value, and it needed zero work.

Normally, I don't buy property like this because I typically add value to homes by rehabbing the ones that really need it. In this case, though, I saw something about the property I really liked. In the backyard, there was a large concrete patio underneath a covered overhang. The property's one bathroom butted right up to the corner of the house near this patio area. The backyard was very large, more space than was needed. The neighborhood was full of working-class families in blue-collar jobs, and the house was less than ten years old.

When I first ran the numbers, the investment worked. The seller was giving me a nice discount on the price, and I had financing with a low interest rate lined up. My big sticking point was I couldn't add value to the house through the rehab. Then it hit me. I remembered the room-addition Upgrade Hack, and I asked my contractor what it would cost to turn that covered patio area into a third bedroom with another bathroom inside.

Because the property's only bathroom was already butting up to this area where the addition would go, we would be able to tap into the existing plumbing for the new bathroom. Because the area was already covered with the existing roofing extended out, the ceiling would be a little lower but not much, and we would save money on the roof (a major expense). Because this portion was near the electrical panel outside, running electrical to the room addition would be much less difficult. Because the concrete pad was already poured, we would save money there too.

Turns out we needed to just put up the walls, run the electrical and the plumbing, build a bathroom, add some flooring, put in insulation, and make French doors out of the existing sliding glass doors, and I could turn a two/one into a three/two. All of this for less than $15,000! While the rent isn't going to jump up right away, you can bet it will be raised to market rent for three-bedroom houses instead of two-bedroom houses. If I decide I want to sell this house, I'll have one that can appeal to many more buyers and will compare with bigger, nicer houses when I choose the listing price. Because I planned to refinance this house anyway, I'll now be pulling out more money than I thought because the house will appraise for more. When the rent readjusts after this lease ends, the increase in rent will pay for the increase in mortgage for the refinance. I will get my money back from the remodel, my cash flow will remain the same, and I will now have a three/two where I once had a two/one. This is a no-brainer and an awesome hack to take advantage of.

In addition to adding new rooms, it can also be beneficial to add a second bathroom to a home with only one. Another personal example: I bought a home a few months ago with three bedrooms and one bathroom. The one bathroom was appealing to me because it had two showers in it, one toilet, and one urinal (yes, a urinal; no idea why). See what I'm seeing here? I plan on putting a wall right down the middle of the two showers, replacing the urinal with a normal toilet, and adding a door to the side that doesn't have one. This will be a cheap and effective way to a turn a three bedroom/one bathroom house into a three bedroom/two bathroom house and add significant value for not much money.

Now that I'm buying in other states, I've found that some houses make this easier to pull off than others do. Buying a house on a concrete slab can make it much more difficult to reroute plumbing or electrical. Raised foundations make this much easier. This isn't something I had ever bothered to learn before I started adding bedrooms, bathrooms, and square footage. I've also learned it's much easier to add rooms when there is already an existing structure that needs to be converted rather than having to build out an entire addition.

Now when I come across a home that could use an extra bedroom or bathroom, I look for sunrooms that I can easily convert into bedrooms. If they are large enough, I can add a bathroom to make it a full suite. While it's clear that these properties would benefit from having more livable space, the owners usually can't afford to make the upgrades themselves, and that's often why I'm able to buy the properties below market value in the first place. Sometimes I'm able to turn one area into a bedroom and then borrow space from an adjoining area that doesn't need it as much (a walk-in closet on the other side of the wall, an oversize laundry room, a living room that could lose the space and nobody would notice, and so on) to give myself an even bigger bedroom or make room for the bathroom I want to add.

This is why communication with your contractor is so important! You need to explain that you want to add the space but are willing to do so only if the increased value of the property can be justified by the price he or she gives you. If the initial price is too high, ask your contractor to come down. If he or she doesn't come down enough, ask what can be taken away from the project so it'll make sense for you. It rarely makes sense to make a single attempt at doing an addition and then give up. Sometimes you have to play Tetris with your contractor, moving pieces around and switching them until you find a match that works. Don't be scared to do this! This is how you learn more about construction and help yourself come up with better ideas in the future to help save you money.

When it comes to adding value to a property, there is massive potential created by adding square footage to the existing structure. There is also potential for major losses. Knowing whether the additional cost, which is often significant, is worth the additional value it will bring is crucial. While it can feel scary to add on to a home, if you think about it, it's really not different from any other upgrade decision you have to make. Don't leave money on the table when it comes to your rehab. Consider all angles, and see what others missed!

FINANCE HACKING

So far, I've given you examples of how to accomplish an Upgrade Hack in various aspects of your rehab. I've given you specific ideas, as well as general examples, of ways I've found success myself. As you can now see, the more creative you can be and the more mental effort you put into your rehab, the more value you can add and the more equity you can create. Equity, not just cash flow, is how you build long-term wealth. Looking for ways to do so will eventually make you wealthy.

In addition to the ways I've already shown you, I'd like to share with you another reason Upgrade Hacking can pay for itself. It refers to the BRRRR strategy coined by Brandon Turner. BRRRR stands for buy, rehab, rent, refinance, repeat—a strategy has been around for a long time. When you use this strategy, you are buying a property below market value, fixing it up, and then pulling your money back out through a refinance. The strength of the BRRRR is that you are adding value through the rehab *before* the house is appraised during the refinance. This alone is a sort of an Upgrade Hack. Perhaps we could call it a finance hack.

By repairing and upgrading your home before it is appraised, you greatly increase your chances of securing a higher appraisal. The higher the appraisal, the more money you can pull back out of the home. When you refinance a home after rehabbing it, the bank you're using to get the loan sends an appraiser to determine the home's worth compared with other homes in the area. If your home has upgraded materials and makes a good impression with the appraiser, he or she will be more likely to compare your home with other, nicer homes in the area. This usually results in a higher appraised value on your home. Why does this matter? Because the bank will be letting you borrow a portion of the appraised price (typically 70–80 percent on most loans). This portion is called the loan-to-value ratio (LTV), and if you need a reminder on this concept, see chapter four.

Because this is the typical refinance process, you can stack the odds in your favor by doing anything possible to increase the value of your house. Indeed, this is how good investors add equity to their properties and are able to get their cash back out to reinvest. If you use nicer materials, you increase your odds of having a higher appraised price. This increases the amount of money you can pull back out.

So what am I getting at here? If you spend an extra $5,000 on better materials than the plain, cheap, standard materials, you could theoretically find that your appraised price is $5,000 to $10,000 higher than if you used cheaper materials. This could cause your house to be compared with nicer homes in the area that share those same upgrades! If you're pulling out 80 percent of the appraised price, and your house appraises for $10,000 higher than it would have, you would be borrowing $8,000 more on the loan than you would be without the upgrades. (Please keep in mind this is extremely market specific, and results can be significantly higher or lower depending on the prices of homes in the area. I've chosen to use these numbers as an example because they are close to what I've found the difference to be in markets conforming to the 1 percent rule, which are where most out-of-state investors are likely to find themselves investing.) That means you spent $5,000 more on the rehab but got to borrow $8,000 more on the loan.

While this isn't "free" money, it is still beneficial in the sense that you leave with more cash in your pocket. Borrowing an extra $8,000 isn't likely to push any deals over the edge in terms of cash flow. If it does, you probably should be looking at flipping the house instead of renting it out. When it comes to investing, cash is king. Cash allows you to buy properties at prices less than your competition's, complete upgrades that the cash-strapped cannot, and even buy more homes when you've saved up enough. Generally, if you can get your cash back out of a deal, you want to!

In my personal business model, hitting a higher appraised price is crucial. I don't want to need to save up $30,000 to $40,000 every time I want to put a down payment on a new property. I started out doing this for years, and the process was cumbersome, inefficient, and held me back in big ways. Nowadays, I want to buy with cash, fix the house up, and then get my cash back out to buy the next one. The quicker I can do this, the better. The more cash I get back, the better. This being the case, it's often in my best interest to use nicer materials than the bare-bottom options that many landlords favor. As long as the neighborhood can support it, using the various Upgrade Hacks I've mentioned usually results in my getting more money back out of the project and being able to add to the next one. Considering I also get a nicer property, better tenants, and more value when I go to sell someday, you can see why I favor this style over other "slumlord type" strategies!

Compound interest is an extremely powerful force when it comes to building wealth. The principles of compounding returns are just as powerful when it comes to other parts of investing. Don't take for granted the power of positive wealth-building decisions slowly repeated over time. Whether those equal saving money, accumulating cash-flowing properties, adding wealth through equity, or getting discounts on upgraded materials, if you keep making solid decisions, you will find yourself much more successful than you thought you would be.

CHAPTER 10

MAXIMIZE ROI

"Never invest in a business you can't understand."

—WARREN BUFFET

As we've discussed so far, finding ways to add value to a project is a huge way to ensure you have a higher likelihood of success and build your net worth and the success of your portfolio much faster. Anybody can buy a house, but it takes a smart investor to learn how to take a property and get every ounce of value out of it he or she can.

After all, isn't that why you're making the effort to invest out of state? If you weren't interested in adding value, you could just buy a turnkey property and be done with it. You're here because *you* want that profit. *You* want to do that work. *You* want to reap the rewards! While learning new things like this can feel overwhelming at first, that's really not different from anything else in the world. Things are almost always difficult, overwhelming, stressful, and inefficient when you first learn them.

Keep this in mind as you try these new strategies I'm providing you with. The more you consistently apply them, the more luck you will start to have finding success with them. It's only through trying and failing in several different ways that I've been able to learn them myself!

BIG LOTS EQUAL BIG OPPORTUNITY

While the size of a lot doesn't often come up when dealing with real estate investing, there is something to be said for considering the size of the backyard when making offers on houses. As I've gotten better at finding distressed properties, I've also been forced to get better at finding creative construction solutions to restore them to a position of value.

I've learned two things during this endeavor.

1. Raised foundations create many more opportunities for creativity in construction than concrete slab foundations allow for.
2. Big backyards do the same.

If you want to get the most value out of your property as possible, you need to consider the fact that you'll likely be adding on to the property in some way or another unless it's already in great shape. It doesn't have to be right away, but at some point while you own a property, it may very well make sense to improve it.

When I first started buying houses in California, the homes were big, new, and impressive. They had everything a buyer could need and didn't require much work other than a carpet cleaning. Now that I'm buying older homes in the Southeast, it's a different situation. Many of the homes have converted garages, Florida rooms, fewer than three bedrooms, or other issues that affect the value of the home's potential in major ways. I've become much better at finding easy ways to add big value to my investment properties.

Many of these ways are dependent on the lot's being large enough to provide me with the opportunity to add space. Adding a master suite onto a two-bedroom, one-bathroom house can be an easy and simple way to add massive value, but it's possible only if the house sits on a lot large enough to allow it. It's also much easier if the house sits on a raised foundation and gives easy access for contractors to run plumbing, electrical, and other conduit under the home. By narrowing my search to look for properties on raised foundations with big lots, I give myself more opportunity to add value, and increase my ROI.

ADDITIONAL DETACHED UNITS

In addition to being able to add on to existing structures, if you're in an area that is popular enough and zoned correctly, you can also build *new* structures to add significantly more value to cash-flowing properties if they can lead to new income opportunities through additional revenue streams. A guesthouse is nice, but when a guesthouse becomes another rental property, you can increase your rent and your ROI in the process by a sizable amount.

Depending on your property's situation, you may have several options when it comes to adding additional revenue through a second structure on your lot. Before you consider any of these options, you'll want to make sure it makes sense to do them. The number one factor that will help determine this is demand.

If your property is in an area with a lot of rental demand, you have a much, much higher probability of finding out that spending money to add more rental income is worth it. Your primary concern with this strategy is very similar to that of other strategies—determining whether the juice is worth the squeeze. By calculating how much yearly rent you expect to earn with this new unit and dividing it by the cost of the conversion/construction, you can quickly determine whether the ROI fits your acceptable parameters or not. The odds of this making sense if you have to build an entire new structure are much lower than the odds if all you have to do is convert something that already exists into an acceptable rental unit.

For example, some properties are built with guesthouses, or in law quarters, in the backyard. If you are purchasing something like this, you may find that all you need to do is split one large bedroom into two smaller bedrooms to have an acceptable rental property. The major expenses involved will be plumbing and electrical. If you've got something that already has this installed, you may be sitting on a value-rich gold mine!

If you have a pool house with running water and electrical already, the same concept can apply. Adding a shower, a toilet, sinks, and other amenities can make a studio-type structure with great value as a rental unit out of a pool house with much less value as a place for kids to store their pool toys.

Having a large backyard gives you options to do things like this that you won't have with smaller backyards. Because this isn't common knowledge, I never knew to look at this when evaluating properties. Now that I know how much the size of a backyard can expand my options, I make sure to consider it when writing my offers. Whenever possible, give yourself opportunity to add value!

WALLS

Another lesser-known trick of the trade when it comes to adding value in real estate investing is knocking down or putting up walls, primarily used by house flippers to modernize houses for resale. But many buy-and-hold investors are missing the boat when it comes to modifying existing structures to add value.

The most commonly exercised method is knocking down walls to expose the kitchen to the rest of the home. Often done to create open floor plans, knocking down walls can be a cheap and easy way to make a house more appealing to today's home buyers to make the space feel bigger.

The compartmentalized look is very dated, and couples prefer an open concept where they can keep an eye on the children or socialize with guests while working in the kitchen. More often than not, when it comes to real estate, we look for ways to tear walls down to improve a home's value as opposed to adding a wall.

While making a floor plan more open is often a good move, another way to add value by tearing down a wall is to look for a way to add space to an area that could use it by taking space away from an area where the space isn't important.

One way I've done this myself is by tearing down a wall that separated a small master bedroom from a large hallway closet. The home was constructed with a very large hall closet right next to a master bedroom. The house was in a great location with high rental demand but was not up to par with newer, more upgraded homes in the area.

I knew that when I wanted to sell the home, buyers would be turned off by the old floor plan and poor use of space by today's standards. Tearing down the wall opened the master bedroom up considerably and made it just big enough that it wasn't noticeably small. The guest bathroom in the same hallway had lots of cabinets and room for storage, and the loss of the hallway cabinet didn't have much of an effect on the tenants of the rental. When I go to sell it, having a master bedroom that's larger than the guest bathrooms will be worth the price of a lost hall closet and the few hundred dollars it cost to tear down the wall.

When you're tearing down walls (or considering doing so), one thing that can make this tricky is whether the wall is constructed to bear weight from the ceiling above. This load-bearing wall either cannot be torn down or modifications must be made to support the weight of the roof if the wall is removed. Your contractor can determine whether a wall is load bearing, and you should consult him or her if you are considering removing or modifying a wall.

While tearing down walls is much more common, I'd like to present you with the concept of adding walls to increase value. While in most cases it's not advisable to add walls to close off floor plans, there are specific instances when adding a wall can increase a home's value. This is primarily found when adding a wall can create an additional bedroom.

If you remember the section on Upgrade Hacks when it came to bedrooms, you may remember how it's often not much money to create a bedroom where there wasn't one before. The key is finding space that isn't being used well. Bedrooms, when needed, are used every day. Dining rooms are commonly used a few times a year.

The same goes for living rooms when there is already a family room. While some families may get use from this space, I'd venture to say that most of them use living rooms as places to store fancy furniture that is rarely ever used and china plates that will never be eaten from. If the family room is large enough to support the needs of a four- or five-person family, and four-bedroom houses are selling for considerably more than three-bedroom houses, I would strongly recommend adding the small cost of a wall to increase your home's overall value by a significant amount.

A strategically placed wall can add major value to your property for the relatively inexpensive price of wood framing, drywall, tape, texture, and paint.

BUYING BAD HOUSES IN NICE AREAS

As you likely already know, the adage "location, location, location" as the most important rule of real estate has stood the test of time and come out on top. When it comes to the long-term value of your investment, nothing will have a bigger impact than the location. Location is the one thing in your investment that can't be changed. It's also the one thing that future buyers will consider before anything else when looking for a new home. Location comes up first in just about every aspect of real estate. That's why you're reading this book! You want to learn how to invest in a location that works better for your goals!

When people contact a Realtor about looking for a new home, the first thing they tell the agent is where they are looking. Number of bedrooms is important but not always set in stone. The same goes for square footage. Beautiful upgrades may entice buyers to pay more than they originally wanted, but it's not going to persuade them to buy a house in an area where they won't want to live. There are so many things you can do to add value to a property or make it more desirable. Unfortunately, there is nothing you can do about the location.

Up to this point in the book, we have discussed many ways you can add value to a property using various techniques. These techniques can be used no matter where the property is located in relation to you, from sea to shining sea. You should be feeling confident that if you buy a property right (something we will discuss more shortly), you can add value to it and increase the value of your investment. This is a good thing.

Considering that we know how to buy houses below market value, and we know how to fix them up below market price, it stands to reason we should be encouraged, not discouraged, by ugly, old, outdated, or smelly homes. Just accept that trying to buy houses in bad areas is not something we can improve, so it's not something we should undertake. After combining the fact that you can improve most properties for less than it would take for others and that the location cannot be improved, it stands to reason our very best chances for success involve buying not so desirable houses in very desirable locations.

This is a trick known by real estate investors for a very, very long time. Some of my very first mentors told me to always buy the smallest house on the block or the ugliest house in the best neighborhood.

They knew they could get a good price on a small or ugly house but benefit from the long-term appreciation of a quality neighborhood. The comparable sales of the nice homes would raise the value of the ugly one, and the rents in the best area would increase faster than the rents for similar small, ugly homes in the not-so-nice areas. This age-old strategy has proved to be successful over and over when it comes to real estate investing.

INCREASE SUCCESS WITH BAD HOUSES
Let's face it, any normal person would prefer to live in a nicer home than a distressed one. Nobody chooses to live in filth or stare at thirty-year-old wallpaper because they like it. When we are targeting old, ugly, smelly, or distressed houses, what we are really targeting are sellers who are much more likely to be motivated. There are three factors that lead to buyers finding good deals.

1. Market distress: when a market is full of inventory or too much supply, and homes can be purchased below market value.
2. Property distress: when a property is in such bad condition that it can be purchased under market value. Think bad houses we are discussing now.
3. Owner distress: when the owner of a property is dealing with financial, emotional, mental, or other problems that allow you to buy a property for below market value because the owner doesn't want to deal with it anymore.

When targeting bad houses in nice areas, we have a much, much better chance of finding properties that exist in categories two and three. Right now, I'd like to focus on why number three, owner distress, is much more likely to be found when targeting bad houses.

The basic premise is that if owners can afford to fix up their houses, they usually will. While this isn't always the case, most people have enough common sense to understand that if they have a property they want to sell, they may need to fix it up a little to get top dollar. If they can do this, most people will. If you're looking at a house that needs some work and it's not being done, there is a good chance this is because the owner cannot afford to do the work or possibly isn't aware the work needs to be done (absentee owners).

If a home is going to sell for top dollar, it is almost always going to be bought by someone using a loan to buy it. When people are borrowing money to buy a house, they can spend more because they are usually primarily interested in what their payments are, not what the total price of the house is. Knowing this, I try to target houses I know will *not* qualify for conventional financing. I want to pay cash for them and get them at a cheaper price because the owner has very few options to sell to other than me. When targeting homes that can be purchased with financing, I am competing with the vast majority of home buyers. When targeting homes that won't qualify for financing, I am competing only with other cash buyers. Makes more sense that I'll find a better deal and get a better price, right?

Eliminating the number of people who can compete with you is a great way to make sure that your aggressive offer gets accepted. Targeting houses that need a lot of work or are in a condition that a bank would not underwrite them is a quick way to help ensure that happens. This is why we look for bad houses! You have a much better chance of finding a home that a property owner either cannot or will not fix up. This is often because of owner distress and is a good target to set your sights on when looking for deals.

What makes this possible when investing out of state is how obvious signs of distress can be when looking at pictures. While some problems like plumbing, electrical, and foundation can't always be seen, others can. A kitchen without cabinets or countertops, a house missing carpet, a roof with tarp on the top, or a house without drywall will show up right away. There are often even notifications given in the online description describing the property as "investor friendly," "cash offers only," or "needs work." Looking for signs like these while scouring the Internet can be a really easy way to find properties that won't qualify for conventional financing.

AREAS WITH A LACK OF INVENTORY THAT BUYERS WANT

I've often found that a key ingredient to doing well in out-of-state investing is in targeting emerging markets that have a lack of the kind of inventory buyers or tenants want. While this can be a great way to target areas likely to appreciate, it often means the houses themselves are outdated. In markets like these, the majority of the buyer's pool is fighting over the few updated, modern houses.

A big reason this happens is that the older houses were built for smaller families than we have today. Today's single professionals want to live in big cities. They want expensive high-rises near tons of modern amenities and restaurants. They want to be close to their place of employment and close to public transportation. This has led to a cycle of businesses that are moving their headquarters into big cities and single professionals who are moving into apartments and condos to follow suit.

Why do I mention this? To point out the contrast between today and forty years ago, when many of the houses we're talking about were built. Forty years ago, people valued different things in a home.

Back then, it was wise to own a home for most people, but it wasn't wise to own a big three- or four-bedroom house with just one person living in it. Hence the market was born for small, two-bedroom, one-bathroom houses with less than a thousand square feet—a starter home, if you will.

There aren't many people looking to follow this pattern today. The first-time buyers of today are now spending ungodly percentages of their salaries on top-of-the-line apartments and rentals rather than buying these starter homes, building equity, and commuting to work in a car instead of using a bike or bus.

So in many of these markets, we were left with renters as the only people having much use for these smaller starter homes. This created a demand for investors to buy them and rent them out and becomes a problem when you want to exit the property, as most people looking to buy them are other investors. Selling a single-family property to another investor is not an ideal strategy to get top dollar because he or she is also looking for the best deals.

This entire situation creates a unique opportunity in certain markets across the country. If you can buy a property only an investor would buy, but then convert it into a property a family would love to purchase and live in, you can maximize your profit potential.

"OVER-UPGRADING"

As I've mentioned previously, one thing you do *not* want to do is upgrade your property so that it's nicer than the surrounding homes.

This is a surefire way to waste your money and efforts.

To help yourself out, invest in nicer areas where the upgrades will be appreciated and valued accordingly. *Don't* be the guy or gal who puts $5,000 spinning chrome rims on a $3,000 car.

That's a foolish move. When you're investing out of state, it can be easier to make mistakes like this because you may be operating under subconscious assumptions based on your own market (where carpeting outside a bedroom is *so* lower class) rather than understanding the market where you're buying (where carpet is a perfectly acceptable flooring option if it's clean and smells nice). The point is, *don't hesitate to ask for help* on things like this from your team of advisers, and don't put yourself into a bad situation by investing in areas that are so cheap, you literally cannot get your money back out of your rehab.

A quick and simple way to make sure you're not over-upgrading a property is by simply looking at the pictures of comparable properties that have sold in the area you're looking to invest in. Ask your agent to send you a list of the comparable homes that have sold within a half mile of your property over the previous six months. Take this list, and thoroughly look through each property's pictures. Note the similarities you see. Are the appliances all white and never stainless steel? Are the countertops always laminate or plain tile and never granite, quartz, or other upgraded materials? Do the cabinets always look like the originals but 35 years old? Is there linoleum in every kitchen and bathroom or wallpaper on most of the walls?

If this is what you're seeing, there's a very good chance you will be finding it very difficult to justify a decent rehab on these properties. Don't plan on increasing the ARV with a fancy remodel.

Unless, of course, the comparable houses you've been looking at sold cheap like the one you're looking at specifically *because* they were so outdated. This is something to consider as well. If you are looking to buy a three-bedroom, two-bathroom house for $65,000 and are looking at all the other homes that sold for $65,000, it would stand to reason it's likely they look a lot like yours, right?

Ask your Realtor for a list of comps in the price range that you're hoping to sell for. If you start seeing nice remodels, upgraded materials, and fresh paint, you should feel much more comfortable that there is a market there for you to rehab this house.

On the other hand, if you're looking at a list of homes in the range of your estimated ARV and you're *still* seeing linoleum, laminate, and wallpaper, that should be a pretty clear indication that you're likely going to be wasting money by doing anything more than the bare-bones repairs the property needs to be rentable or sellable. As the old saying goes, if a car runs, it has value. Sometimes just getting your property in good enough shape to live in is the most efficient way you can use it.

A last bit of advice: If it looks as though there is no room to justify upgrades, ask your Realtor whether the neighborhood is up-and-coming or whether there is reason to believe there may be demand there in the future. Realtors have access to their multiple listing service that will allow them to see whether prices have been rising, falling, or staying the same over a period of time. If a specific area is seeing rising prices and shorter days on market, a metric used to measure how long a property is listed for sale before it goes pending, you may just have found an area where demand for upgrades may be on the way.

In all reality, if you're considering investing out of state, there is a good chance you're going to be targeting these up-an-coming areas anyway. One of my go-to strategies is to ask my Realtor who works with the most buyer clients in his office. Once I get in touch with the Realtor who works with the most buyers, I ask which neighborhoods the agent is seeing the most demand for and in which areas the houses go under contract fastest. There is simply no better way to understand which areas are likely to see the most demand other than asking the boots-on-the-ground agents, whose job it is to find properties for clients. They know what clients want, and they know what their experiences are in trying to find them houses. The same is true for property managers. They know where tenants want to live, they know how quickly properties go off the market, and they know where the demand is growing.

Find out where these areas are and have your agent, wholesaler, or deal finder start to aggressively look for something to buy. Focus on these areas, and you are much, much more likely to end up buying a property that will justify nice upgrades and may even increase in value during the rehab process to help you out on the appraisal when it's finished! Holding costs during a project can be a pesky drain on your budget. If you can find a way to buy a property in an area that is appreciating, you may find the higher appraisal helps offset the holding costs when you go to sell or refinance. This will definitely help your bottom line!

CHAPTER 11

TRICKS TO FIND MORE DEALS OUT OF STATE

If past history was all that is needed to play the game of money, the richest people would be librarians.

—WARREN BUFFETT

While everything I've shared about finding projects on the MLS up to this point has been good stuff, I'd like to go ahead and hit you with the big guns now. When it comes to finding distressed property where you have the best chance possible to buy it for under-market value, nothing is going to beat offering on REO, short sales, NODs, and half-finished projects. Not only are these easy for your Realtor to search for, but they are also highly likely to sell for under-market value—if you're willing to pay the price.

   1. **REO:** REO stands for "real estate owned." This is property owned by a bank that has had a title transferred back to the

bank when the owner stopped paying the mortgage. Often used synonymously with *foreclosure*, REO refers to the state of a property after the foreclosure process has been completed.

2. **Short sale**: A short sale refers to a seller's attempting to sell his or her property for less than the amount owed on the mortgage. The process is called short because the seller is short the amount of money he or she would need to pay off the note. The word *short* definitely does not refer to the amount of time it takes the sale to close. Infamous for their frustrating lack of communication between seller, note holder, and buyer, short sales turn many people off who want a relatively good chance at remaining sane during the transaction.

3. **NOD**: NOD stands for "notice of default." A notice of default is issued by a bank when a note holder becomes delinquent on his or her payment. Required to be made public knowledge in many states, NODs can be great ways to find motivated sellers because they indicate the foreclosure process is beginning and the seller is facing a nasty credit hit if something isn't done soon.

4. **Half-finished projects**: This one isn't a technical term; I just didn't have a fancy way to refer to these properties. A half-finished project is just as it sounds. Somebody attempted a rehab but did not finish, and the house is now being sold. Often these are coupled with short sales or REO inventory. In this category, you can also include partially burned houses, hazard material situations, and abandoned properties that need serious work. Ineligible for traditional financing and unappealing to anyone but the most experienced investor or contractor, these projects can be gold mines or money pits.

As you can guess, these four different methods for targeting distressed properties have high success rates because the various people involved in owning properties in these conditions are very likely to have a high motivation to sell. As you know by now, targeting sellers who are more likely to be highly motivated to sell will increase your odds of finding a good deal and will save you time in the process.

REAL ESTATE OWNED

Homes that have been taken back by banks and are sitting on banks' asset sheets are almost always going to be a good way to find a deal, regardless of the state. Because banking regulations and the foreclosure process are similar throughout the United States, you'll find that usually you just need to learn some subtle nuances about the way each state works. If you're going to target REO property, it's best to use a real estate agent. Agents are familiar with the process and have connections with other people who can find answers to questions they may not already know.

If you have already found an agent you like and feel comfortable with, simply have him or her search the MLS for any property listed as an REO. I also ask agents to look through the list of what they find and send me the ones they believe look like the best opportunity. Once I've got this list, it's a fairly straightforward process to find the homes I want to offer on. Evaluating properties is a pretty consistent process, regardless of where they are. What's important is that you know what you're looking for.

Depending on the area you're looking in, you may find a whole bunch of inventory or not much at all. If you're not finding much inventory, your job of evaluating the properties is much easier. The bad news is, you are less likely to find something that matches your investing criteria if there isn't much to pick from. While REO isn't the only way to find good deals, it has traditionally been a solid, consistent way to buy homes under market value. If you don't have much foreclosure inventory where you are looking, odds are your options may be more limited.

If you *do* get a lot of options to choose from, your odds of finding something to buy will increase. It's much better to sort through too much inventory than not enough! When it comes to evaluating REO properties, you'll want to consider a few different factors every single time.

1. Are there any county/city/government/mechanic/etc. liens against the property that the buyer will need to pay?
2. What is the age and condition of the roof?
3. Is there WDO (wood destroying organisms) damage of significant value?

4. How many other offers have been made on the property?
5. Will you be allowed an inspection period if your offer is chosen?

While this is far from every question you should be asking, I've found that when it comes to REOs, and specifically out-of-state REOs, these five points are the most pertinent.

1. You'll want to know whether there are any liens for obvious reasons, as you'll have to pay them, and this will affect your bottom line. This is information the listing agent will provide you, and if he or she doesn't, it is information that will come up during the escrow period when the title search is done. If you are provided with this information up front, it's usually safe to assume the bank is expecting you to have included it in your offering price. It is tough to get the bank to negotiate the price lower post-acceptance based on this information. It is best if you had it up front.

2. I live in California; it's no secret we don't get much rain. Where I invest in Arizona, it's also no surprise that there isn't much rain. Because there is very little rain in these areas, roof inspections can become almost an afterthought. Roofs last for a long time, to say the least. Additionally, prices are high enough to justify materials like tile to cover roofs, and tile can last for very long periods of time. My point? Roofs aren't a very big deal in those areas.

   Where I invest in Florida, however, it's a different story. Florida gets a lot of rain, which can cause some roofing wear and tear much faster. Florida also gets a lot of wind-driven rain, which is even worse for roofs. The result is the life expectancy of a roof is much, much shorter in Florida than it is in California or Arizona. Additionally, homes in North Florida aren't as expensive and typically can't support the price of an upgraded tile roof. Why do I mention this? Because when you're investing in an area you don't live in, it can be very easy to overlook things like this.

   The roof is the example I'm giving, but it can be many different things. Be sure to ask your agent about the biggest housing expenses in the area you are investing in. A roof is a common one. So are frozen pipes. In certain areas of the country (the cold ones!), if a home has been sitting vacant too long and the temperature of the home drops too low, the pipes can freeze and then burst. *Expensive.* In parts of the South, if a home has been vacant too long and the air-conditioning is not running, the humidity can lead to mold or fungus growing on the walls. *Not good.* Different geographic locations present different challenges, and it's important to make sure you are receiving counsel from the right team members about the things you may be ignorant of. This is crucial in out-of-state investing, especially in the beginning.

As I've learned to implement my system in more and more areas, I've learned the value of asking more and more people what concerns they have with different projects. I ask my property manager what issues he or she is having with other rental units so I can make sure my Realtor looks into them. I ask my contractor what issues he or she is finding with vacant properties so I can make sure I account for this in my offer. I ask other investors on BiggerPockets what kinds of things newbies tend to overlook so I can make sure I'm not that newbie myself. Ask, ask, ask. Don't let pride or vanity cost you money when you have to learn something the hard way. Out-of-state investing is awesome, but you need to make sure you're taking advantage of as many other resources as possible to reduce the number of mistakes you'll make.

3. Wood-destroying organisms (WDO) can turn a good deal bad real quick. Keep in mind that when I mention WDO, I'm not referring to just the insects themselves. WDO typically covers other things like dry rot or other types of fungus that damage wood and foundations. While this is something you'll typically discover during the inspection phase, you can cut that step out a lot of the time in the beginning. In many states, if a listing agent has been notified of the presence of any WDO damage (or any other significant defects for that matter), he or she is required to disclose this to subsequent buyers.

4. Finding out how many offers have been made on a property will help you determine how aggressive you want to be, as well as whether you need to adjust your strategy overall. In general, the more people who are bidding on a property, the higher

you'll have to bid to get it. While it can be a cause of concern if no one else is bidding on the same properties you are (maybe these people know something you don't), it can be just as bad for your business if you are competing with twenty other investors on properties you like.

I recently found one of these spots for myself. A great neighborhood with above-average schools, really good rental returns, and increasing home prices. There are not a lot of investors working the area, as there are very few other offers when I bid on houses, but there also isn't a lot of inventory. What am I going to do? I ordered a special printer than can print out envelopes with addresses printed on them. Next, I'm going to look up addresses for homes in that area purchased during a certain time frame and start mailing letters saying I buy homes to every single one of them. If I can't find the inventory, I'll make the inventory. You can too!

It doesn't matter where you live—a letter can travel anywhere. Once you've got the team in place, there are a lot of options available to you to find the deals. That's what makes out-of-state investing so great!

5. In just about every case I have seen, there has been a period when buyers who changed their mind after an inspection could get their money back. While these inspection periods can vary in length or name (sometimes they are called due diligence periods or other names like that), the basic gist of them is usually the same. Your offer gets accepted, you order inspections, and then you either back out of the deal, ask for repairs/credits, or move forward with the deal.

It's important to clarify up front whether an inspection period will be allowed. In some cases, sellers expect buyers to perform these inspections before making offers. If you're operating under the assumption that you have a period of time to back out and recover your deposit, and it turns out you don't, this can be bad news. A good rule of thumb is to ask whether a house has an inspection period right off the bat. If it does, make sure you give yourself enough time to perform the inspections. If it doesn't, ask whether offers have already been made.

If the house already has offers in and the seller will be choosing one soon, you may not want to pay for an inspection before you even know whether you will win the house. If the house does not have offers on it yet, it may be worth it to order the inspection before you make an offer and base it on the inspection report. If this works out, you can include the inspection report as well as an estimate for repairs from your contractor along with your offer to help take the sting out of an offer below asking price. Just keep in mind that many Realtors may not even open the inspection report if they are required to disclose what's in it to future buyers. Yes, that feels shady, but that's part of the business of real estate. Better to understand it and use it to your advantage than be taken advantage of.

HOMEPATH

HomePath.com is an awesome tool. This website is a place where Fannie Mae sells its foreclosure inventory directly to investors. I use it often after I found my primary residence on this website (in a stroke of great luck, I was able to buy a home for $280,000 that appraised at $415,000 after it closed).

A brief explanation of how HomePath works: Fannie Mae, or FNMA, is a part-private, part-public government-sponsored enterprise. It serves the purpose of purchasing or guaranteeing mortgages after they have already originated from a financial institution. By buying or guaranteeing these mortgages from banks, Fannie Mae frees up the banks' money and enables them to make more loans. This is intended to assist the real estate market and help make obtaining mortgages easier for home buyers (if you haven't understood this yet, just know that the U.S. government is *constantly* trying to inflate the housing market and spur it forward in this country).

When a mortgage owned or guaranteed by FNMA defaults, Fannie Mae gets the home on its balance sheet as a bank that held the note would. While Fannie Mae can let a Realtor attempt to sell the listing, it often sells these homes directly to consumers. That's where we investors come in.

While investors need to wait to let owner-occupants get first crack at the inventory, much of this inventory doesn't sell right away and becomes eligible for investor purchase. You can find these houses directly from the website, or you can ask your agent to look for you.

This is a great tool because Fannie Mae offers these homes in all fifty states! Talk about an out-of-state investor's dream. If you are looking to find only REO inventory and don't have a direct connection, this website can be a huge help.

SHORT SALES

A short sale, as defined earlier, is a term used for when the amount the seller is trying to sell his or her house for is less than the amount owed on the loan. While these sales are almost always trickier than traditional sales, the complexity of the transaction can absolutely be manipulated to work in your favor.

When a seller is attempting to sell his or her property for less than the amount owed, the note holder (typically a bank) has to give its permission for this to take place. After all, the note holder is taking a bath here, and it would be illegal for people to sell a home if they were unable to pay off the balance of the note used to secure it. It is this multifaceted communication situation that makes short sales one of the absolute most frustrating elements of real estate investing.

The process goes something like this:

1. Seller Mary wants to sell her home for a fair market value of $200,000. The home is in great shape and in a desirable area. Unfortunately, when Mary bought the home, she paid $300,000 for it and put down only 10 percent. This left Mary with a note holding a balance of $270,000. Mary has paid this note down to $260,000 at the time she wants to sell the house.

2. Mary hires real estate agent Joe to sell her home. Joe contacts the bank holding Mary's mortgage note and informs it he will be attempting to sell Mary's home for a fair market price of $200,000. The bank tells Joe to let it know when he gets an offer.

3. Joe lists the home for sale. Buyer Bobby likes the house and wants to pay $180,000 for the home. As Bobby is the only interested buyer, Mary accepts Bobby's offer, and agent Joe presents it to the bank for approval.

4. Buyer Bobby then waits so long to hear back from the bank that

he finds another house to buy and moves on with his life. Mary is unable to sell her home, as each subsequent buyer follows suit, and agent Joe begins to hate his job.

This is how the average short sale works. Because the buyer needs acceptance not only from the seller but also from the bank, it can be an extremely long, frustrating, and inefficient way to buy a home. For the average home buyer, short sales are usually just not worth the headache they create.

But you, fellow investors, are not the average home buyer, and you have tools at your disposal that owner-occupants don't! A short sale can work in an investor's favor because we are planning to use the property in a way that owner-occupants aren't. When owner-occupants buy a property, they are buying a home. They want something they can feel comfortable living in. When an investor buys a property, they aren't buying a home. They are buying an income stream.

When you consider that we are buying an income stream, it becomes much easier to deal with the headache of waiting to hear back from the bank about whether our offer has been accepted. I made an offer on a townhome in North Florida early in 2016. At the time of this writing, it is about eight months later, and I still have not received an answer. Were I trying to arrange my life around this purchase because I'd planned to live there, this would be a difficult situation! Luckily for me, I am not. And I'm more than happy to sit and wait. Here's why.

When the sellers accepted my offer, I was more than happy to buy it at the price they accepted. Since then, prices have been slowly going up every month for the past eight months. Were the bank to accept my offer now, I would be getting a property worth even more than it was worth when I first offered. I'll be able to obtain a higher appraisal and pull more of my capital back out if I keep it to rent, and I'll be able to sell it for more than I thought I could should I choose to flip it.

On the other side of that story, there is the possibility that the price could decrease from the time the sellers accepted my offer. If the market were to turn around, I could find myself in a situation where the house is worth less than I believed it to be when I bought it. My ARV could have dropped, and my appraisal could have come back worse than I expected. This would be bad. Very bad, and it would make buying a short sale as an investor a risky proposition.

But thankfully, it is not so! The awesome thing about a short sale is that if it doesn't hold its value, or worse yet loses value, I can call the deal off before the bank answers me! As an investor buying a short sale, I hold all the cards. If I like where the price goes while I'm waiting, I can stay in the game and get an even better deal than I thought. If I don't like where the price goes, I can call the deal off. Like buying an option in the stock market, short sales put power in the hands of the investor while they take power away from the hands of the owner-occupant. For this reason alone, I believe short sales are much better suited to investors.

A short sale falls under the umbrella of "owner distress" of the three ways investors find deals (market distress, property distress, and owner distress). Knowing this, I look to actively target short sales in my acquisition strategy to find good properties for my portfolio.

If you've got the stomach for it, you should too.

NOD

A NOD, or notice of default, is a notice banks send to homeowners when they've fallen behind on their payment and the bank is preparing to initiate the foreclosure process. Because by law NODs must be made public, it isn't very difficult to learn how to find when they've happened and send the sellers a note stating that you'd like to buy their home. Personally, I haven't been able to find the time to do this, but I do let my agent know I'd like to target NODs in my search for properties that work for me.

While the home is not *yet* in distress, you can still get good deals on NODs. The reason is that the sellers know they are staring down the barrel of a financial gun and may not want to stick around to see how that's going to turn out. If people have fallen far enough behind on their mortgage payment that a NOD has been issued, there is a really good chance they have fallen on some financial hard times. As a good investor, you need to figure out what that is and decide whether you can come up with a solution to help them.

A foreclosure will wreak havoc on people's credit and is a big source of embarrassment. It takes some sensitivity in dealing with these folks because they aren't too likely to be happy with your knowing so much of their personal financial situation. Overcoming the initial defensiveness and awkwardness of this situation is going to be crucial if you want to find success here.

In my opinion, it's best to be honest. Simply explain that banks are required to post their NODs in a public place and you saw this property while looking through them. Quickly transition into the part where you explain you would like to help these people, and ask them whether they wouldn't mind hearing you out. For many of these people, they are stressed and want a way out. That's what you're trying to provide, and that's what you need to be ready to show.

The value you bring to this situation is your ability to buy their house before they are foreclosed on. Once the property goes into foreclosure and is typically auctioned on the courthouse steps, both you and the homeowners lose. You won't be able to buy it unless you compete with everyone else, and they won't be able to avoid the ding their credit is going to receive as well as the lost equity they may have had in the house.

Now that I've mentioned equity, it's important to note why that matters. If the homeowners have equity, you stand a great chance of being able to buy this property if they're willing to sell, and you also have much more bargaining room when it comes to explaining to them how you can help them.

If the home in question is worth $150,000, and the homeowner owes $100,000 on the mortgage, you can offer to buy the place for $105,000. You get a property well below market value, and the homeowner gets to save his or her credit, can buy time from you to move out of the house without being forcibly kicked out by the courts, and gets a clean $5,000 to start a new life. When there is equity, there are options. And options are what builds wealth.

You may be asking why someone wouldn't simply list his or her house with a Realtor if the house had $50,000 in equity. I often asked this question myself. The truth is, many people don't realize how deep underwater they are until it's too late. If their home is twenty to thirty days away from being foreclosed on, it may just not be feasible to try to work out a traditional sale with a buyer who needs the traditional time of an escrow period to get inspections, due diligence, and loan requirements in order. As the wise investor with your finances already in order, you're able to move swiftly and within the time frame that keeps the sellers' credit safe. This is the value you bring, and you should be sure to communicate that. It's much better for the sellers to get a little cash in their pocket and save their credit than to lose everything with nothing to show for it. That's your angle, and that's what you need to convey!

NODs are another sign of seller distress and can offer you the opportunity to buy something before other investors get their hands on it. They also typically allow you the opportunity to buy a property that's in much better shape than it would be after the foreclosure process! If you've ever seen a home that ticked-off homeowners have destroyed before the bank took it back, then you know what I'm talking about. Get the property under contract while the homeowners are still living there, and you can save yourself the trouble of having to fix all the damage they may do later!

HALF-FINISHED HOMES

Ah, the half-finished home. This one brings a tear to my eye. Of the ways to find a distressed property through the MLS, this one is probably my personal favorite. A half-finished home is exactly what it sounds like—a flip or a rehab that someone started and ran out of money or lost the desire to complete. I just can't pass it by without stopping to show it a little attention.

The half-finished home can be awesome for many reasons. One of the most obvious is that it's not very likely to be eligible for a conventional loan. For a home to qualify for conventional financing, it needs to be livable.

1. Homes with no carpet are not livable.
2. Homes with no stove are not livable.
3. Homes with missing drywall are not livable.
4. Homes with missing chunks of roof are not livable.
5. Homes without working plumbing and electrical, counter space, windows, and a host of other problems likely to be found in a half-finished home are not livable.

This is good for you! As a cash buyer, you can go in and write an offer on a house that others with less cash cannot. Same goes for others with less experience with managing rehabs. A house without a kitchen is a huge problem for a lot of investors, especially those turnkey folks looking to invest out of state without having to do any work! But for those of you reading this book, who have learned how to hire and manage contractors from *anywhere*, this should not scare or intimidate you. If anything, it opens doors that others can't access!

A half-finished home would fall under the category of property distress. Targeting half-finished homes gives a cash buyer a unique advantage to find a property that can be purchased significantly under market value. If you are going to use this strategy, it works best if you target areas that don't already have a large amount of house flippers looking for deals. Ask your Realtor to search for half-finished homes in areas where homes have been sitting on the market for longer periods of time than in the surrounding areas. This is a good way to hedge your bet that fewer investors are looking for deals here.

In addition to saving you big money on the acquisition, half-finished homes can save you good money on the construction side too. While most of the old, distressed properties I buy need to be torn down and updated anyway, a half-finished home is theoretically already halfway torn down! Because the first phase in just about any project is the demolition, you are almost assured that a big chunk of the demolition has already been started or is totally completed. You will find yourself much more likely to save on demolition when someone else has taken the liberty of performing it for you.

Your contractor will also have a much easier time figuring out what needs to be done when the walls are torn down and the previous owner's work is exposed. A good contractor can put together the pieces of what the previous one was doing and tell you before you even write your offer what some of the big expenses are going to be. Ever watch those HGTV shows and hear the contractors say, "We won't know how bad it is until we open it up and see what's going on"? They say that because contractors don't have x-ray vision and can't see through walls or know where the electrical system is compromised. However, if the previous owner's contractor has already opened the wall to repair the plumbing or started work on the electrical system, your contractor may be able to figure out right away what expenses you may be looking at other than the cosmetic ones you've already budgeted for.

While every half-finished house is going to be different, your odds of knowing ahead of time what you're getting into are better with a half-finished house than they are with any other kind of distressed property. This is a major reason I love buying homes that are not livable when someone else has already started the project but could not complete it.

But make sure you are very careful about getting a full inspection on these homes. There could very well be a reason the previous owner chose to take the loss and not finish the project, and it might not just be because he or she ran out of money. Costly electrical, pool, plumbing, or, God forbid, foundation issues can ruin many deals, regardless of how low the purchase price was. If you're going to go this route (which I suggest you do if you can), *make sure you get a thorough inspection of the property*. Know what you're walking into, know what it will cost, and run your numbers accordingly.

If you are new to investing and looking to land your first deal (possibly with partners as a joint venture), this can be a really great way for you to find an opportunity to get yourself into the game by combining money with others to be able to write an all-cash offer. Because these properties will almost always require all-cash offers, joining funds with others can give you the upper hand when it comes to negotiating a good price and getting your foot in the door. The key to finding success in this strategy is to have a good contractor who can let you know what the previous owners were trying to do and what you can do to build on that work to save you money and time. Don't neglect this awesome and effective way to find homes on the cheap with motivated sellers needing to sell them below market value!

LEVERAGING THE LISTING AGENT

If you don't have an agent you're thrilled about, or you want to work a strategy that may save you a little money, you can attempt to leverage the listing agent to help push your offer to the front of the pack. While this strategy can work, it's usually best suited for those with a little more experience searching, investigating, negotiating, and evaluating properties.

The upside to this strategy is it can help you get a better deal—sometimes. The downside is you likely won't be getting the same representation in the process. If you're newer (in real estate investing in general or in this area specifically), I recommend you shy away from this strategy and focus on finding an agent you like who can do a little hand-holding until you get your feet underneath you.

However, if you feel as if you can handle the risk and are comfortable with the situation, this strategy can pay off big. When using this strategy, you'll be doing most of the heavy lifting yourself. This means you'll be searching for properties, evaluating them, and doing your research all by your lonesome for the most part. Some people don't mind this because they like doing that anyway. For others, this becomes too burdensome and intimidating. Only you know your personality and skill set, so only you can determine how comfortable you'll be with this.

If you're OK with it, you'll be using the Internet to find properties for sale that interest you. Once you've found one that meets your investing criteria (which you now have learned is easier than ever before with advances in technology!), you will be contacting the listing agent directly and presenting an offer that is likely to pique his or her interest. Here's why:

In standard real estate sales, the seller of the house pays a commission that is divided between the two agents (listing and buying agents). Depending on the price of the house, this can be a sizable or much more modest amount for the agents. In many states, real estate agents can represent *both* parties in a transaction as long as this fact is disclosed. Where I live, this is referred to as double-ending a deal. It allows the listing agent to be able to keep the entire commission check without having to split it. Obviously, many agents will like that.

This practice is viewed unfavorably in many areas because the perception is if an agent is representing both parties, he or she is representing neither party. There is an obvious conflict of interest involved. In a standard transaction, each party has an agent who negotiates for his or her interests. The perception is that this is a healthier way to handle the stresses of an escrow period as the dueling agents bring "balance to the Force." Because the potential for one party to feel taken advantage of—justified or not—is so high, many states will not allow a Realtor to represent both parties.

In my opinion, having two agents can screw up a deal just as much as it can make one work.

Most of the time, clients have no idea it even happened. They are just told, "They didn't accept our terms," by their own agent and never know it's because the two agents got into a personal ego war over who was going to bend for the other. As someone who has been a buyer, a seller, and an agent of real estate deals, I've seen it all from a unique perspective. I can tell you with zero doubt in my mind that many agents are not win-win types. They are insecure, ego-driven people who are more interested in "winning" than serving their client's needs. In fact, I've seen this enough to know that having my own agent can help, but at times it can also hurt.

If there is only one agent involved in the deal, the potential for unscrupulous behavior does increase but so does the potential for a can-do attitude that sincerely fosters communication in a way that all parties can get what they want. If you find the right agent, having only one agent can genuinely make everything go smoother, not harder. With no ego to get in the way, and much less opportunity for botched communication, the agent can act in the role of facilitator and adviser more than hard-bargain negotiator and make the deal come together much easier.

In the end, isn't this what we really want? As investors, we should already know what our numbers are. We should already know what our time frame is. We should always be able to ask questions of our agent, but if we are relying on our agent to tell us what to do, odds are we shouldn't be trying to buy the property anyway. If you had two agents in the deal, and yours was representing only you, would you really rely on his or her advice for what to do in this situation from beginning to end? Odds are you already know. As first-time home buyers, we rely on our agents to handle our wavering emotions and guide us through the process as if it's our first time learning to ski or surf. But as investors who already know how to, we need them only to help us find the mountain or get us to the beach. Once we are there, we should know how to make it on our own!

If this is the situation you find yourself in (and it likely is or at least will be when you're ready to invest out of state), I find it less necessary to have your own agent represent you in a deal. It's for this reason that I feel comfortable letting an agent double-end my own deals much of the time and why I can confidently share this as a legitimate strategy to save yourself some money. Now that you know more of the dangers and the perks of this method, I'll tell you why it works so well.

To put it bluntly, as investors, we are typically offering less than asking price much of the time. For us to be able to find a property that meets our investment criteria, we need to hunt for bargains. If it were easy, everyone would do it, and there would be nothing to buy, right? Because of this, most of our deals get shot down. We will hear no much more often than yes. If that's not the case for you, you're probably offering way too much money in the first place!

Allowing an agent the opportunity to represent both parties is an immediate and effective way to give him or her incentive to push your deal over anyone else's. If you're the only person offering, it gives the agent an incentive to push for the buyer to take your offer, or at least work with you, which he or she may not have been inclined to do had the agent been splitting the commission with another one.

If you don't think the agent makes a difference in getting your offer accepted, I've got news for you, friend. You've been grossly misled. Selling a house is *stressful*. Many sellers are alternating between a state of greed in getting top dollar for their home and a state of fear that no one will buy it. These swings in emotion can take place daily or even hourly! It can be so unpleasant that most sellers will rely on their real estate agents to help them decide what is best for them. They will do this *even though they know the agent is getting paid only if the house sells*. There is nothing wrong with the fact that the agent receives a commission, nothing at all. But think about whether this same strategy would fly in other businesses. Would you rely on your car salesperson to tell you how much to pay for a car?

It is the stress of home buying and selling that forges the bond between agent and client, and it's a unique relationship. The person you're trying to buy the house from is under stress, just as you are. For every ounce of energy you spend worrying whether the seller will take your offer, he or she is spending it worrying about whether an offer will come in. This stress will cause the seller to lean on the advice of the agent for questions like how to counter a offer, how to structure the deal, and when to accept an offer. We want to take advantage of this compromised emotional state to get our offer accepted and a deal in our portfolio!

Now that I've laid the groundwork for you a little, I hope you can see what I'm getting at. When you approach listing agents and express interest in their property, they will begin to get excited. When you tell them you don't have an agent you're working with, they will start to drool a little. When you tell them you'd like them to represent you in the transaction, as well, they will start to feel the urge to break out in song and dance right there on the phone. I've seen it both in person and via third party. It's real.

If you can get agents to want to work with you and keep the commission, that excitement is going to transfer from them to their seller in a very organic way. Your agents will now be extra-motivated to get this deal put together and will even be able to sweeten the conditions for their sellers a little because they'll be getting more of the commission themselves. If I can use that leverage to increase my chances of getting the property, you can bet I'm going to do it. If the only risk I'm taking on is that I will have less hand-holding, well, I had just better make sure I'm comfortable buying in that area and know what questions to ask.

Now that you can see the benefits, here's an easy script you can use when reaching out to listing agents of properties you've found. I typically e-mail agents because of the time difference when looking at properties out of state, but you can use it on the phone through a voice mail just as easily.

Hello. My name is David, and I'm an investor in California looking for investment opportunities in [*agent's town*]. I'm looking to buy cash-flowing rental property at about 70–75 percent of market value that I can fix up and rent out. I'm an [*all-cash or type of loan and down payment*] buyer and looking to buy X amount of properties there this year.

I really love your listing on [123 *Main Street*]. It seems to have great bones, is in a neighborhood I love, and appears to have a lot of potential as a rental property. I'm not working with an agent right now and was wondering whether you would mind representing me as well as your seller in this transaction. I have a few questions for you, but I think I'd like to write an offer on this one when you have some time. I can be reached by text or phone at [*phone number*] or at [*e-mail address*]. Thank you very much, and I look forward to hearing from you!

—David

This is the script I use over and over when I'm looking for properties to buy on my own. Whether I'm using Zillow, my Keller Williams app, or an agent's website, I copy and paste this e-mail to every agent with a property I think has some potential. Once the agent e-mails you back, you can disclose the purchase price and terms you had in mind, how you came to that number, and what you're hoping to accomplish long term. If the agent agrees that is a good possibility, you're off to a great start! If he or she tells you flat out it just won't work, the agent will typically follow that up by trying to set you up on a search. If you allow the agent to, your in-box will quickly become flooded with search after search of e-mail drip campaigns.

It's at this stage when I usually tell the agent what my exact criteria are, what I will buy, what I won't, and how many I can buy at one time. I ask to not set me up on an automatic drip campaign but to please keep me in mind if he or she comes across any properties that meet my criteria. I then let the agent know that for anything he or she brings me that I flip, I will let him or her list the sale. If you do this enough, you'll come across the hard-working agents who really want to succeed and will pound the pavement to find you property.

This strategy worked for me recently on a townhome in North Florida. I found one I liked, made an offer about 25 percent below asking price, and was turned down. I then checked in with that agent every two weeks for the next two months to see whether the seller had changed his mind. After two months, I stopped checking.

Approximately two months after that, the agent e-mailed me again to see whether I still wanted to buy the house. Because she knew she wouldn't have to split the commission, she remembered me and reached out to see whether I was still interested. One week later, and she'd convinced the seller I was his best option because

I could close, had proof of funds, and wanted the property badly. Fourteen days later, the house was in my name for the original price I had offered.

Do you think the agent would have been as likely to remember me if I had my own agent representing me? It's possible but much less likely. What's also less likely would be the agent's pushing her seller to take my offer, which was significantly below asking price. Because she didn't have to split the commission, she was much more likely to present the benefits of my offer more favorably rather than focusing on the drawbacks or negatives. Understanding that agents, just like you, are people, and just like you, these people have interests they are after, will help give you an advantage in real estate investing that others miss because their head is buried in the numbers.

PAYING YOUR REAL ESTATE AGENT A BONUS

While your first thought may have been to cringe at the thought of paying a real estate agent even more money than the commission he or she will be receiving from the seller, I've never regretted it once. I myself have used this method to motivate my agent to use his or her own leverage with other deal finders in the office. While it's great to have several agents working for you and keeping an eye out for deals, it's even better to have several *taking advantage of their entire office* to help find you deals. Let me explain just how I do this.

First off, it's important to understand how a real estate agency works. Most real estate agents work in an office with other agents under the supervision of a common broker. These agents don't spend all their time in the office, but they do tend to check in on a semi-frequent basis. At Keller Williams, where I work, I see the same familiar faces just about every time I walk in. As these agents get to know me, they have started to learn that I'm really interested in buying properties to flip (in Northern California, where I live, buying and holding is just not an option). As more people in my office begin to associate me as the agent who buys distressed property, my odds of buying more flips gets better and better.

What I've come to learn is that I don't need to reduce the effectiveness of this system to just one office where I work. As I've learned more about how agents work, think, and network, I've learned new strategies for how to leverage this system across the country. By teaching the agents who are looking for houses for me to replicate what I do in my own office, I can systematically increase my odds of having deals brought right to me. All I've had to do is find a way to give every party involved an incentive and a reason to keep their ear out for me. It works like this:

I tell my real estate agent in Arizona that I'd like him to have a talk with the members of his office at the agency's next meeting (agents are required to attend sporadic training or office meet-ups throughout the year). During this meeting, I ask him get up in front of the group and explain to them that he has a buyer in California who is looking for houses to buy, renovate, and then sell or rent. He explains that his buyer will pay all cash, close in two weeks, and write the cleanest offer possible. I ask him to give examples of houses we've closed on to let his peers know how I work.

Then I ask him to let everyone know that I'd like to buy houses from the other agents in the office too. For every agent who brings me a deal (that my agent vets first to make sure it meets my requirements), I will let that agent represent me in the transaction and collect the commission of the buyer's agent. Essentially, he's telling all the agents in the office that they can get a very good shot at a full commission if they keep me in mind when they find deals and bring them to him before anyone else. He reminds them that I have an excellent record of closing and am a very good buyer to work with.

In exchange for doing this, I give my agent a bonus. I pay him $1,000 (in this specific area, that's a good chunk of change, but in different areas, I would pay different amounts) for every property he shows me that one of the agents in his office brought to him. Then, once the property is rehabbed, I let my agent list it if I'm going to flip it. Make sense?

My agent gets a free-and-clear $1,000 bonus for doing nothing but announcing my intentions to his office and vetting the deal before presenting it to me. He also gets the opportunity to list anything I buy to flip, essentially giving him the ability to use the other agents in his office to find him listings in addition to earning a bonus for doing pretty much nothing.

The other agents in the office know they have a surefire sale if they get a hot deal with a buyer who has already been vetted by one of the top agents in the office and will do all the communication with me if they can't. This is about as much of a win-win-win as I can imagine.

Me? I make $24,000 on a flip I would normally have made $25,000 on. That "bonus" barely even makes a dent in the overall financial picture, but it makes a big difference to my agent, who doesn't need to worry about my "cheating" on him and knows I want to get him paid too.

Now, imagine if you grew to the point where you had two different agents in seven different states who were bringing you up every two months at their office meetings. Imagine the amount of deals you would be considering that were brought your way. Are you having trouble finding properties that make sense to invest where you live? Consider using this technique to leverage the hard work, network, and experience of real estate professionals all over the country. The results could very well shock you!

In addition to asking my agent to have these discussions with his office, I also ask him to have them with his team. In addition to that, I also ask him to send out sporadic Facebook and Twitter posts letting all his followers and colleagues know he has a client who is looking for distressed property. Think about the amount of people who will see that—it's not just agents. Grandma with that rental she is so tired of managing after Grandpa passed away. Aunt Mary who got divorced and is stuck with the house she never wanted. Cousin Jessica with the vacation cabin she rarely uses and needs a new septic tank she doesn't want to pay for.

See how powerful this can become? Your agent likely has no idea how influential he or she is or how much untapped potential he or she has when it comes to finding you deals. *You* have to teach them! Your agent is your partner in making you wealthy; help him or her understand better ways to do it. Once your agent starts getting paid, he or she won't mind that you did! Using these techniques consistently over time will help you build a team and, better yet, a system that will increase the amount of people working on your behalf and subsequently the amount of leads you get brought your way.

CHAPTER 12

THE LONG-DISTANCE INVESTOR

Fears are educated into us and can, if we wish, be educated out.

—KARL AUGUSTUS MENNINGER

As I'm sure you've seen by now, many of the concepts, strategies, and tips in this book are no different from what investors are already doing when running businesses in their hometown. Whether they center on finding deals, rehabbing properties, or managing rentals, the fundamentals of real estate do not change no matter where you're buying!

The difference between out-of-state investing and investing locally is almost completely in our own heads. If we see out-of-state investing as something incredibly difficult, risky, or daunting, then it will be. Real estate affords enough challenges on its own that at any point, the whole process can seem overwhelming. But if we take an objective look at the work required to successfully invest out of state versus investing locally, we'll quickly see how the two processes are virtually identical.

The problem with out-of-state investing is found in the mind and in our emotional response to it, not in the process itself. I hope by now you can see that the way I buy houses out of state really isn't any different from the way you have been buying them locally. I hope you can see that in some ways, buying out of state removes me from the process and makes the whole thing run more efficiently! Most business owners (i.e., all investors) mess things up by trying to do too much. When our inner "control monster" rears its ugly head, we become less effective and less efficient and burn out much more quickly. The best business owners focus on what they're good at and leave the rest to others who do it better.

Investing out of state forces you to focus on acquisition and building a team, and it gets you out of changing door locks and screening tenants. In addition to removing you from the temptation to manage each project completely on your own, out-of-state investing offers you an even bigger advantage: *the opportunity to buy where it makes sense to buy.* How many people do you think are out there, spinning their wheels looking for properties nearby and spending time they don't have trying to find a deal close by, simply for convenience? You don't have to anymore! Investing out of state offers you the ability to buy where the buying is good and increases your odds of success by locating target-rich areas in which to spend your time hunting.

Sports are a lot more fun when you score. Sales are a lot more fun when you get paid. Shopping is a lot more fun when you buy something on sale. Real estate investing is a lot more fun when you buy properties under market value and watch your cash flow grow! If you find your interest waning and you're losing focus and desire to keep looking for deals, it may very well be because you haven't bought anything recently.

My advice to you is to fish where the fish are biting. The same goes for writing offers. If houses are all selling at prices that don't make sense to cash-flow, don't keep mindlessly writing offers. Go to where the prices make sense! When you have confidence to invest anywhere, this becomes a very real possibility for you (and it makes real estate investing a *lot* more fun).

I've done very well in real estate because I've focused on earning money at jobs I can do well and investing in markets that have done well. I've built up cash flow through acquiring properties in areas that are known for cash flow. I've built up equity by improving the properties I buy each time. This has enabled me to not rely on future appreciation but still see my net worth grow each time I purchase a property.

Investing in real estate, no matter where you buy it, works the same way. The fundamentals are the same, the process is the same, and the numbers are the same. When you understand the logistics and the steps involved, it really doesn't matter where the house is located. The process doesn't change.

I've been able to successfully find lenders, property managers, and rehab teams across several different cities in different states, and I've found out that no matter where I go, the fundamentals are the same. Real estate is real estate. The prices change, the markets change, but the process is always the same. My hope is that you, in reading this, find yourself encouraged to replicate my success and see the fire of excitement that can so quickly die renewed again inside as you successfully purchase properties you're excited about and that meet your standards.

Don't let the fact that you live in an expensive location become an excuse to keep you from getting involved in investing. Living in an expensive location is often a huge blessing because your wages are also high.

Technology is making the world smaller and smaller every day. We currently live in a time when information is readily available within seconds, and most of us are *not* taking advantage. Don't become a part of that statistic! Start realizing the power that the Internet and modern technology has given us and harness it to help you achieve your investing goals.

There is a world out there of hungry agents looking for clients who want to buy houses. Eager contractors ready to go to work for you. Driven property managers who want to add to their portfolios. *These people are willing to do the worst parts of real estate on your behalf, freeing you up to do the fun part!* Hunting down deals and buying properties is every investor's primary job. Let the people who want to do the other work for you, do the other work. Learn how to find deals in areas where the deals can be found, and you'll find real estate investing becomes a lot more fun and very addicting!

Markets are always changing. At some point, the area where you live will become affordable, and you'll likely be able to buy there. Until then, build your portfolio by buying in cash-flow-rich, growing, and solid communities where you will reap the benefits for years to come.

Don't be the investors who are so one-dimensional that they can buy only where they live—be the investor who has the knowledge, skill set, and ability to invest anywhere!

> *I will tell you how to become rich. Close the doors. Be fearful when others are greedy. Be greedy when others are fearful.*
>
> —WARREN BUFFETT

ACKNOWLEDGMENTS

This book would never have happened without Allison Leung's encouragement and support. Thank you for taking an interest in me! Also for Brandon Turner's guidance and Katie Askew's diligence. Thank you, Josh Dorkin, for letting me be part of your family here. Thank you to the readers and listeners of BiggerPockets for liking what I've had to say.

Also thank you to Tim Rhode for convincing me I was more than I thought, Dave Osborn for challenging me to dream bigger, Daniel Del Real for setting an amazing example to follow, and Andrew Cushman for your friendship and professional guidance. You guys give me the confidence to take on bigger challenges and seek bigger rewards. Special thanks to Wendy Dunning for the stunning interior design. Finally, thank you you to my editors, Urmila Ramakrishnan, Paul Silverman, and Michael Lavrisha, for helping bring this to fruition.

More from
BiggerPockets Publishing

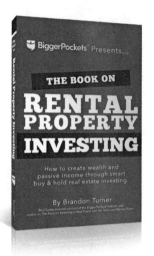

The Book on Rental Property Investing

With nearly 400 pages of in-depth advice and strategies for building wealth through rental properties, *The Book on Rental Property Investing* by BiggerPockets podcast cohost Brandon Turner will teach you how to build an achievable plan, find incredible deals, pay for your rentals, and much more! If you ever thought of using rental properties to build wealth or obtain financial freedom, this book is for you.

Finding and Funding Great Deals

Learn to find great deals in any market with help from seasoned real estate investor, agent, and author Anson Young. In *Finding and Funding Great Deals*, learn tried-and-true methods for finding deals anywhere, ways to improve your real estate business, and smart negotiation tactics. With this practical guide to several deal-finding approaches, new and seasoned investors alike will learn new techniques!

If you enjoyed this book, we hope you'll take a moment to check out some of the other great material BiggerPockets offers. BiggerPockets is the real estate investing social network, marketplace, and information hub, designed to help make you a smarter real estate investor through podcasts, books, blog posts, videos, forums, and more. Sign up today—it's free! **Visit www.BiggerPockets.com.**

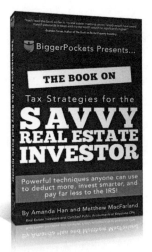

The Book on Tax Strategies for the Savvy Real Estate Investor

Taxes! Boring and irritating, right? Perhaps. But if you want to succeed in real estate, your tax strategy will play a huge role in how fast you grow. A great tax strategy can save you thousands of dollars a year. A bad strategy could land you in legal trouble. *The Book on Tax Strategies for the Savvy Real Estate Investor* will teach you ways to deduct more, invest smarter, and pay far less to the IRS!

Set for Life: Dominate Life, Money, and the American Dream

Looking for a plan to achieve financial freedom in just five to ten years? *Set for Life* is a detailed fiscal plan targeted at the median-income earner starting with few or no assets. It walks you through three stages of finance, guiding you to your first $25,000 in tangible net worth, then to your first $100,000, and then to financial freedom. *Set for Life* teaches you how to build a lifestyle, career, and investment portfolio capable of letting you live the life of your dreams.

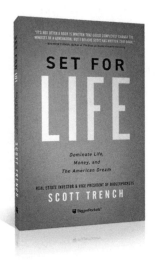

Property tax rate
WalkScore.com
Crime stats. Trulia's crime heat maps
Rentometer.com
Mortgage Calculator plus